COLLINS
WEEKEND
DIY
PROJECTS

COLLINS

WEEKEND
DIY
PROJECTS

JACKSON · DAY

TED SMART

**COLLINS
DIY PROJECTS
IN A WEEKEND**
Conceived, edited and
designed at Inklink,
Greenwich, London,
England

Text:
Albert Jackson and David Day

Design and art direction:
Simon Jennings

Text editor:
Peter Leek

Illustrators:
Robin Harris and David Day

Studio photography:
Ben Jennings

Editorial photography:
*For a full list of photographers
and copyright owners see
acknowledgments page 256*

**First published in 1997
by HarperCollins Publishers,
London**

For HarperCollins
Editorial director: Polly Powell

A CIP catalogue record is available
from the British Library

Text set in Copperplate and Sabon by
Inklink, London

Printed in Singapore

Jacket design: Simon Jennings
Jacket photograph: Ben Jennings

Some of the text
and illustrations in
*Collins
DIY Projects in a Weekend*
were previously published in
Collins Complete DIY Manual

This edition produced for The Book People Ltd,
Hall Wood Avenue, Haydock, St Helens, WA ll 9 UL

CONTENTS

ALLOW A COUPLE OF HOURS

1 A COUPLE OF HOURS

New life
for an old door
10

Clearing a blocked
sink or basin
14

Curing a dripping
overflow
17

Insulating a
hot-water cylinder
19

Lagging your pipes
20

Stopping that
tap dripping
21

Fixing a cold
radiator
23

Making your
front door safe
24

Facelift for an old
fireplace
25

2 A MORNING'S WORK

Putting up curtain
rails
28

Hanging blinds
31

Fitting a better
lock
34

Getting a toilet
cistern
to flush
36

Fitting a new carpet
38

New flooring for
your kitchen or
bathroom
40

Stripping old
wallpaper
44

Reviving your
furniture
46

Looking after
garden furniture
47

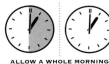

ALLOW A WHOLE MORNING

3 A WHOLE DAY

ALLOW A WHOLE DAY

Making windows
burglarproof
50

Papering the ceiling
54

Painting the ceiling
56

Mending creaking
stairs
58

Draughtproofing
your doors
62

Sealing up draughty
windows
66

Putting up new
shelving
68

Patching up
damaged plaster
74

Insulating your loft
78

Quick-and-easy
double glazing
81

4 THE COMPLETE WEEKEND

Laying a small patio
84

Making a real stone
pathway
90

Painting the living
room
92

Refurbishing your
kitchen cabinets
102

Papering the spare
room
104

Blocking out noisy
neighbours
114

Tiling the bathroom
117

ALLOW THE COMPLETE WEEKEND

CONTENTS

OUTDOORS

ALLOW A COUPLE OF HOURS

ALLOW A WHOLE MORNING

ALLOW THE COMPLETE WEEKEND

1 A COUPLE OF HOURS

Tips for planning your garden
128

Quick fix for a rotting fence
134

Stopping your pond overflowing
135

Camouflaging an ugly wall
136

Levelling a loose paving slab
138

Lopping branches
139

Saving rainwater
140

Plant protection
142

Making a garden incinerator
144

2 A MORNING'S WORK

Laying stepping stones across your lawn
148

Laying decorative cobblestones
149

Maintaining garden steps
150

Replacing a fence post
152

Making a hanging bird table
156

A nesting box for garden birds
158

Window boxes and planters
160

Storing your garden tools
163

3 A WHOLE DAY

Making a compost bin
168

Hanging a garden gate
172

Creating a water feature for your patio
177

Laying on a water supply
180

Protecting your fish from cats
181

Refurbishing an old wall
182

Smartening up a tarmac drive
189

Making a gravel garden
192

4 THE COMPLETE WEEKEND

Erecting a panel fence
196

Screening off a patio
200

Building a dry-stone wall
204

Terracing a steep garden
208

Laying a log path
210

Making steps from logs
211

Building a flight of strong steps
212

Laying out a parking space
214

Constructing a rockery
218

Making a small pond
220

ALLOW A WHOLE DAY

Building a cascade
226
Laying a firm base
for a tool shed
228
A new life for the
garage floor
232
Patching up
rendered walls
234
Brighten up a
dull wall
236

Glossary of terms
241
Index
246
Notes
254
Acknowledgments
256

INTRODUCTION

Nowadays so many things compete for time and attention that our so-called free time has to be managed as carefully as the working day if we are to fit everything into our busy lives. Doing up our homes often takes second place to more pressing needs, even though there are jobs that have been on our 'must do' lists for months. By giving you attainable targets to aim for and simple instructions to follow, this book will help you break the log jam.

So that you can organize your weekends better, we have selected some of the more essential and popular DIY projects and suggested how much time you need to put aside to complete them. Some are very simple and should take you no longer than an hour or two. Other jobs are more time-consuming, and you may have to put in a whole day or even allow for the entire weekend.

In any case, not everybody works at the same speed. If you are fairly experienced, you will be able to cruise through some of these tasks in less time than we suggest; but if you are tackling a project for the first time, you are bound to be a little hesitant and may find yourself taking longer. And then there are the unforeseen snags that can turn an hour's work into a day of misery! For these reasons, we have suggested sensible cut-off points for those jobs where time matters. If you can see yourself running out of time, try to pace the work so that you can leave a project at a stage where you can conveniently pick it up again the next weekend or over a couple of evenings during the following week.

You can easily waste half a day or more unless you remember to buy all the materials you need in advance. Similarly, check our list of essential tools for each project and make sure you have them to hand and in good working order for the weekend.

INDOORS

1

A
COUPLE
OF HOURS

New life
for an old door
10

Clearing a blocked
sink or basin
14

Curing a dripping overflow
17

Insulating a
hot-water cylinder
19

Lagging your pipes
20

Stopping that
tap dripping
21

Fixing a cold radiator
23

Making your
front door safe
24

Facelift for an old fireplace
25

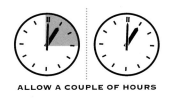

NEW LIFE FOR AN OLD DOOR

The first impression any visitor gets of your home is the front door. If it is smartly painted, with gleaming door pull, knocker and letter plate, the entrance to your house or flat looks attractive and welcoming, but it soon starts to look neglected if you leave the fittings to go dull or rusty and the paintwork becomes chipped or badly weathered. Painting the door with a nice bright colour is easy, but what is the best treatment for the door fittings? Cast-iron door knockers, for example, are usually painted black; but it seems a pity to paint over brass or chrome door furniture, especially as there are clear lacquers to protect them once you've got the metal shining to perfection.

WARNING

Follow manufacturers' safety advice when using paint strippers and wear protective gloves when handling cleaning fluids.

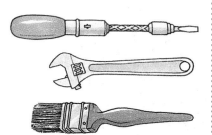

Essential tools

Goggles

Large artist's brush

Paintbrush

Protective gloves

Screwdriver

Spanner

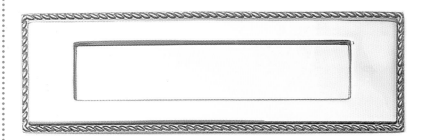

DOOR FURNITURE IS THE COMMON EXPRESSION USED TO DESCRIBE KNOBS, KNOCKERS, LETTERPLATES, NUMERALS, AND BELL PUSHES.

10

CLEANING BRASS FITTINGS

Brass weathers to a dull brown colour, but it is usually simple enough to buff up dirty fittings with a metal polish. However, if exterior door fittings have been left unprotected, you may have to use a solution of salt and vinegar to soften heavy corrosion before you can start polishing.

Washing with salt and vinegar
Mix one level tablespoonful each of salt and vinegar in 275ml (½ pint) of hot water. Use a ball of very fine wire wool to apply liberal washes of the solution to brass fittings, then wash the metal in hot water containing a little detergent. Rinse and dry the fittings before polishing.

Getting rid of verdigris
Badly weathered brass can develop green deposits called verdigris. This heavy corrosion may leave the metal pitted, so clean it off as soon as possible.

Line a plastic bowl with ordinary aluminium cooking foil. Attach a piece of string to each item of brassware, then place it in the bowl on top of the foil. Dissolve a cup of washing soda in 2.5 litres (4 pints) of hot water and pour it into the bowl to cover the metalware.

Leave the solution to fizz and bubble for a couple of minutes, then lift out the metal fittings with the string. Replace any that are still corroded. If necessary, the process can be repeated using fresh solution and new foil.

Rinse the brass with hot water, dry it with a soft cloth, then polish.

BRASS IS A COMMON MATERIAL USED FOR DOOR FURNITURE AND IF WELL CARED FOR AND POLISHED IT WILL BRIGHTEN ANY ENTRANCE.

POLISHING YOUR DOOR FITTINGS

Burnish brass door furniture with a 'long-term' brass polish that leaves an invisible chemical barrier on the metal. This inhibits corrosion so that the metal needs cleaning less frequently.

Clean grimy chrome-plated door furniture with lighter fluid, or wash it in warm soapy water containing a few drops of household ammonia. Then burnish the metal with a mild cream chrome polish. Metal polishes should be used sparingly on plated fittings, as consistent polishing will eventually wear through to the base metal.

Lacquering polished brass or chrome
Having polished the metal to a high gloss, use a nailbrush to scrub it with warm water containing some liquid detergent. Rinse the fittings in clean water, then dry them thoroughly with an absorbent cloth.

Paint on acrylic lacquer with a large, soft artist's brush, working swiftly from the top. Let the lacquer flow naturally, and work all round the object to keep the wet edge moving. If you do leave a brush stroke in partially set lacquer, finish the job, then warm the metal (if possible, by standing it on a radiator). As soon as the blemish disappears, remove the object from the heat and allow it to cool gradually in a dust-free atmosphere. If lacquer becomes discoloured or chipped, remove it with acetone, repolish the metal, and then apply fresh lacquer.

TIP ● ● ● ● ● ● ● ● ● ● ● ● ● ● ● ● ●
Saving time when polishing
Clearly, it would be a chore to remove your door fittings every time you want to polish them, but metal polishes tend to discolour the surrounding paintwork. However, you can protect the paint from abrasive cleaners by using a template cut from thin card which you slip over each fitting. Alternatively, stick low-adhesive masking tape over the paintwork.

You don't have to remove a door fitting, such as a letter plate that has raised edges. The next time you repaint the door, allow the paint to coat the edges, but wipe it from the surface of the fitting with a cloth dampened with white spirit. Once the paint is dry, you can polish the exposed metal without touching the painted woodwork.

CLEANING AND PAINTING CAST-IRON FITTINGS

You can't do a lot with rusty cast-iron door knockers or letter plates until you have soaked them in paraffin for several hours to soften the corrosion. Then you can clean the metal with fine wire wool and paint the bare metal with a rust-inhibiting primer or, alternatively, a proprietary rust-killing jelly or liquid that will remove and neutralize rust.

Some rust killers are self-priming, so no additional primer is required. Otherwise, work a suitable primer into crevices and fixings, and make sure sharp edges and corners are coated generously. Finish the metal with semi-matt black paint.

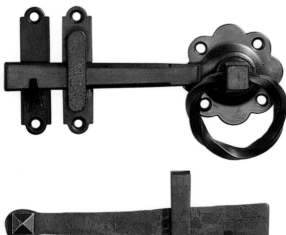

STRIPPING OLD PAINT FROM DOOR FITTINGS

After years of redecorating, door fittings can become so clogged with paint that it is no longer possible to distinguish their true form and detail. At this stage, it pays to remove the layers of old paint with a proprietary chemical stripper.

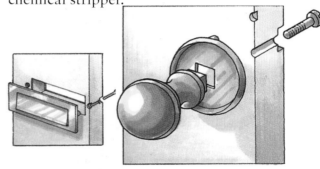

DOOR FITTINGS ARE USUALLY ATTACHED WITH BOLTS

Removing the paint
Even if you intend to strip the paint from the door, it's best to remove the fittings and strip them separately. Arrange them in one or more metal-foil dishes and pour chemical paint stripper into each dish. Stipple the stripper onto the fittings with an old paintbrush to ensure that the chemicals penetrate all the crevices. Leave the stripper to do its work for 10 to 15 minutes, then check that the paint has begun to soften.

Wearing protective gloves and goggles, remove the softened paint from each item with fine wire wool. If there is still paint adhering to a fitting, return it to the dish and apply fresh stripper.

Wash the stripped metal with hot water and dry it thoroughly with thick paper towels. If the fitting is hollow, stand it on a wad of newspaper to allow any water trapped inside to drain away.

CLEARING A BLOCKED SINK OR BASIN

Essential tools

Sink plunger

Hydraulic pump

Adjustable wrench

Don't ignore the early signs of an imminent blockage of the wastepipe from a sink or basin – it only gets worse. If the water drains away slowly, use a proprietary chemical drain cleaner to remove a partial blockage before you are faced with clearing a serious obstruction. Regular cleaning with a similar cleaner also keeps the waste system clear and sweet-smelling. If a wastepipe blocks without warning, try a series of measures to locate and clear the obstruction.

IF THE WATER FROM THE KITCHEN SINK DRAINS AWAY SLOWLY THIS IS USUALLY THE SIGN OF A BLOCKED WASTEPIPE OFTEN CAUSED BY AN ACCUMULATION OF FAT AND FOOD DEBRIS. TRY ONE OF THE REMEDIES OPPOSITE TO RESTORE NORMAL DRAINAGE FUNCTION.

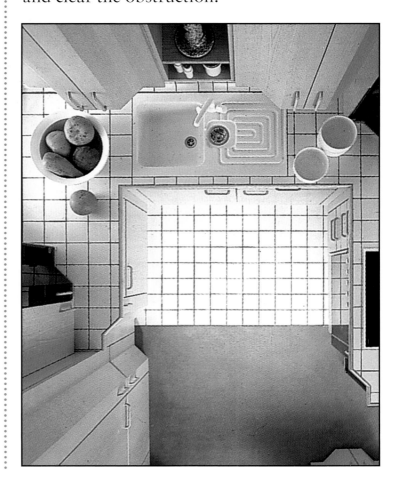

CLEANING THE WASTE-PIPE AND TRAP

In most cases, blockages occur because grease, hair and particles of kitchen debris build up gradually within traps and wastepipes. If water drains away sluggishly, use a cleaner immediately. Follow the manufacturer's instructions carefully, with particular regard to safety. Always wear protective gloves and goggles when handling chemical cleaners, and keep them out of the reach of children.

If unpleasant odours linger after you have cleaned the waste, pour a little disinfectant into the basin overflow.

Using a plunger

If one basin fails to empty while others are functioning normally, the blockage must be somewhere along its individual branch pipe. Before you attempt to locate the blockage, try forcing it out of the pipe with a sink plunger. Smear the rim of the rubber cup with petroleum jelly, then lower it into the blocked basin to cover the waste outlet. Make sure there is enough water in the basin to cover the cup. Block the overflow with a wet cloth, held in one hand, while you pump the handle of the plunger up and down a few times. The waste may not clear immediately if the blockage is merely forced further along the pipe, so repeat the process until the water drains away. If it will not clear after several attempts, try clearing the trap.

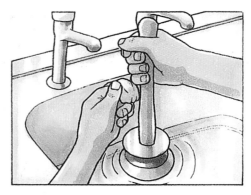

USE A PLUNGER TO FORCE OUT A BLOCKAGE

Now clear the trap

The trap, situated immediately below the waste outlet of a sink or basin, is basically a bent tube designed to hold water that seals out drain odours. Traps become blocked when debris collects at the lowest point of the bend. Place a bucket under the basin to catch the water, then use a wrench to release the cleaning eye at the base of a standard trap. Alternatively, remove the large access cap on a bottle trap by hand. If there is no provision for gaining access to the trap, unscrew the connecting nuts and remove the entire trap.

Let the contents of the trap drain into the bucket, then bend a hook on the end of a length of wire and use it to probe the section of wastepipe beyond the trap. (It is also worth checking outside to see if the other end of the pipe is blocked with leaves.) If you have to remove the trap, take the opportunity to scrub it out with detergent before replacing it.

UNSCREW THE ACCESS CAP ON A BOTTLE TRAP

Another way to clear the branch pipe

Quite often, a vertical pipe from the trap joins a virtually horizontal section of the wastepipe. There should be an access plug built into the joint so that you can clear the horizontal pipe. Have a bowl ready to collect any trapped water, then unscrew the plug by hand. Use a length of hooked wire to probe the branch pipe. If you locate a blockage that seems very firmly lodged, rent a drain auger from a tool-hire company to clear the pipe.

If there is no access plug, remove the trap and probe the pipe with an auger. If the wastepipe is constructed with push-fit joints, you can dismantle it.

TIP ● ● ● ● ● ● ● ● ● ● ● ● ● ●

The last resort

If a plunger is ineffective in clearing a blocked waste outlet, use a simple hand-operated hydraulic pump. A downward stroke on the tool forces a powerful jet of water along the pipe to disperse the blockage. If it is lodged firmly, an upward stroke may create enough suction to pull it free.

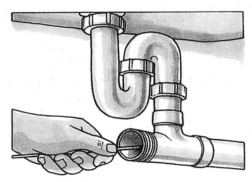

USE HOOKED WIRE TO PROBE A BRANCH PIPE

Tubular trap
If the access cap to the cleaning eye is stiff, use a wrench to remove it.

Bottle trap
A bottle trap can be cleared easily, because the whole base of the trap unscrews by hand.

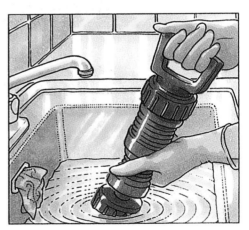

Using a hydraulic pump
Block the sink overflow with a wet cloth. Fill the pump with water from the tap, then hold its nozzle over the outlet, pressing down firmly. Pump up and down until the obstruction is cleared.

CURING A DRIPPING OVERFLOW

The level of water in a toilet cistern or in the water-storage cistern in the loft is controlled by a hollow float attached to one end of a rigid arm fitted to the water-inlet valve. As the level rises, the water lifts the float until the other end of the arm eventually closes the valve, shutting off the incoming water. If the arm is not adjusted correctly, water continues to flow into the cistern until it escapes to the outside through an overflow pipe. Usually, the solution is to adjust the float arm.

ALLOW A COUPLE OF HOURS

Essential tools
Screwdriver

THE FLOAT ARM WILL ALWAYS BE FOUND IN THE CISTERN BEHIND THE TOILET. IN THIS CASE THE CISTERN IS PANELLED IN BUT IS ACCESSIBLE THROUGH A REMOVABLE SHELF.

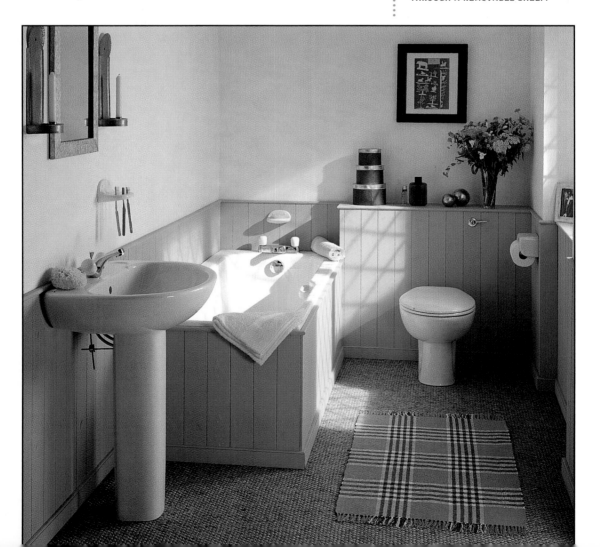

ADJUSTING THE FLOAT ARM

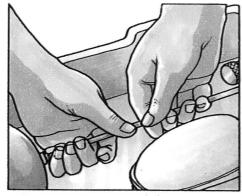

STRAIGHTEN OR BEND A METAL FLOAT ARM

1 Adjust the float to maintain the optimum level of water, which is about 25mm (1in) below the outlet of the overflow pipe. On some valves the arm is a solid-metal rod. Bend it downward slightly to reduce the water level.

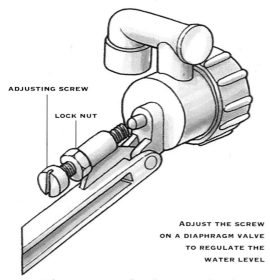

ADJUSTING SCREW

LOCK NUT

ADJUST THE SCREW ON A DIAPHRAGM VALVE TO REGULATE THE WATER LEVEL

2 The arm on a diaphragm valve has an adjusting screw that presses on the end of a piston. Release the lock nut and turn the screw towards the valve to lower the water level, or away from it to allow the water to rise.

REPLACING A DAMAGED FLOAT

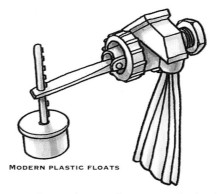

MODERN PLASTIC FLOATS

Modern plastic floats rarely leak, but old-style metal floats eventually corrode and allow water to seep into the hollow ball. The float gradually sinks until it won't ride high enough to close the valve.

Emergency measures
Unscrew the float and shake it to test whether there is water inside. If you can't replace it for several days, lay the ball on a bench and enlarge the leaking hole with a screwdriver. Pour out the water and replace the float, then cover it with a plastic bag, tying the neck tightly around the float arm.

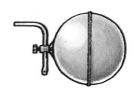

Thumb-screw adjustment
Some float arms are cranked, and the float is attached with a thumb-screw clamp. To adjust the water level in the cistern, slide the float up or down the rod.

INSULATING A HOT-WATER CYLINDER

ALLOW A COUPLE OF HOURS

Many people think that an unlagged cylinder has the advantage of providing a useful source of heat in an airing cupboard – but in fact it squanders a surprising amount of energy. Even a lagged cylinder should provide ample heat in an enclosed airing cupboard; if not, an uninsulated pipe will do so.

Choosing the jacket
Proprietary water-cylinder jackets are made from segments of mineral-fibre insulation, 80 to 100mm (3¼ to 4in) thick, wrapped in plastic. Measure the approximate height and circumference of the cylinder to choose the right size. If need be, buy a jacket that is too large, rather than one that is too small. Make sure the quality is adequate by checking that it is marked with the British Standard kite mark (BS 5615).

Fitting the jacket
Thread the tapered ends of the jacket segments onto a length of string and tie it round the pipe at the top of the cylinder. Distribute the segments evenly around the cylinder and wrap the straps or tapes provided around it to hold the jacket in place. Spread out the segments to make sure the edges are butted together, and tuck the insulation around the pipes and the cylinder thermostat.

    If you should ever have to replace the cylinder itself, consider substituting a preinsulated version, of which there are various types on the market.

Essential tools

No tools required

TIP ● ● ● ● ● ● ● ● ●

It is also a good idea to insulate hot-water pipes in those parts of the house where their radiant heat is not contributing to the warmth of the rooms (see Lagging your pipes, page 20).

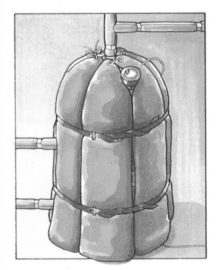

Lagging a hot-water cylinder
Fit a jacket snugly around the cylinder and wrap foamed-plastic tubes around the pipework, especially the vent pipe directly above the cylinder.

Essential tools

Scissors

Craft knife

**Lagging pipes with
foamed-plastic tubes** ☞

*1 Most tubes are pre-
slit along their length
so that they can be
sprung over the pipe . Butt
successive lengths of foam
tube end-to-end, and seal
the joints with PVC
adhesive tape.*

*2 At a bend, cut small
segments out of the
split edge so that the
tube will bend without
crimping. Fit it around the
pipe and seal the closed
joints with tape.*

*3 Where two pipes are
joined with an elbow
fitting, mitre the
ends of the two lengths of
tube, butt them together
and seal with tape.*

*4 Cut lengths of tube
to fit snugly around
a T-joint, linking
them with a wedge-shaped
butt joint, and seal with
tape as before.*

LAGGING
YOUR PIPES

When water in a plumbing system is allowed
to freeze, it expands and sometimes splits the
wall of the pipe or forces a joint apart, with
the result that water pours into the house as
soon as the ice melts. It therefore pays to
insulate cold-water pipes in unheated areas of
the building.

CHOOSING INSULATION FOR PIPES

You can wrap pipework in lagging bandages (there are
several types, some of which are self-adhesive), but it is
generally more convenient to use foamed-plastic tubes
designed for the purpose. This is especially true for
pipes close to a wall, which may be awkward to wrap.

Foamed-plastic tubes are made in sizes to fit pipes of
various diameters: the tube walls vary in thickness
from 12 to 20mm (½ to ¾in). More expensive varieties
incorporate a metallic-foil backing that reflects some
of the heat back into hot-water pipes.

1 SPRING THE TUBE
ONTO A PIPE

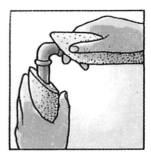

3 CUT MITRES TO ACCOMMODATE
A SOLDERED ELBOW

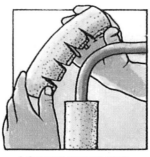

2 CUT THE PLASTIC TUBE
TO FIT A BEND

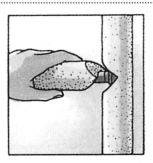

4 CUT A WEDGE-SHAPE BUTT
AT A T-JOINT

STOPPING THAT TAP DRIPPING

There is no need to put up with a dripping tap when it is so easy to replace the washer. Before you dismantle the tap, insert the plug and lay a towel in the bottom of the sink or bath to catch small objects.

TURNING OFF THE WATER

On a modern plumbing system there should be a valve on the supply pipe to the tap which will allow you to turn off the water. On an older system, turn off the main stopcock in order to service the cold-water tap in the kitchen (and other taps under mains pressure). To isolate bathroom taps, cut off the water supply to the storage cistern in the loft by turning off the main stopcock, then open up the taps to drain the cold water.

   To work on a hot-water tap, first turn off the boiler or immersion heater and close the valve on the cold-feed pipe to the hot-water cylinder (usually situated in the airing cupboard). Run the hot taps.

INSIDE A
TRADITIONAL TAP
1 CAPSTAN HEAD
2 METAL SHROUD
3 GLAND NUT
4 SPINDLE
5 HEADGEAR NUT
6 JUMPER
7 WASHER
8 TAP BODY
9 SEAT
10 TAIL

Essential tools
Adjustable wrench
Spanner
Screwdriver

Removing a shrouded head from a tap
On most modern taps the head and cover is in one piece. You will have to remove it to expose the headgear nut. Often a retaining screw is hidden beneath the coloured hot/cold disc in the centre of the head. Prise out the disc with the point of a knife. If there's no retaining screw, simply pull the head off.

FITTING A
NEW WASHER

If the tap is shrouded with a metal cover, unscrew it by hand or use a wrench, taping the jaws in order to protect the chrome finish.

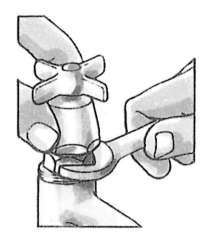

1 Lift up the cover to reveal the headgear nut just above the body of the tap. Slip a narrow spanner onto the nut and unscrew it until you can lift out the entire headgear assembly.

2 The jumper to which the washer is fixed fits into the bottom of the headgear. In some taps the jumper is removed along with the headgear, but in other types it will be lying inside the tap body.

3 The washer itself may be pressed over a small button in the centre of the jumper; in which case, prise it off with a screwdriver.

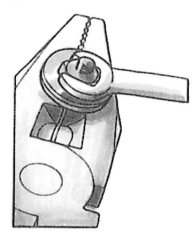

4 If the washer is held in place by a nut, it can be difficult to remove. Allow penetrating oil to soften any corrosion; then, holding the jumper stem with pliers, unscrew the nut with a snug-fitting spanner. (If the nut will not budge, replace both the jumper and the washer.)

Fit a new washer and retaining nut, then reassemble the tap.

FIXING A COLD RADIATOR

If one of your radiators feels cooler at the top than at the bottom, it's likely that a pocket of air has formed in it and is impeding the circulation of the water. Trapped air stops radiators heating up fully, and regular intake of air can cause corrosion. Getting the air out – 'bleeding the radiator' – is a simple matter.

Releasing the air

First switch off the circulation pump – and preferably turn off the boiler too, although that is not vital.

Each radiator has a bleed valve at one of its top corners, identifiable by a square-section shank in the centre of the round blanking plug. You should have been given a key to fit these shanks by the installer; but if not, or if you have inherited an old system, you can buy a key for bleeding radiators at any DIY shop or ironmonger's.

Use the key to turn the shank of the valve anticlockwise about a quarter of a turn. It shouldn't be necessary to turn it further – but have a small container handy to catch spurting water, in case you open the valve too far, plus some rags to mop up water dribbling from the valve. Don't be tempted to speed up the process by opening the valve further than necessary to let the air out – that is likely to produce a deluge of water.

Clearing a blocked valve

If no water or air comes out when you attempt to bleed a radiator, check whether the feed-and-expansion tank in the loft is empty. If the tank is full of water, then the bleed valve is probably blocked with paint.

Close the inlet and outlet valves, at each end of the radiator, then remove the screw from the centre of the bleed valve. Clear the hole with a piece of wire and reopen one of the radiator valves slightly to eject some water from the hole. Close the radiator valve again and refit the screw in the bleed valve. Open both radiator valves and test the bleed valve again.

ALLOW A COUPLE OF HOURS

Essential tools
Radiator key

Dispersing the air pocket in a radiator
You will hear a hissing sound as the air escapes. Keep the key on the shank of the valve – then when the hissing stops and the first dribble of water appears, close the valve tightly.

ALLOW A COUPLE OF HOURS

Essential tools

Tape measure

Brace or power drill

Wood bits

Screwdriver

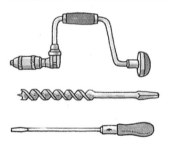

USE A DOOR VIEWER TO CHECK THE IDENTITY OF A CALLER BEFORE OPENING THE DOOR.

MAKING YOUR FRONT DOOR SAFE

It is not a good idea to open your front door to anyone until you know who is calling. It will take you no more than an hour or two to fix a simple peephole viewer that will enable you to see visitors without opening the door, and a strong security chain which will allow you to check their identification before you admit them.

Fitting a viewer

Select a viewer with as wide an angle of vision as possible: you should be able to see someone standing to the side of the door or even crouching below the viewer. Choose one that is adjustable to fit any thickness of door.

Drill a hole the recommended size – usually 12mm (½in) – right through the centre of the door at a comfortable eye level. Insert the barrel of the viewer into the hole from the outside, then screw on the eyepiece from inside.

Attaching a security chain

No special skills are needed to fit a door chain. Fix it securely, just below the lock, by screwing the metal plates to the door and frame.

FACELIFT FOR AN OLD FIREPLACE

A traditional fireplace comprises a wooden or painted-metal surround which usually encloses a cast-iron grate. When open fires were the only form of heating, the grate was polished daily with 'black lead', a soft paste made with graphite which nowadays is supplied in toothpaste-like tubes. It produces an attractive silver-black finish that is ideal for highlighting decorative details, but it is not a permanent or durable finish and will have to be renewed periodically. However, since it is easy to apply this is not an arduous chore.

ALLOW A COUPLE OF HOURS

Essential tools
Old toothbrush

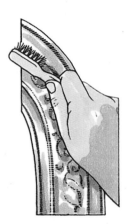

Applying grate polish
Squeeze some polish onto a soft cloth and spread it onto the metal; for best coverage, use an old toothbrush to scrub it into decorative details.

When you have covered the grate, buff the polish to a satin sheen with a clean, dry cloth. Several applications of grate polish makes for a moisture-resistant finish, but it won't prevent rust spots forming if, for example, you accidentally spray the grate when watering pot plants.

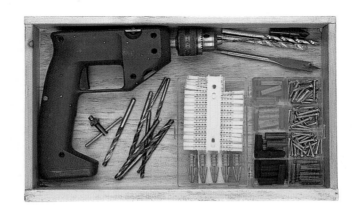

2

A MORNING'S WORK

Putting up curtain rails
28
Hanging blinds
31
Fitting a better lock
34
Getting a toilet cistern
to flush
36
Fitting a new carpet
38
New flooring for your
kitchen or bathroom
40
Stripping old wallpaper
44
Reviving your furniture
46
Looking after
garden furniture
47

Essential tools

Hammer

Masonry bit

Power drill

Screwdriver

Spirit level

Tape measure

Wood bits

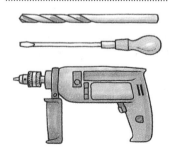

A TRADITIONAL-STYLE BRASS CURTAIN POLE CAN SUPPORT HEAVY DRAPES AND LEND PERIOD CHARM TO AN INTERIOR SCHEME.

PUTTING UP CURTAIN RAILS

Window treatments play an important part in the design of any interior and, although the overall size and shape of your windows are fixed, you can emphasize or modify their proportions by careful dressing with curtains. Curtains also provide privacy and help to insulate a room from the sun, cold draughts and noise. Curtains can be bought ready-made in a variety of fabrics and sizes, or you can make your own.

The fabrics you choose for curtaining can make a dramatic difference to an interior, but the method you adopt for hanging curtains can contribute to the decorative style and overall effect, too.

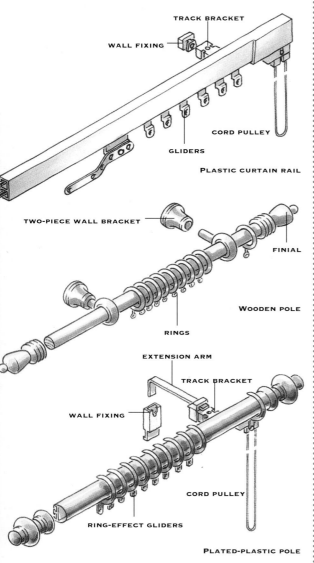

TRACK BRACKET

WALL FIXING

CORD PULLEY

GLIDERS

PLASTIC CURTAIN RAIL

TWO-PIECE WALL BRACKET

FINIAL

WOODEN POLE

RINGS

EXTENSION ARM

TRACK BRACKET

WALL FIXING

CORD PULLEY

RING-EFFECT GLIDERS

PLATED-PLASTIC POLE

Modern curtain rails

Modern rails are made from plastic, aluminium or painted steel. They are available in various styles and lengths and come complete with fixing brackets and glider rings or hooks. Some are supplied ready-corded, which makes drawing curtains easier and protects them from hand soiling.

Although typically used in straight lengths, most rails can be shaped to fit a bay window. Depending on the tightness of the bends, more brackets may be required when fitting a plastic rail into a bay than for metal types. Rails vary in rigidity, which dictates the minimum radius to which they can be bent. Plastic bends more easily when warm.

Traditional-style poles

The curtain poles that were a feature of heavily draped Victorian interiors have become a popular alternative to the low-key track systems of modern times. Made from metal, plastic or wood, they come in a range of plated, painted or polished finishes. Traditional poles are supported on decoratively shaped brackets and are fitted with end-stop finials and large curtain rings. Some designs now conceal corded tracks to provide the convenience of modern curtain rails while retaining old-world charm.

Two wall-mounted decorative brackets are normally used to support curtain poles, but a central bracket may be required to support heavy fabrics or long poles. Plated-plastic tracked versions with ring-effect gliders are available in a range of lengths and are mounted on angle brackets. Light-weight slim poles are also made for sheer curtains or nets. These are fitted with side-fixing or face-fixing sockets.

SCREWING A RAIL OR POLE TO THE WALL

Draw a guideline at a suitable height above the window opening, then plot the positions for the brackets along the line. Drill holes for wall plugs when you are fixing into masonry walls. The screws must penetrate right into the structural material, not just into the plaster. Screw directly into the wood framing of a partition wall, and use self-tapping screws or cavity fixings for metal lintels.

If it proves difficult to get a secure fixing at all the marked positions, screw a 25mm (1in) thick batten to the wall on which to mount the brackets. You can paint the batten to match the wall or cover it with wallpaper.

In some cases, you can screw light-weight fixing brackets directly to the wooden architrave of a traditional sliding sash or casement window.

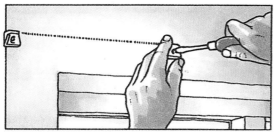

ALIGN THE BRACKETS WITH A LINE MARKED ON THE WALL

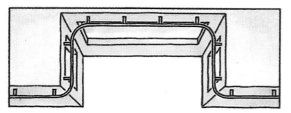

SUPPORTING THE RAIL IN A BAY WINDOW
FIX A RAIL-SUPPORT BRACKET ON EACH SIDE OF A BEND.

FIXING TO THE CEILING

In a modern house it may be more convenient to mount curtain track on the ceiling.

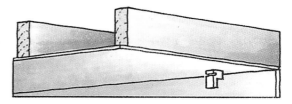

1 Joists that run at right angles to the wall provide a fixing for placing curtain track at any distance from the wall. Drill pilot holes into the joists and screw the brackets in place.

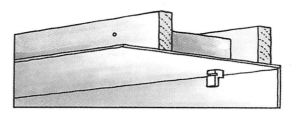

NAIL NOGGINGS BETWEEN JOISTS

2 Joists that run parallel to the wall need noggings nailed between them at the required fixing points. Skew-nail the noggings flush with the ceiling.

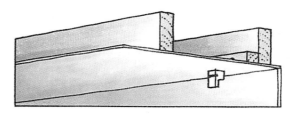

NAIL A BATTEN TO THE JOIST

3 If the required position is close to the original joist, nail a 50 x 50mm (2 x 2in) batten to the face of the joist to provide fixing points for the curtain track.

HANGING BLINDS

ALLOW A WHOLE MORNING

Blinds provide simple, attractive and sometimes sophisticated ways of screening windows. Most are available in standard sizes, but they can be made to measure or cut to size at home. Although simple in appearance, some blinds incorporate refined opening-and-closing mechanisms.

YOU CAN BUY ROLLER BLIND MATERIAL TO EITHER DIFFUSE OUTSIDE LIGHT OR TO BLOCK IT COMPLETELY. VENETIAN BLINDS PROVIDED MORE CONTROL OF THE LIGHT LEVEL BUT ARE OFTEN MORE EXPENSIVE.

Essential tools

Tape measure

Spirit level

Power drill

Masonry bits

Wood bits

Screwdriver

Hammer

Pliers

Tenon saw

Scissors

EASY-TO-FIT ROLLER BLINDS

A wide range of low-cost roller blinds can be bought in kit form. A typical kit consists of a wooden roller with two end caps, one of them spring-loaded to work the blind, two support brackets, a narrow lath, and a pull cord with a knob. Similar kits have aluminium rollers with a different type of return mechanism. Rollers come in several lengths; unless you find one that fits your window exactly, get the next largest size and cut it to the required length. You can buy fabric separately and cut it to width and length.

Fitting a wooden roller
If you decide to fit the roller inside the window recess, place the brackets in the top corners of the window frame. Remove the right-hand end cap by pulling out the round pin from the roller. Cut the roller to fit between the brackets, replace the cap and drive in the pin.

If you want to hang the roller outside the window recess, cut the roller 100mm (4in) longer than the width of the opening. Fit the brackets by drilling and plugging the wall.

Attaching the fabric
Roller-blind fabric must be non-fraying to avoid hems at the sides, and it should be cut precisely or it will not run evenly on the roller. Cut the width to fit between the two end caps, and the length to cover the window plus an extra 200mm (8in).

Make a bottom hem 6mm (¼in) wide, then turn it up to form a sleeve for the lath. Glue and tack the other end of the fabric to the roller, taking care to align the top edge with the roller's axis. Fix the pull cord to the lath with the small screws provided.

Adjusting the roller action
To adjust a spring-loaded action, hold the roller with its flat peg on the left and roll the fabric up so that it hangs from the roller's far side. Place the roller in the brackets and unroll the blind completely; then make it return by giving it a slight pull to release the spring catch. If it returns sluggishly, pull it halfway down, then lift it off the brackets, roll it up fully by hand and replace it. If it now flies back too violently, take the rolled-up blind off the brackets, unwind it a little and replace it.

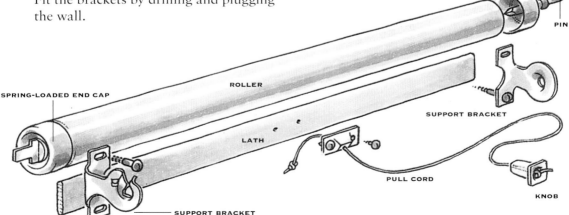

PLAIN END CAP

PIN

ROLLER

SPRING-LOADED END CAP

SUPPORT BRACKET

LATH

PULL CORD

KNOB

SUPPORT BRACKET

COMPONENTS OF A TYPICAL SPRING-LOADED ROLLER KIT

VENETIAN BLINDS

Horizontal blinds, or Venetian blinds as they are more often called, provide a stylish treatment for most windows. They come in a range of standard sizes, and can be made to measure. They are usually made of metal and are available in a range of coloured finishes, including special effects such as mirror, marble and perforated slats. Wooden-slat versions are also made.

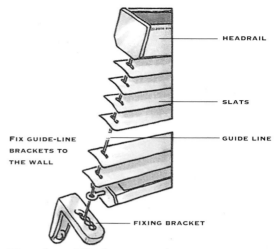

HEADRAIL

SLATS

GUIDE LINE

FIX GUIDE-LINE BRACKETS TO THE WALL

FIXING BRACKET

Hanging a blind at an angle
Venetian blinds can be specified for use on a sloping window. Thread the guide lines (they prevent the blind sagging) through holes punched in the slats. These lines are fixed at each end to the headrail and are held taut by fixing brackets at the bottom.

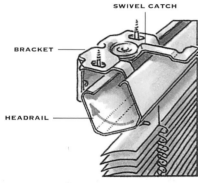

SWIVEL CATCH

BRACKET

HEADRAIL

LOCATE THE HEADRAIL ON BRACKETS

Putting up a Venetian blind
If you plan to hang the blind in a window recess, measure the width at the top and bottom of the opening. If the dimensions differ, use the smaller one. Allow about 9mm (⅜in) clearance at each end. Screw the fixing brackets in place so that the blind, when hanging, will clear any window catches or handles. Set the end brackets about 75mm (3in) in from the ends of the blind's headrail.

Mount the headrail in the brackets. Some are simply clamped, while others are locked in place by a swivel catch on each bracket. Raise and lower the blind to check the mechanism is working freely. To lower the blind, pull the cord across the front of the blind, to release the lock mechanism, and let it slide through your hand. Tilt the slats by rotating the control wand.

SOGHISTICATED VERTICAL BLINDS
Like Venetian blinds, vertical blinds suit simple modern interiors and work well with large picture windows and patio doors. The blinds hang from an aluminium headtrack that houses the mechanism and is fixed to brackets screwed to the wall or ceiling; the vanes are simply clipped into hooks on the headtrack and linked together by short chains at the bottom. Weights fitted into bottom pockets ensure that the vanes hang straight.

Fixing the track
Mark a guide line on the wall, ceiling or window soffit. Allow sufficient clearance for the rotating vanes to clear obstacles such as window or door handles. Drill, plug and screw the mounting brackets in place and clip the track into the brackets.

Hang the preassembled vanes on the headtrack hooks, first checking that the hooks are facing the same way and that you are attaching the vanes with the seams facing in the same direction.

Essential tools

Brace or power drill
Bradawl
Chisel
Craft knife
G-cramp
Mallet
Marking gauge
Padsaw or jigsaw
Screwdriver
Try square
Wood bits

Night latch

This type of lock alone does not provide adequate security.

Mortise sashlock

Suitable for back and side doors that are used frequently.

FITTING A BETTER LOCK

The door by which you leave the house – usually the front door – needs a particularly strong lock, because it can't be bolted from inside except when you are at home. Don't rely entirely on an old-fashioned night latch, which offers no security at all – it is only as strong as the screws holding it to the door, and a thief can easily break a pane of glass to operate it or simply slide back the bolt with a credit card. Fit a mortise lock, inserted into a slot cut in the edge of the door, where it cannot easily be tampered with. There are various patterns to suit the width of the door stile and the location of the door.

Mortise lock
Use this type of lock on your front door.
1 LOCK BODY
2 FACEPLATE
3 STRIKING PLATE

Selecting the right mortise lock

A mortise sashlock is suitable for back and side doors. It has a handle on each side that operates a springbolt, and a key-operated deadbolt which can't be pushed back once the door is closed. Purely key-operated mortise locks are best for final-exit doors where no handle is necessary. Any exterior-door lock should conform to BS 3621: this is a British Standard which ensures that the lock has a minimum of 1000 key variations, is proof against 'picking' and is strong enough to resist drilling, cutting or forcing. Some locks are intended for right-hand opening doors.

INSERTING THE LOCK

Wedge the door open, so that you can work conveniently on the closing edge.

1 Scribe a line centrally on the edge of the door with a marking gauge, and use the lock body as a template to mark the top and bottom of the mortise.

2 Choose a drill bit that matches the thickness of the lock-body and drill out the majority of the waste wood within marked lines. Square up the edges of the mortise with a chisel until the lock fits snugly in the slot.

3 Mark around the edge of the faceplate with a knife, then chop a series of shallow cuts across the waste wood with a chisel. Pare out the recess until the faceplate (including its thin brass coverplate, if fitted) is flush with the edge of the door.

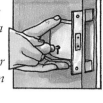

4 Hold the lock against the face of the door and mark the centre of the keyhole with a bradawl. Clamp a block of scrap timber to the other side of the door over the keyhole position and drill right through on the centre mark (the block prevents the drill bit splintering the face of the door as it bursts through on the other side). Using a padsaw or power jigsaw, cut out a slot for the keyhole on both sides of the door.

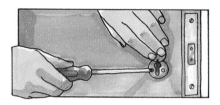

5 Screw the lock into its recess and check its operation, then attach its coverplate. Finally, screw the escutcheons over the keyholes.

6 With the door closed, operate the bolt; it may incorporate a marking device to gauge the position of the striking plate on the doorframe. If it doesn't have a marking device, shoot the bolt fully open, then push the door to and draw round the bolt on the face of the frame.

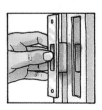

7 Mark out and cut the mortise and recess for the striking plate, as described for the mortise lock itself.

ALLOW A WHOLE MORNING

Essential tools

Adjustable wrench

Pliers

Three-part siphon
This type of siphon can be dismantled for replacement of the flap valve without having to shut off the water or drain the cistern.

Inside your cistern☞
The components of a direct-action WC cistern.

1 OVERFLOW
2 FLOAT
3 FLOAT ARM
4 FLOAT VALVE
5 ONE-PIECE SIPHON
6 WIRE LINK
7 FLUSHING LEVER
8 FLAP VALVE
9 PERFORATED PLATE
10 SEALING WASHER
11 RETAINING NUT
12 FLUSH-PIPE CONNECTOR

GETTING A TOILET CISTERN TO FLUSH

When you depress the flushing lever on your toilet cistern, it lifts a perforated plastic or metal plate at the bottom of an inverted U-bend tube (siphon) that is fixed to the base of the cistern. As the plate rises, the perforations are sealed by a flexible plastic diaphragm (flap valve), so that the plate can displace a body of water over the U-bend to promote a siphoning action. The water pressure behind the diaphragm lifts it again so that the contents of the cistern flow up through the perforations in the plate, over the U-bend and down the flush pipe. As the water level in the cistern drops, so does the float, opening the float valve to refill the cistern.

If the cistern will not flush until the lever is operated several times, the flap valve probably needs replacing. If the flushing lever feels slack, check that the wire link at the end of the flushing arm is intact.

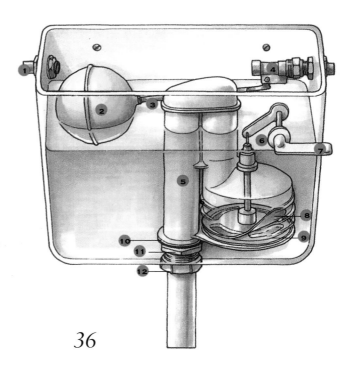

CHANGING THE FLAP VALVE

If the WC cistern will not flush first time, take off the lid and check that the water level is up to the internal mark and that the flushing lever is actually operating the mechanism. If it seems to be working normally, replace the flap valve in the siphon.

1 Before you service a one-piece siphon, shut off the water by tying the float arm to a stout batten placed across the cistern. Flush the cistern.

2 Use a large wrench to unscrew the nut that holds the flush pipe to the underside of the cistern. Move the pipe to one side.

3 Release the remaining nut which clamps the siphon to the base of the cistern. A little water will run out as you loosen the nut, so have a bucket handy. (The siphon may be bolted to the base of the cistern instead of being clamped by a single retaining nut.) Disconnect the flushing arm and ease the siphon out of the cistern.

4 Lift the plastic diaphragm off the metal plate and replace it with one of the same size. Reassemble the entire flushing mechanism in the reverse order and attach the flush pipe to the cistern.

TIP ● ● ● ● ● ● ● ● ● ● ● ● ● ●
Making a new wire link
Retrieve the pieces of broken link from the cistern, then bend a new link from a piece of thick wire. If you have thin wire only, twist the ends together with pliers to make a temporary repair.

Essential tools

Bolster

Craft knife

Hammer

Junior hacksaw

Knee kicker

Scissors

Straightedge

Using a knee kicker
The only special tool required for laying carpet is a knee kicker for stretching it. It has a toothed head, which is pressed into the carpet while you nudge the end with your knee. You can hire a knee kicker from a carpet supplier.

FITTING A NEW CARPET

Some people prefer to loose-lay carpet, relying on the weight of furniture to stop it moving around. However, a properly stretched and fixed carpet looks much better and, provided you are carpeting a fairly simple rectangular room, it isn't difficult to accomplish.

WHY UNDERLAY IS IMPORTANT

A carpet benefits from a resilient cushion laid between it and the floor – it is more comfortable to walk on and the carpet lasts longer. Without an underlay, the divisions between the floorboards will begin to show as dirty marks on a pale carpet as dust from the gaps begins to emerge.

An underlay can be a thick felt or a layer of foamed rubber or plastic. When you buy a foam-backed or rubber-backed carpet, the underlay is an integral part of the floorcovering. In theory, rubber-backed or foam-backed carpets need no additional underlay, but floorboards can still show through cheaper qualities.

In addition, it is worth laying rolls of brown paper or synthetic-fibre sheet over the floor to stop dust and grit working their way into an underlay and to prevent rubber-backed carpet sticking to the floor.

HOW TO FIX YOUR CARPET TO THE FLOOR

LAYING THE CARPET

There are different methods for holding a carpet firmly in place, depending on the type of carpet you are laying.

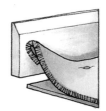

Carpet tacks
Along each edge of the carpet, a 50mm (2in) strip is folded under and nailed to a wooden floor with improved cut tacks about every 200mm (8in). You can usually cover the tack head by rubbing the pile with your fingertips. When using this method, the underlay should be laid 50mm (2in) short of the skirting to allow the carpet to lie flat along the edge.

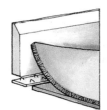

Gripper strips
These wooden or metal strips have fine metal teeth which grip the woven foundation. They are not really suitable for rubber-backed carpets, although they are used. Nail the strips to the floor, 6mm (¼in) from the skirting, with the teeth pointing towards the wall. Cut short strips to fit carpet into doorways and alcoves. Glue gripper strips to a concrete floor. Cut underlay up to the edge of each strip.

Double-sided tape
Use adhesive tape for rubber-backed carpets only. Stick 50mm (2in) tape around the perimeter of the room; then, when you are ready to fix the carpet, peel off the protective paper layer from the adhesive tape.

If you are laying a separate underlay, join neighbouring sections with short strips of carpet tape or secure them with a few tacks to stop them moving.

Roll out the carpet, butting one machine-cut edge against a wall, and fix that edge to the floor; make sure that any pattern runs parallel to the main axis of the room.

Stretch the carpet to the wall directly opposite and temporarily fix it with tacks, or slip it onto gripper strips. Don't cut the carpet yet. Work from the centre towards each corner, stretching and fixing the carpet, then do the same at the other sides of the room.

Cut a triangular notch at each corner so that the carpet will lie flat. Adjust the carpet until it is stretched evenly, then fix it permanently. When you are using tape or gripper strips, press the carpet into the angle between skirting and floor with a bolster chisel; trim with a knife held at 45 degrees to the skirting. Tuck the cut edge behind the strip with the bolster.

Fitting a threshold bar across the door
Cut the carpet to fit around the doorframe on both sides of the opening, and make a straight cut from one side to the other. Fit a single- or double-sided threshold bar over the cut edge of the carpet.

TOP
DOUBLE THRESHOLD BAR
BOTTOM
SINGLE THRESHOLD BAR

Essential tools

Adhesive spreader

Bolster

Craft knife

Home-made scriber

Scissors

Straightedge

Sheet vinyl is available in a wide range of colours and patterns. To ensure it lays as flat as possible, leave the vinyl in the room for 24 to 48 hours before laying it, preferably opened flat or at least stood on end, loosely rolled.

NEW FLOORING FOR YOUR KITCHEN OR BATHROOM

Sheet vinyl is ideal wall-to-wall floorcovering for kitchens, utility rooms and bathrooms, where you are bound to spill water from time to time. It is straightforward to lay if you follow a systematic routine.

Unbacked vinyl

Sheet vinyl is made by sandwiching the printed pattern between a base of PVC and a clear protective PVC covering. All vinyls are relatively hard-wearing, but some have a thicker, reinforced protective layer to increase their durability; ask your supplier which type will suit your needs best. There is a vast range of colours, patterns and textures from which to choose.

Backed vinyl

Backed vinyl has similar properties to the unbacked type, with the addition of a resilient underlay to make it softer and warmer to walk on. The backing is usually a cushion of foamed PVC.

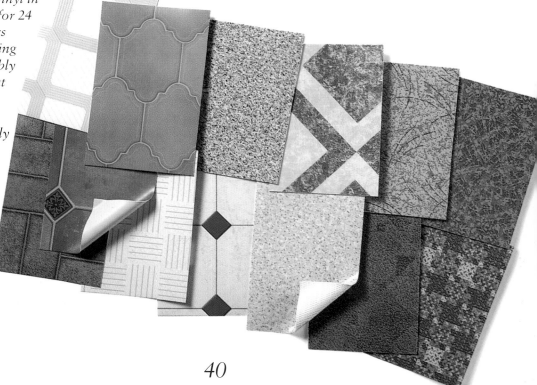

LAYING SHEET VINYL

Before you lay a sheet of vinyl floor-covering, make sure the floor is flat and dry. Vacuum the surface and nail down any loose floorboards. Take out any unevenness by screeding a concrete floor or hardboarding a wooden one. A concrete floor must have a damp-proof membrane; a ground-level wooden floor must be ventilated below. Don't lay vinyl over boards that have recently been treated with wood preserver.

1 Assuming there are no seams, start by fitting the vinyl against the longest wall first. Pull the vinyl away from the wall by approximately 35mm (1½in); make sure it is parallel with the wall or the main axis of the room. Drive a nail through a wooden lath about 50mm (2in) from one end, and use the nailed lath to scribe a line following the skirting. Cut the vinyl with a knife or scissors and slide the sheet up against the wall.

To get the rest of the sheet to lie as flat as possible, cut a triangular notch at each corner. Make a straight cut down to the floor at external corners. Remove as much waste as possible, leaving 50 to 75mm (2 to 3in) turned up all round.

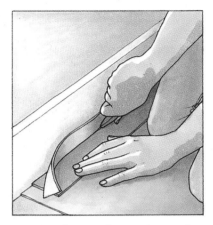

2 Press the vinyl into the angle between skirting and floor with a bolster. Align a metal straightedge with the crease and run along it with a sharp knife held at a slight angle to the skirting. If your trimming is less than perfect, nail a cover strip of quadrant moulding to the skirting.

Fit the vinyl around the doorframe by creasing it against the floor and trimming the waste. Make a straight cut across the opening and fit a threshold bar over the edge of the sheet.

Modern vinyls can be loose-laid but you may prefer to glue the edges, especially along a door opening. Peel back the edge and spread a band of the recommended flooring adhesive with a toothed spreader, or use a 50mm (2in) wide double-sided adhesive tape.

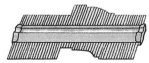

Profile gauge
A profile gauge is a useful tool for copying the shape of door mouldings or pipework; it provides a pattern that helps you fit soft flooring accurately.

Fitting vinyl flooring around doorways
Cut a notch at each of the corners and trim around the doorframe.

Cutting around a toilet or washbasin
To fit around a WC pan or basin pedestal, fold back the sheet and pierce it with a knife just above floor level; draw the blade up towards the edge of the sheet. Make triangular cuts around the base, gradually working around the curve until the vinyl sheet can lie flat on the floor. Crease and cut off the waste.

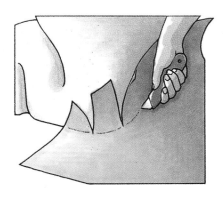

Joining strips of vinyl
If you have to join widths of vinyl, scribe one edge to the wall, then overlap the free edge with the second sheet until the pattern matches exactly. Cut through both pieces with a knife, then remove the waste strips. Without moving the sheets, fold back both cut edges, apply tape or flooring adhesive and press the join together.

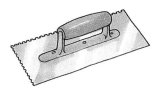

SERRATED TROWEL

VINYL FLOORING IS THE IDEAL CHOICE FOR KITCHENS.
SOME MANUFACTURERS, PARTICULARLY OF THE MORE
EXPENSIVE RANGES, RECOMMEND THAT YOU HAVE IT
PROFESSIONALLY FITTED. HOWEVER, IF YOU FOLLOW
THE INSTRUCTIONS SET OUT ON THE PREVIOUS PAGES
SHEET VINYL IS VERY SIMPLE TO CUT AND LAY.

ALLOW A WHOLE MORNING

Essential tools

Large paintbrush

Scraper

Paper scorer

Steam stripper

Steam stripper
You can hire a large industrial model or buy a lightweight steam stripper with its own reservoir. Hold the tool's sole plate against the wall until the steam penetrates and softens the wallpaper, then remove it with a scraper. Wash the stripped wall to remove traces of paste.

See also:
Painting the ceiling, page 56
Painting the living room, page 92
Papering the ceiling, page 54
Papering the spare room, page 104
Patching up damaged plaster, page 74

STRIPPING OLD WALLPAPER

Because scraping off old wallcoverings is a necessary preliminary to practically all decorating schemes, it is included here as a project in its own right. Provided the room is not too big and there are no unexpected snags, it should not take you more than half a day to scrape off conventional wallpaper. Stripping specialized wallcoverings or painted wallpaper may take a little longer. Add an appropriate length of time to your decorating schedule.

Eradicating mould growth
Where mould growth is affecting wallpaper, soak it with a warm water-and-bleach solution, then scrape off the paper and burn it. Wash the wall with fresh bleach solution.

SCRAPING OFF THE PAPER

To soften the old wallpaper paste, soak the paper with warm water mixed with a little washing-up liquid, or use a proprietary stripping powder or liquid.

Conventional wallpaper

Apply the water with a sponge or house-plant sprayer. Repeat and leave the water to penetrate for 15 to 20 minutes.

Use a wide metal-bladed scraper to lift the softened paper, starting at the seams. Take care not to dig the points of the blade into the plaster. Resoak stubborn areas of paper and leave them for a few minutes before stripping.

Electricity and water are a lethal combination: where possible, dry-strip around switches and sockets. If the paper cannot be stripped dry, switch off the power at the consumer unit when you come to strip around electrical fittings, and unscrew the faceplates so that you can get at the paper trapped behind them. Do not use a sprayer near electrical accessories.

Collect all the stripped paper in plastic sacks, then wash the wall with warm water containing a little detergent.

Scoring a washable wallpaper

Washable wallpaper has an impervious surface film, which you must break through to allow the water to penetrate to the adhesive.

Use a wire brush or a serrated scraper to score the surface, then soak it with warm water and stripper. It may take several applications of the liquid before the paper begins to lift.

Stripping painted wallcoverings

Use a wire brush or home-made scorer to scratch the surface, then soak the paper with warm water plus a little paper stripper. Painted papers (and washables, too) can easily be stripped using a steam stripper (see opposite). Hold the stripper's sole plate against the paper until the steam penetrates, then remove the soaked paper with a wide-bladed scraper.

Peeling vinyl wallcoverings

Vinyl wallcovering consists of a thin layer of vinyl fused with a paper backing. To remove the vinyl, lift both bottom corners of the top layer of the wallcovering, then pull firmly and steadily away from the wall. Either soak and scrape off the backing paper or, if you want to leave it as a lining paper, smooth the seams with medium-grade abrasive paper, using very light pressure to avoid wearing a hole.

Painting over old wallpaper

For best results, it is always best to strip off an old wallcovering before you hang a new one. However, if the existing paper is perfectly sound, you can paint it with emulsion or oil paints (but be warned: it will be more difficult to remove in the future). Strong reds, greens or blues may show through the paint, as will a pattern printed with metallic inks; mask them by applying an aluminium spirit-based sealer. Do not paint vinyl wallcoverings, except for blown vinyl.

A home-made wallpaper scorer
Drive some nails through a block of softwood measuring about 150 x 125 x 25mm (6 x 5 x 1in), so that the points just protrude.

Essential tools
Paintbrush

Choosing polish
A good polish should be a blend of beeswax and a hard polishing wax such as carnauba. Some contain silicones to make it easier to achieve a high gloss. Polishes range from practically colourless to various shades of brown, which are used to darken the wood.

You can buy flat tins of polish with a thick paste-like consistency. Alternatively, use a liquid wax polish which you can brush onto the wood.

Although it is very attractive, wax polish is not a hard-wearing finish and should be used indoors only.

REVIVING YOUR FURNITURE

It is no secret that a lot of DIY projects represent hard work, but wax polishing furniture is not one of them. It's a rewarding job, and one that is so easy to accomplish that even complete beginners are able to achieve excellent results. A wax polish will preserve and maintain another finish, or can be used as a finish itself.

Polishing new wood
If you want to wax-polish a new piece of furniture or a piece you have stripped back to bare wood, seal it first with one coat of clear varnish (or French polish on fine furniture). This will stop the wax polish being absorbed too deeply into the wood and provides a slightly more durable finish.

Cleaning off old polish
Before waxing old furniture, clean it first to remove deposits of dirt and possibly an old wax dressing. Dip very fine wire wool into white spirit and rub in the direction of the grain. Don't press too hard – as you want only to remove wax and dirt, without damaging the finish below. Wipe the cleaned surface with a cloth dampened with white spirit, and leave to dry before repolishing.

Applying the polish
Apply one coat of paste wax polish with a soft-cloth pad. About 15 minutes later, use a ball of very fine wire wool to apply another coat, rubbing in the direction of the grain. After about four or five coats, leave the wax to harden overnight before burnishing with a duster.

If you prefer to use liquid wax, brush on an initial sealer coat; then an hour later pour more polish onto a cloth pad and rub it in with a circular motion. Follow up by rubbing parallel with the wood grain. Add a third coat if required. Leave the polish to harden overnight, then bring to a high gloss by burnishing vigorously with a soft duster.

LOOKING AFTER GARDEN FURNITURE

Good-quality wooden furniture is made to stand outside for years without any noticeable deterioration. However, it pays to check it over during early spring to make sure it is in good condition, so you can enjoy the garden as soon as the weather warms up.

Make sure the joints are sound and tighten up any bolts or screw fixings. Use fine wire wool or an abrasive nylon pad to remove traces of mould growth or tree resin, and then touch up the finish if it is showing signs of wear or looks dry and dowdy.

If old varnish or paint is starting to flake or split, it may be worth stripping it with a chemical paint remover so you can apply a finishing oil instead (see right). A modern oil finish is ideal for exterior furniture and joinery: it is easy to apply and requires no more than annual maintenance to protect any wood from weathering and to preserve its appearance. Suitable finishes are usually marketed as Danish oil or teak oil.

If your furniture is already oiled, treat all surfaces with one coat of fresh oil and wipe off the excess immediately.

ALLOW A WHOLE MORNING

Essential tools
Paintbrush

Oiling stripped wood
The most efficient way to apply a finishing oil to bare wood is to rub it in with a pad of soft, lint-free rag. Don't store oily rags: keep them in a sealed tin while the job is in progress, then unfold them and leave them outside to dry before throwing them away.

A brush is a convenient way to spread oil over large surfaces and into carvings or mouldings.

Rub or brush a generous coating of oil into the wood grain. Leave it to soak in for 10 to 15 minutes, then wipe off excess oil with a clean cloth. After about six hours, coat the wood with oil once more. The next day, apply a third and final coat; raise a faint sheen by burnishing with a soft duster.

3

A WHOLE DAY

Making windows
burglarproof
50

Papering the ceiling
54

Painting the ceiling
56

Mending creaking stairs
58

Draughtproofing your doors
62

Sealing up draughty
windows
66

Putting up new shelving
68

Patching up damaged
plaster
74

Insulating your loft
78

Quick-and-easy double
glazing
81

ALLOW ONE WHOLE DAY

Essential tools

Chisel

Drill bits

Hammer

Mallet

Marking gauge

Power drill

Screwdriver

Try square

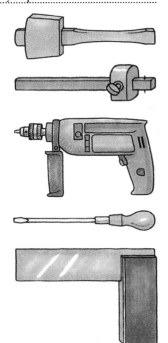

MAKING WINDOWS BURGLARPROOF

Windows are a common means of entry for burglars – so make sure they are adequately secured, especially if they are on the ground floor or can be reached easily. There are all sorts of locks for wooden and metal windows, including some that lock automatically when you close the window. Locks for attaching to metal window frames are rather more difficult to fit, as you may have to cut threads for the screw fixings.

CHOOSING THE RIGHT LOCK

The type of lock suitable for a window depends on how the window opens. Sliding sashes are normally secured by locking them together, whereas casements – which open like doors – should be fastened to the outer window frame or locked by rendering the catches and stays immovable. Whichever type of lock you choose, it makes sense to buy the best you can afford for the more vulnerable windows and to spend less on ones that are especially difficult to reach.

Any window lock must be strong enough to resist forcing and has to be situated correctly for optimum security. On small windows, for example, fit a single lock as close as possible to the centre of the meeting rail or vertical stile; on larger windows, you will need two locks, spaced apart.

Locks that can only be released by a removable key are the most secure. Some keys will open any lock of the same design (an advantage in that you need fewer keys, although some burglars may carry a range of standard keys). With other locks, there will be several key variations.

Wooden windows need to be fairly substantial to accommodate mortise locks, so surface-mounted locks are often used. These are quite adequate and, being visible, act as a deterrent.

If the fixing screws are not concealed when the lock is in place, drill out the centre of the screws once fitted, so they cannot be withdrawn.

LOCKING A SASH WINDOW

There are two effective ways to prevent a forced entry through a sliding sash window. You can either use dual screws to immobilize both sashes or restrict their movement with sash stops.

Fitting dual screws
A dual screw consists of a bolt that passes through both meeting rails. The screw is operated by a special key, and there is little to see when the window is closed.

BOLT RECEIVERS   BOLT   KEY

1 To fit a dual screw, with the window shut and the catch engaged, drill through the inner meeting rail into the outer one. Wrap tape around the drill bit to gauge the depth accurately.

2 Slide the sashes apart and tap the two bolt-receiving devices into their respective holes. Close the window and insert the threaded bolt with the key until it is flush with the window frame. If need be, saw the bolt to length.

Installing sash stops
When the bolt is withdrawn with a key, a sash stop fitted to each side of a window allows it to be opened slightly for ventilation. As well as deterring burglars, sash stops prevent small children from opening the window any further.

1 To fit a stop, drill a hole in the upper sash for the bolt then screw the faceplate over it (on close-fitting sashes, you will probably have to recess the faceplate).

2 Screw the protective plate to the top edge of the lower sash to prevent the bolt bruising the wood.

Where to place window locks
The arrows indicate the best positions for window locks.

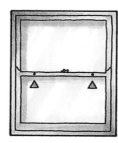

LOCKING A CASEMENT WINDOW

A locking bolt can be fitted to a wooden window frame: the bolt is engaged by turning a simple catch, but it can only be released with a removable key.

Fitting a surface-mounted casement lock
With the lock body screwed to the part of the window that opens, mark and cut a small mortise in the fixed frame for the bolt; then screw on the coverplate.

A similar device for metal windows is a clamp which, when fixed to the opening part of the casement, shoots a bolt that hooks over the fixed frame.

Locking the handle
A cockspur handle, which secures the opening edge of the casement to the fixed frame, can be locked by means of an extending bolt that you screw to the frame, just below the handle. However, ensure that the handle is not worn or loose – otherwise the lock may be ineffective.

Lockable handles, that will allow you to secure a window which is left ajar for ventilation, can be substituted in place of a standard handle.

LOCKING FANLIGHT WINDOWS

You can buy a variety of casement-type locks, as well as devices that secure the stay to the window frame. The simplest kind is screwed below the stay arm to receive a key-operated bolt passed through one of the holes in the stay arm. Purpose-made lockable stays are also available.

A better alternative is a device that clamps the window itself to the surrounding frame. Attach the lock first, then use it to position the staple.

THIS TYPE OF LOCK BOLTS THE STAY TO THE WINDOW FRAME

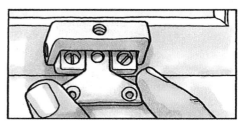

ATTACH THIS TYPE OF LOCK FIRST, THEN SCREW THE STAPLE TO THE FRAME

SECURING FRENCH WINDOWS WITH RACK BOLTS

French windows and other glazed doors are fairly easy to force open – a burglar only has to break a pane to reach the handle inside. Key-operated locks are essential to prevent a break-in.

Fit two rack bolts in the closing edge of a single glazed door. Locate one bolt near the top of the door, the other close to the bottom.

Each door of a double French window needs a bolt at the top and bottom, positioned so that one bolt shoots into the upper frame and the other into the threshold below. It is necessary to take each door off its hinges in order to fit the lower bolt.

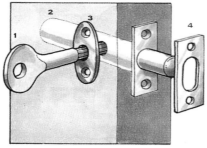

STANDARD
RACK BOLT
1 KEY
2 BARREL
3 KEYHOLE
PLATE
4 LOCKING
PLATE

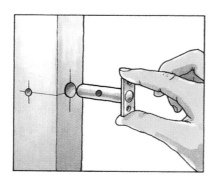

1 Drill a hole – usually 16mm (⅝in) in diameter – for the barrel of the bolt in the edge of the door. Use a try square to transfer the centre of the hole to the inside face of the door. Mark the keyhole and drill it with a 10mm (⅜in) bit, then insert the bolt.

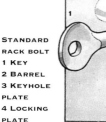

2 With the key holding the bolt in place, mark the recess for the faceplate; then pare out the recess with a chisel. Screw the bolt and keyhole plate to the door. Operate the bolt to mark the frame, then drill a 16mm (⅝in) diameter hole to a depth that matches the length of the bolt. Fit the locking plate over the hole.

TIP • • • • • • • • • • • • • • • •

Locking sliding doors
If you have aluminium sliding doors, fit additional locks at the top and bottom to prevent the sliding frame from being lifted off its track. These locks are costly, but they offer at least a thousand key variations and provide good security.

Essential tools

Craft knife

Paperhanger's brush

Paste brush

Pasting table

Scissors

Seam roller

Tape measure

See also:
Applying the paste, page 107

PAPERING THE CEILING

Papering a ceiling isn't as difficult as you may think: the techniques are basically the same as for papering a wall, except that the strips of paper are usually longer and more unwieldy to hold while you brush them into place. Set up a strong, secure work platform – it's virtually impossible to work from a single stepladder – and enlist a helper to support the folded paper while you position one end and progress backwards across the room. If you have marked out the ceiling first, the result should be faultless.

Marking out the ceiling

If possible, construct a work platform that spans the width of the room. The best type of platform to use is a purpose-made decorator's trestle, but you can manage with a pair of scaffold boards spanning two stepladders.

Now mark the ceiling to give a visual guide to positioning the strips of paper. Ideally, aim to work parallel with the window and away from the light, so you can see what you are doing and so that the light will not highlight the seams between strips. However, if the distance is shorter the other way, you may find it easier to hang the strips in that direction.

Mark a guide line along the ceiling, one roll width minus 12mm (½in) from the side wall, so that the first strip of paper will lap onto the wall.

PUTTING UP THE PAPER

Paste the paper and fold it concertina-fashion. Drape the folded length over a spare roll and carry it to the work platform. You will find it easier if a helper supports the folded paper, leaving both your hands free for brushing it into place.

Hold the strip against the guide line, using a paperhanger's brush to stroke it onto the ceiling. Tap it into the wall angle, then gradually work backwards along the scaffold board, brushing on the paper as your helper unfolds it.

If the ceiling has a cornice, crease and trim the paper at the ends. Otherwise, allow the ceiling paper to lap the walls by 12mm (½in) so that it will be covered by the wallcovering. Work across the ceiling in the same way, butting the lengths of paper together. Cut the final strip roughly to width, and trim into the wall angle.

Papering a ceiling
*The job is much easier
if two people work
together.*

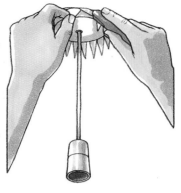

Cutting around a pendant light
Where the paper passes over a ceiling rose, cut several triangular flaps so you can pass the light fitting through the hole. Tap the paper all round the rose with a paperhanger's brush and continue on to the end of the length. Return to the rose and cut off the flaps with a knife.

Papering around a centrepiece
If your ceiling has a decorative plaster centrepiece, work out the position of the strips of paper so that one of the seams will pass through the middle. If you cut long flaps from the side of each strip, you can tuck the paper in all round the plaster moulding and cut the flaps off later.

Supporting pasted paper
If you have to work from a stepladder, your assistant can support the paper on a cardboard tube taped to a broom.

ALLOW ONE WHOLE DAY

Essential tools

Paintbrushes

Paint roller or pad

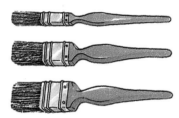

PAINTING THE CEILING

Even the most experienced decorator can't help dripping a little paint – so, unless you are planning to decorate the ceiling and walls of the room with the same colour paint, always paint the ceiling first. Cover the floor with dust sheets, and erect a work platform so you can cover as much of the surface as possible without changing position. For a first-class job, paper the ceiling with lining paper before you paint it.

A LIGHT CEILING CREATES A FEELING OF SPACE AND AIRINESS (ABOVE). DARK DRAMATIC TONES HAVE BEEN USED TO GREAT EFFECT (RIGHT), WHILE THE WHITE-PAINTED CORNICE ADDS LIGHT RELIEF AND DEFINES THE CEILING AREA.

See also:
Painting the living room, page 92
Papering the ceiling, page 54

APPLYING THE PAINT

Seal a dirty, stained ceiling with a general-purpose primer before you apply emulsion; cover heavy nicotine stains with an aluminium spirit-based sealer. You should bind powdery distemper to the ceiling with a white or clear stabilizing primer.

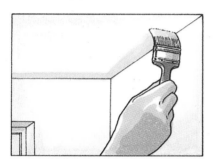

1 Start in a corner near the window and carefully paint along the edges with a small paintbrush. If you are going to paper the walls, brush paint well into the corners between walls and ceiling, covering the top 50mm (2in) of each wall.

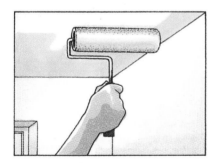

2 Working from the wet edges, paint in bands 600mm (2ft) wide, working away from the light. Whether you use a brush, pad or roller, apply each fresh load of paint just clear of the previous application, then blend in the junctions for even coverage.

If you are using conventional emulsion paint, you will need to apply a second coat to achieve an even coverage.

3 Switch off at the mains before unscrewing a ceiling-rose cover, since you will be exposing electrical connections. With the cover unscrewed, you can paint right up to the backplate with a small brush.

TIP ● ● ● ● ● ● ● ● ● ● ●

Reaching the ceiling
Painting a ceiling is far less tiring if you erect a work platform, using stepladders and planks (see page 54). Alternatively, hire slot-together scaffold frames to construct mobile platforms or fixed towers. Build a tower that compensates for the slope of the staircase when painting the ceiling above a stairwell.

ALLOW ONE WHOLE DAY

Essential tools

Brace or power drill

Chisel

Countersink bit

Hammer

Mallet

Nail punch (nail set)

Plug cutter

Screwdriver

Tenon saw

Wood bits

EXPOSED WOODEN STAIRS ARE VERY
ATTRACTIVE BUT IT IS IMPORTANT TO
CURE CREAKING AND FLEXING
PROBLEMS BEFORE YOU DISPENSE
WITH THE CUSHIONING AND
INSULATION BENEFITS PROVIDED
BY CARPET.

MENDING CREAKING STAIRS

A creaking staircase is an extremely irritating problem, caused by loose boards flexing and rubbing together. The most satisfactory repairs can be achieved by working from underneath the stairs, but if the underside of your staircase is plastered, it is simpler to work from above.

While you are working on the stairs, check the landings for loose floorboards.

WORKING FROM UNDERNEATH THE STAIRS

If it is possible to get to the underside of the staircase, have someone walk slowly up the stairs, counting them out loud. From your position under the stairs, note any loose steps and mark them with chalk. Have your assistant step on and off the ones you've marked while you inspect them to discover the source of the creaking.

Fixing a loose housing joint

If the end of a tread or riser (the vertical part of the step) is loose in its housing, the glued wedges that hold it in place may have worked loose.

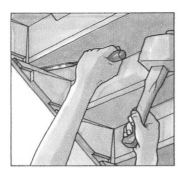

1 Prise out the loose wedges with a chisel. Clean the wedges with sandpaper or, if they are damaged, make new ones from hardwood.

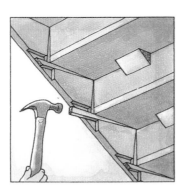

2 Apply woodworking adhesive to the joints and tap the wedges home with a hammer.

Replacing loose blocks

Check the triangular blocks that fit in the angle between the tread and riser. If the adhesive has failed on any of the faces, remove the blocks and clean off the old glue.

1 Before replacing the blocks, prise the shoulder of the tread-to-riser joint slightly open with a chisel, apply new adhesive to it, then pull the joint up tight, using 38mm (1½in) countersunk screws.

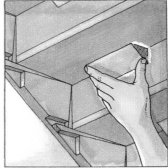

2 Rub the glued blocks into the angle. If suction alone proves to be insufficient, use panel pins to hold the blocks in place while the adhesive sets (try to avoid treading on the repaired steps in the meantime). If some of the blocks are missing, cut new ones from a length of 50 x 50mm (2 x 2in) softwood.

WORKING FROM ABOVE THE STAIRS

To identify where the problems occur, remove the stair carpet and walk slowly up the stairs. When you reach a creaking tread, shift your weight to and fro to discover which part is moving and mark it with chalk.

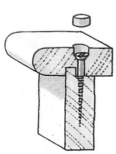

Screwing the nosing

A likely weakness will be the joint between the nosing (front edge of the tread) and the riser. This is normally a tongue-and-groove joint, or possibly a butt joint with a wooden moulding set into the angle between the two.

The easiest solution is to drill clearance holes for 38mm (1½in) countersunk screws directly over the centre line of the riser. Inject woodworking adhesive into the holes and work the joint a little to encourage the glue to spread into it, then pull the joint up tight with the screws. If the screws cannot be concealed by stair carpet, counterbore the holes to set the screw heads below the surface of the tread, then plug the holes with matching wood.

Gluing a loose riser joint

A loose joint at the back of the tread cannot be repaired easily from above. You can try working water-thinned PVA woodworking adhesive into the joint, but you cannot use woodscrews to pull the joint together.

As an alternative, reinforce the joint by gluing a section of 12 x 12mm (½ x ½in) triangular moulding into the angle between the tread and the riser – but for safety's sake don't make the depth of the tread less than 220mm (8¾in). Unless the stair carpet covers the full width of the treads, cut the moulding slightly shorter than the width of the carpet.

Another option is to glue a similar moulding to each step and apply a wood dye to unify the colour.

TIP ●

Curing squeaking floorboards

Over a period of time the flexing of the floor or expansion and contraction of the wood can loosen floorboard nails. The resulting movement of the wood against the nails or adjacent boards produces the annoying squeaks.

Use a nail punch (nail set) and hammer to drive the floorboard nails deeper; this allows the tapered edges of the nails to grip the wood firmly. If nails are missing, secure loose boards with ring-shank nails.

If nailing is not sufficient to hold a warped board in place, use countersunk woodscrews; dampening the wood thoroughly before fixing may help a board to 'give' as you screw it down. Bury the screw heads and cover them with plugs of wood if the floorboards are exposed.

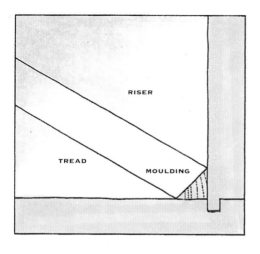

RISER

TREAD

MOULDING

GLUING A LOOSE RISER JOINT

DRAUGHTPROOFING YOUR DOORS

Draughts account for quite a large proportion of the heat lost from your home and are also responsible for a good deal of discomfort. It is therefore worth spending a little money and effort to exclude them from your home. Locate draughts by running the flat of your hand along likely gaps. If you dampen your skin, it will enhance its sensitivity to the cold draughts. Otherwise, wait for a very windy day to conduct your search.

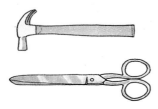

Essential tools

Hacksaw

Hammer

Power drill

Scissors

Screwdriver

Wood bits

EXTERIOR DOORS ARE A NOTORIOUS SOURCE OF HEAT LOSS AND THESE SHOULD BE DRAUGHTPROOFED FIRST. IN ADDITION TO THE EDGES AND THE BOTTOM OF THE DOOR PAY ATTENTION TO KEYHOLES AND LETTERPLATES.

FILLING THE GAP BENEATH THE DOOR

If the gap between the door and floor is very large, it is bound to admit fierce draughts, so it pays to use a threshold excluder to seal the gap. If you fit an excluder to an exterior door, make sure it is suitable; and if you can't buy an excluder that fits the opening exactly, cut a longer one down to size.

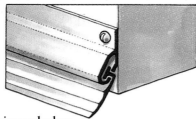

Flexible-strip excluders
The simplest form of threshold excluder is a flexible strip of plastic or rubber that sweeps against the floorcovering to form a seal. The most basic versions are self-adhesive strips that are simply pressed along the bottom of the door, but other types have a rigid-plastic or aluminium extrusion screwed to the door to hold the strip in contact with the floor. This kind of excluder is rarely suitable for exterior doors and quickly wears out. However, it is inexpensive and easy to fit. Most types work best over smooth flooring.

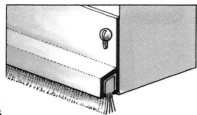

Brush seals
A long nylon-bristle brush set into either a metal or plastic extrusion can be used to exclude draughts under doors. This kind of excluder is suitable for slightly uneven or textured floorcoverings, and can be fitted to hinged or sliding doors.

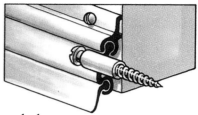

Automatic excluder
The plastic strip and its extruded clip are spring-loaded, so they lift from the floor as the door is opened. When you close the door, the excluder is pressed against the floor by a stop screwed to the doorframe. Suitable for both interior and exterior doors, automatic excluders inflict little wear on floorcoverings.

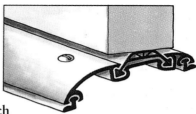

Flexible arch
The aluminium extrusion with its arched vinyl insert presses against the bottom edge of the door. As it has to be nailed or screwed to the floor, it is difficult to use a flexible-arch excluder on a solid-concrete floor. If you plan to fit one on an external door, buy a version that has additional underseals to prevent rain from seeping beneath it. You may have to plane the bottom of the door.

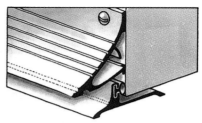

Door kits
The best solution for an exterior door is a kit combining an aluminium weather trim designed to shed rainwater, which is fitted to the door, and a weather bar with a tubular rubber or plastic draught excluder for screwing to the threshold.

SEALING AROUND THE DOOR

A well-fitting door requires a gap of 2mm (1/16in) at top and sides so that it can be operated smoothly. However, a gap this large loses a great deal of heat. There are several ways to seal it, some of which are described here. The cheaper excluders have to be renewed regularly.

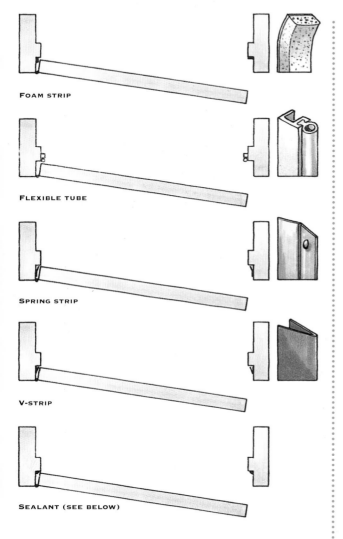

FOAM STRIP

FLEXIBLE TUBE

SPRING STRIP

V-STRIP

SEALANT (SEE BELOW)

FROM TOP TO BOTTOM

Stick-on foam strips
The most straightforward excluder is a self-adhesive foamed-plastic strip, which you stick around the rebate: the strip is compressed by the door, forming a seal. The cheapest polyurethane foam will be good for one or two seasons (although it's useless if painted), but is suitable for interior doors only. The better-quality vinyl-coated polyurethane, rubber or PVC foams are more durable and do not perish on exposure to sunlight, as their cheaper counterparts do. Don't stretch foam excluders when applying them, as that reduces their efficiency. The door may be difficult to close at first, but the excluder will adjust after a short period of use.

Flexible-tube excluders
A small vinyl tube held in a plastic or metal extrusion compresses to fill the gap around the door. The cheapest versions have an integrally moulded flange, which can be stapled to the doorframe, but they are not as neat.

Sprung-leaf strips
Thin metal or plastic strips that have a sprung leaf are either pinned or glued to the doorframe. The top and closing edges of the door brush past the sprung leaf, sealing the gap, while the hinged edge compresses a leaf on that side of the door. This type of draught excluder cannot cope with uneven surfaces unless a foam strip is incorporated on the flexible leaf.

V-strips
A variation on the sprung strip, the leaf is bent right back to form a V-shape. The strip can be mounted to fill the gap around the door or attached to the door stop so that the door closes against it. Most types are cheap and unobtrusive.

● TIP

Draughtproofing sealant
You can effectively seal gaps with a bead of flexible sealant squeezed onto the door stop; a low-tack tape is applied to the surface of the door to act as a release agent. As the door is closed, it flattens the bead, filling the gap perfectly. When the sealant has set, the parting layer of tape is peeled from the door. You can also buy flexible tubing for bonding with sealant to compensate for movement.

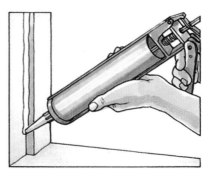

DRAUGHT-PROOFING KEYHOLES AND LETTERBOXES

Make sure the external keyhole for a mortise lock is fitted with a pivoting coverplate to seal out draughts during the winter.

You can buy a hinged flap that screws onto the inner side of the door to cover a letter box. Some types have a brush seal mounted behind the flap to reduce draughts.

Keyhole coverplate
The coverplate is part of the escutcheon.

Brush-seal excluder
*A brush seal neatly draughtproofs
a letter box.*

HAVING DRAUGHTPROOFED THE EXTERIOR DOORS, SEAL ONLY THOSE INTERIOR DOORS THAT CAUSE NOTICEABLE DRAUGHTS (THERE SHOULD BE SOME 'TRICKLE' VENTILATION FROM ROOM TO ROOM).

ALLOW ONE WHOLE DAY

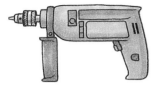

Essential tools

Hacksaw

Hammer

Power drill

Scissors

Screwdriver

Wood bits

HINGED CASEMENT WINDOWS (ABOVE) ARE EASY TO SEAL, USING ANY OF THE EXCLUDERS SUGGESTED FOR FITTING AROUND A DOOR; BUT DRAUGHT-PROOFING A SLIDING SASH WINDOW (RIGHT) PRESENTS A MORE COMPLEX PROBLEM.

See also:
Draughtproofing doors, page 62

SEALING UP DRAUGHTY WINDOWS

Because they can affect every room in the house, draughty windows waste even more heat than a badly fitting door. As part of an energy-saving scheme, it is imperative to seal at least the worst offenders with effective draught excluders.

Draughtproofing a sash window

The top and bottom closing rails of a sash window can be sealed with any form of compressible excluder. The sliding edges usually admit fewer draughts, but they can be sealed with a brush seal fixed to the frame – inside for the lower sash, outside for the top one. A springy V-strip or a compressible plastic strip can be used to seal the gap between the sloping faces of the central meeting rails of a traditional sash window. For square rails, use a blade seal.

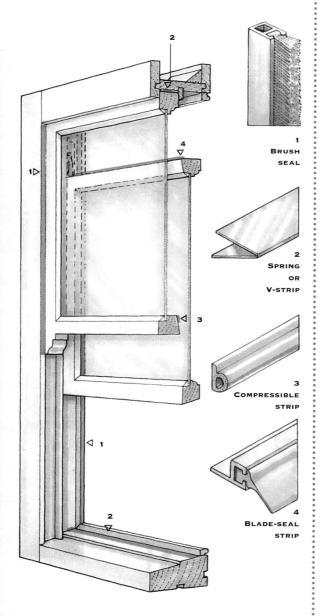

1
BRUSH
SEAL

2
SPRING
OR
V-STRIP

3
COMPRESSIBLE
STRIP

4
BLADE-SEAL
STRIP

Sealing a pivot window

When you close a pivot window, the movable frame comes to rest against fixed stops. Fitting excluders to these stops will seal off the worst of the draughts. You can use compressible spring or V-strip draughtproofing, or a good-quality flexible-tube strip, so long as they are weatherproof.

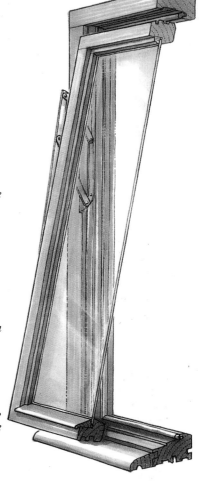

TIP ● ● ● ● ● ● ● ● ● ● ● ● ● ● ● ● ●
Filling large gaps

Large gaps left around newly fitted window frames (and doorframes) will be a source of draughts. Use an expanding-foam filler to seal these gaps. When the filler has set, repoint the masonry on the outside.

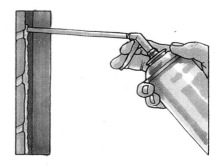

SEAL LARGE GAPS WITH EXPANDING FOAM

ALLOW ONE WHOLE DAY

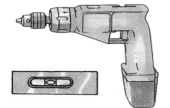

Essential tools

Hammer

Masonry bit

Plumb line

Power drill

Screwdriver

Spirit level

Tenon saw

Wood bits

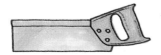

IT SHOULD TAKE ABOUT A
DAY TO PUT UP A BANK
OF ADJUSTABLE SHELVES IN YOUR
LIVING ROOM OR IN A CHILD'S
BEDROOM.

PUTTING UP NEW SHELVING

Why is it that when you move into a new house or flat, there are never enough shelves for all your books or other possessions? And even when you think you have put up sufficient shelving for your future needs, the shelves always seem to be overflowing after just a couple of years. Thankfully, shelving is relatively inexpensive and easy to install.

Depending on where it is and what it is to be used for, shelving can be anything from a set of planks on functional-looking brackets in a garage to elegant spans of solid wood or plate glass on apparently delicate supports made of light alloy.

WHAT MATERIALS TO USE FOR YOUR SHELVES

Ready-cut shelves, in a wide variety of sizes, are usually made from solid wood or man-made boards, but shelves manufactured from glass or painted pressed steel are also available. Man-made-board shelves are painted or finished with wood or plastic veneer. If the standard range of shelves does not meet your requirements, you can make your own using the following materials.

Solid wood
Softwoods such as pine usually contain knots unless specially selected. Parana pine is generally knot-free and available in wide boards, but is more expensive.

You can buy hardwoods such as oak, beech and ash from some timber merchants, but their relatively high cost limits their use to special features and built-in furniture.

Blockboard
Blockboard is a stable man-made board constructed from strips of softwood glued and sandwiched between two layers of plywood-grade veneer.

The board is as strong as solid wood, provided the shelving is cut with the core running lengthways. You will need to lip the raw edges with veneer or solid wood to cover the core.

Plywood
Plywood is built up from veneers with their grain alternating at right angles to one another in order to provide strength and stability. The edges of plywood shelves can be left exposed or covered as for blockboard.

Chipboard
Chipboard, the cheapest man-made board, is most often used for the core of manufactured veneered shelving. Chipboard shelves are liable to bend under load unless they are supported properly.

Medium-density fibreboard
Medium-density fibreboard (MDF) is a dense and stable man-made board that is easy to cut and machine. It finishes smoothly on all edges and does not need to be lipped. MDF is ideal for painting or veneering.

Glass
Plate glass is an elegant material for display shelving. Use toughened glass, which is available to special order. Have it cut to size and the edges ground and polished by the supplier. Textured or wired glass can be used for added interest.

MAKING SURE YOUR SHELVES WON'T SAG

Solid timber or blockboard, with its core running lengthways, are best for sturdy shelving – but a shelf made from either material will still sag if its supports are too far apart. Veneered chipboard, though popular because of its low cost, availability and appearance, will eventually sag under relatively light loads, so it needs supporting at closer intervals than solid wood. Moving the supports in from each end of a shelf helps distribute the load and reduces the risk of sagging.

Material	Thickness	Light load	Medium load	Heavy load
Solid wood	18mm (¾in)	800mm (2ft 8in)	750mm (2ft 6in)	700mm (2ft 4in)
Blockboard	18mm (¾in)	800mm (2ft 8in)	750mm (2ft 6in)	700mm (2ft 4in)
Chipboard	16mm (⅝in)	750mm (2ft 6in)	600mm (2ft)	450mm (1ft 6in)
MDF	18mm (¾in)	800mm (2ft 8in)	750mm (2ft 6in)	700mm (2ft 4in)
Glass	6mm (¼in)	700mm(2ft 4in)	Not applicable	Not applicable

RECOMMENDED SHELF SPANS

The chart shows recommended maximum spans for shelves made from different materials. If you want to increase the length of any shelf, either move the supports closer together, add another bracket, use thicker material for the shelf, or stiffen its front edge.

Stiffening your shelves

Wooden battens, lippings or metal extrusions can be fixed to the underside or front edges of a shelf to increase its stiffness. A wall-fixed batten may also be used to support the back edge in some cases. A deep wooden front rail will conceal a strip-light fitting; a metal reinforcement can be slimmer and less noticeable.

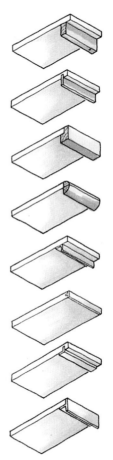

FROM TOP TO BOTTOM
WOODEN BATTEN
PLYWOOD STRIP
REBATED BATTEN
HALF-ROUND LIPPING
SCREWED METAL ANGLE
GROOVED METAL T-SECTION
GROOVED METAL ANGLE
SCREWED METAL T-SECTION

CHOOSING THE BEST SHELF-SUPPORT SYSTEM

The method you use to support a bank of shelving depends a great deal on your chosen location. It is often possible, for example, to span a fireside alcove with fixed built-in shelves that have no apparent means of support. Adjustable shelf brackets offer a greater degree of flexibility, allowing you to redesign your storage system at some time in the future as your collection or library expands. Furthermore, this type of shelving does not rely on side walls for support and can be cantilevered off a straight wall. The brackets may be made from pressed, cast or wrought steel, or from extruded alloy.

Shelf brackets
There are many systems on the market with brackets which slot or clip into metal upright supports that are screwed to the wall. Most uprights have holes or slots at close intervals that accommodate lugs on the rear of each bracket. In one system the upright has a continuous groove over its entire length, so that the brackets may be placed at any level.

One advantage of such systems is that the weight and stress of loaded shelves are distributed down the supporting uprights. Another factor in their favour is that, once the uprights are in place, shelving arrangements can be changed easily and further shelves added, as the need arises, without the necessity for more fixings.

Use the cheap and functional pressed-metal types for utilitarian shelving in a garage or workshop, and choose the more expensive and attractive brackets for your storage needs around the house.

Built-in shelves
Made-to-measure shelving tends to look more substantial and permanent than even the best bracket system. However, it invariably means more work, since you have to cut and fit each shelf individually. You must also make your own supports, usually battens screwed to the walls or vertical side panels made from solid wood or man-made boards. And unless you incorporate a library-style adjustable system, built-in shelves tend to be fixed and therefore less adaptable for future needs.

FIXED PRESSED-STEEL BRACKETS

ADJUSTABLE BRACKET WITH SLOTTED UPRIGHT

ADJUSTABLE BRACKET WITH GROOVED UPRIGHT

PUTTING UP WALL-MOUNTED SHELVING

The construction of the walls will to some extent determine the type of fixing and the positioning of your shelves. On masonry walls, for example, you can place shelf supports almost anywhere; on a timber-framed wall shelves should ideally be fixed to the studs or noggings, but you can use special cavity fixings provided the loads are not excessive.

Loads cantilevered from wall brackets impose great stress on the fixing screws, especially the top ones. If the screws are too small, or if the wall plugs are inadequate, the fixing may be torn out. This is even more likely when you are erecting deep shelves. The fixings for a built-in shelf, with its ends supported on battens within a masonry alcove, are not so highly stressed.

For most ordinary shelving, brackets fixed to a wall of masonry with 50mm (2in) screws and wall plugs should be adequate. Deep shelves intended for a heavy load such as a television set or stack of records may need more robust fixings such as wall bolts, though extra brackets to prevent the shelf sagging will also share the weight. Brackets must be long enough to support almost the entire depth of a shelf.

Fixing individual shelf brackets

When fixing pairs of individual brackets to a solid wall, first mark two vertical guide lines. Hold one bracket at the required height and mark the wall through the fixing holes.

1 Drill into the wall with a masonry bit, insert wall plugs and screw the bracket in place. Using one of the shelves and a spirit level, position the second bracket, then mark and fix it similarly.

2 When fixing brackets to a timber-framed wall, locate the studs and drill pilot holes for the screws. Lightly lubricate screws that are difficult to insert. If you use cavity-wall fixings, drill adequate clearance holes through the plaster lining in order to insert the fittings.

When you are erecting a bank of shelving, fix all the brackets first and simply place the shelves on them. Use a plumb line or spirit level to align the ends of the shelves before you fix them to the brackets.

Fitting a shelving system

Strong wall fixings are essential, since even one loose upright could jeopardize the safety of the whole bank of shelving.

1 The upright supports must be vertical, and the best way of ensuring this is to fix each one lightly to the wall by its top screw, then, holding it vertical with the aid of a spirit level, mark the position of the bottom screw.

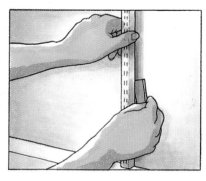

2 With that screw in place, you can check that the upright is vertical in its other plane, not sloping outwards because the wall is out of true. If required, place packing behind the upright to correct it. Also insert packing wherever hollows occur close to fixing points.

Clip one bracket to the upright, then another to the second upright while you hold it against the wall. Get a helper to lay a shelf across the brackets, then use a spirit level to check that the shelf is horizontal.

Mark the top hole of the second upright, and fix that upright as you did the first one. Locate brackets in both uprights and fix the shelves to them. A gap between the back of the shelves and the wall may provide a useful space for cables leading to lamps or equipment.

Making built-in shelves

The simplest way to make built-in open shelves is to fit them into alcoves such as those flanking a chimney breast. However, the surface of the walls is unlikely to be perfectly regular, and some trimming of the shelves may be needed to make them a good fit. Mark the height of the shelves and draw levelled lines from the marks, using a spirit level. Cut wooden support battens to suit the depth of the shelves.

If the shelves are not fitted with a deep lipping, cut the front ends of the supports to a 45-degree angle; you will hardly notice them once you have filled the shelves with books or other items.

For a better appearance, apply deep lippings to the front edges of the shelves. These make the shelving look more substantial and hide the supports.

For a more refined look, make your shelf supports from L-section metal extrusion. Fix the supports securely to the wall with countersunk screws.

Essential tools

Bolster chisel

Filling knife

Hammer

Paintbrush

Plasterer's trowel

Tinsnips

Wallpaper scraper

PATCHING UP DAMAGED PLASTER

Whatever you intend to use as a decorative finish, plastered walls or ceilings must be made good by filling cracks and holes. Patching plasterwork can be a messy job and if you are not careful you can end up with white footprints all round the house. Cover the floor around the work area with dust sheets, particularly if you are unable to remove the carpets. If you are working overhead also cover the furniture. You don't need to be an expert plasterer unless you are faced with repairing large areas of loose plaster, in which case it is worth hiring a professional. There are easy-to-use fine fillers available, but if you need to make good a thick coating you can use the traditional undercoat and top-coat plasters or one of the newer one-coat plasters. Let plaster and fillers dry out thoroughly before you begin to apply paint or wallcoverings.

TIP
Levelling the repair
Uneven plaster can spoil any decorative finish. Use a straight-edged batten to help level the surface of a plaster patch before finishing with a trowel.

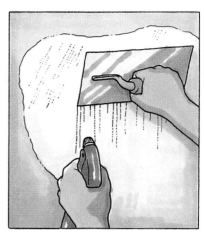

LEVEL THE REPAIR WITH A BATTEN THEN SMOOTH OFF WITH A TROWEL. SPRAY PLASTER OCCASIONALLY AS YOU SMOOTH IT.

FILLING CRACKS AND HOLES

Special flexible emulsions and textured paints are designed to cover hairline cracks, but larger ones will reappear in a relatively short time if they are not filled adequately.

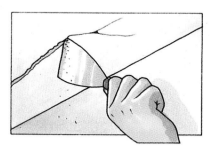

1 Rake loose material from a crack with the blade of a scraper or filling knife. Undercut the edges of larger cracks in order to provide a key for the filling. Mix up interior-grade cellulose filler to a stiff consistency or use a pre-mixed filler.

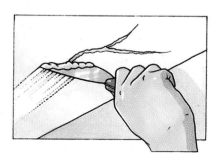

2 Dampen the crack with a paintbrush, then press the filler in with a filling knife. Drag the blade across the crack to force the filler in, then draw it along the crack to smooth the filler. Leave the filler standing slightly proud of the surface, ready for sanding flush with abrasive paper. Fill shallow cracks in one go; but build up the filler in stages in deep cracks, letting each application set before adding more.

Fill and rub down small holes and dents in solid plasterwork, using the methods recommended for filling cracks.

TIP ● ● ● ● ● ● ● ● ● ● ● ● ● ● ● ● ● ● ●

Gaps between skirting boards
Large gaps can open up between your skirting boards and the wall plaster. Cellulose filler simply falls into the cavity behind, so bridge the gap with a roll of press-in-place butyl sealant.

PATCHING UP DAMAGED CORNERS

Cracks sometimes appear in the corner between walls or between the wall and ceiling; fill these by running your finger dipped in filler along the crack. When the filler has hardened, rub it down with medium-grade abrasive paper.

1 To build up a chipped external corner, dampen the plaster and use a filling knife to scrape the filler onto the damaged edge, working from both sides of the corner.

2 Let the filler stiffen, then shape it with a wet finger until it closely resembles the original profile. When the filler is dry, smooth it with abrasive paper.

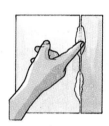

PATCHING A LATH-AND-PLASTER WALL

If you live in an older house, you might find that a wall between two rooms is hollow. This type of partition wall is made with a timber framework covered with thin strips of wood known as laths which serve as a base for the plaster. If the laths are intact, just fill any holes in the plaster with cellulose filler or fresh plaster. If some laths are broken, you need to reinforce the repair with a piece of fine expanded-metal mesh.

1 Rake out loose plaster and undercut the edge of the hole with a bolster chisel. Use tinsnips to cut the metal mesh to the shape of the hole, but a little larger.

2 The mesh is flexible, so you can easily bend it in order to tuck the edge behind the sound plaster all round.

3 Flatten the mesh against the laths with light taps from a hammer and, if possible, staple the mesh to a wall stud to hold it.

4 Apply one thin coat of backing plaster and let it dry for about an hour before you fill the hole flush with more plaster.

FILLING HOLES IN PLASTER-BOARD

Use plasterer's glass-fibre patching tape when mending holes up to about 75mm (3in) across.

1 Stick on the self-adhesive strips in a star shape over the hole, then apply cellulose filler and feather the edges.

2 Alternatively, use an offcut of plasterboard just larger than the hole yet narrow enough to slot through. Bore a hole in the middle and thread a length of string through. Tie a galvanized nail to one end of the string.

3 Butter the ends of the offcut with filler, then feed it into the hole. Pull on the string to force it against the back of the cladding, then press filler into the hole so that it is not quite flush with the surface. When the filler is hard, cut off the string and apply a thin coat of filler for a flush finish.

PATCHING LARGER HOLES

A large hole punched through a plasterboard wall or ceiling cannot be patched with wet plaster only.

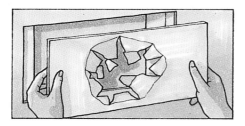

1 Using a sharp craft knife and a straightedge, cut back the damaged board to the nearest studs or joists at each side of the hole. Cut a new panel of plasterboard to fit snugly within the hole and nail it to the joists or studs using galvanized plasterboard nails.

2 Use a steel plasterer's trowel to spread finish plaster over the panel, forcing it well into the edges. Allow the plaster to stiffen, then smooth it with a dry trowel. You may have to add another layer to bring the patch to the level of the wall or ceiling.

PLASTER AND PLASTERBOARD SURFACES ARE FAIRLY TOUGH, BUT VULNERABLE AREAS SUCH AS SLOPING CEILINGS, ALCOVES AND EXTERNAL CORNERS CAN SUFFER DAMAGE.

STEEL PLASTERER'S TROWEL

ALLOW ONE WHOLE DAY

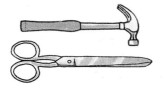

Essential tools

For blanket insulation:

Large pair of scissors

Sharp kitchen knife

For loose-fill insulation:

Broom

Hammer

Home-made spreader

Scissors

Screwdriver

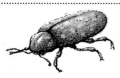

**Check roof timbers
for woodworm**
*Woodworm is the
common name for a
variety of woodboring
insects. Familiar species
are the deathwatch beetle
(top) and the furniture
beetle (below).*

See also:
Lagging your pipes, page 20

INSULATING YOUR LOFT

Approximately a quarter of the heat lost from an average house goes through the roof, so preventing this should be one of your priorities when it comes to insulating your home. Provided that you are able to gain access to your loft space, reducing heat loss through the roof is simply a matter of laying insulating material between the joists, which is cheap, quick and effective.

On inspection, you may find that your roof space has existing but inadequate insulation – at one time even 25mm (1in) of insulation was considered to be acceptable. It is worth installing extra material to bring the insulation up to the recommended thickness of 150mm (6in).

GETTING READY

Check roof timbers for woodworm or signs of rot, so they can be treated first. Make sure that all the electrical wiring is sound, and lift it clear so that you can lay insulation beneath it.

The plaster or plasterboard ceiling below will not support your weight. You therefore need to lay a plank or two, or a chipboard panel, across the joists so you can move about safely.

If there is no permanent lighting in the loft, rig up an inspection lamp on an extension lead and move it wherever it is needed – or hang the lamp high up to provide an overall light.

Most attics are very dusty, so wear old clothes and a gauze face mask. It is also wise to wear protective gloves, especially if you're handling glass-fibre batts or blanket insulation, which may irritate sensitive skin.

LAYING BLANKET INSULATION

Blanket insulation is made from glass fibre, mineral fibre or rock fibre – it is widely available in the form of rolls that fit snugly between the joists. Before starting to lay blanket insulation, seal gaps around pipes, vents or wiring entering the loft with flexible mastic.

Remove the blanket wrapping in the loft (the insulation is compressed for storage and transportation, but swells to its true thickness when released).

Begin by placing one end of a roll into the eaves – make sure you don't cover the ventilation gap (trim the end of the blanket to a wedge shape so that it does not obstruct the airflow).

Unroll the blanket between the joists, pressing it down to form a snug fit – but don't compress it. If you have bought a roll that's slightly wider than the joist spacing, allow it to curl up against the timbers on each side.

Continue at the opposite side of the loft with another roll. Cut it to butt up against the end of the first one, using either a large kitchen knife or a pair of long-bladed scissors. Continue across the loft till all the spaces are filled. Trim the insulation to fit odd spaces.

Do not cover the casings of light fittings that protrude into the loft space. Also, avoid covering electrical cables in case they overheat – lay the cables on top of the blanket or clip them to the sides of the joists above it.

Do not insulate the area immediately below a cold-water cistern (the heat rising from the room below will help to prevent freezing during the winter).

Cut a piece of blanket to fit the cover of the entrance hatch, and attach it with PVA adhesive or with cloth tapes and drawing pins. Fit foam draught excluder around the edges of the hatch.

Insulating with glass-fibre blanket
Place the end of a roll against the eaves and trim at an angle (1) or fit eaves vents (2). Lay rolls between joists (3), and trim ends to fit with scissors (4). Clip cables to joists (5) or lay them over the blankets. Don't place insulation below a cistern. Insulate cistern and cold-water pipes separately.

Loose-fill insulation in either pellet or granular form is poured between the joists, up to the recommended depth of 150mm (6in). Exfoliated vermiculite, made from the mineral mica, is the most common form of loose-fill insulation on the market – but other types, such as mineral wool, cork granules and cellulose fibre, are also available. Run electrical cable over the insulation or along the joists as suggested for glass-fibre blankets.

Seal all gaps around pipes and vents to prevent condensation.

When laying loose-fill insulation, to avoid blocking the eaves, wedge strips of plywood or thick cardboard between the joists, or install proprietary eaves vents as recommended for blanket insulation.

Pour insulation onto the ceiling and distribute it roughly with a broom. Level it with a spreader cut from hardboard. If the joists are shallow, nail on lengths of wood to build up their height to at least 150mm (6in), if only to support walkway boarding in specific areas of the loft.

Cover cold-water pipes with cardboard before pouring insulation.

To insulate the entrance hatch, screw battens around the outer edge of the cover, then fill with granules and pin on a hard-board lid to contain them.

Lagging cold-water cisterns
To comply with current bylaws, your cold-water-storage cistern must be insulated. Buy a Bylaw 30 kit, which includes a jacket and all the other equipment that is required. Insulate your central-heating expansion tank at the same time.

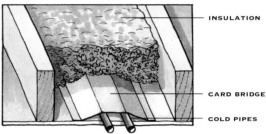

INSULATION

CARD BRIDGE

COLD PIPES

Insulating the pipes
If there are cold-water pipes running between the joists, lay blanket insulation over them to prevent them from freezing. If that is not practical, insulate each pipe run separately with foamed-plastic tubes.

Before pouring loose-fill insulation, lay a bridge made from thin card over cold-water pipes running between the joists, so they will benefit from warmth rising from the room below. If the joists are shallow, cover the pipes with foam tubes before pouring the insulation.

Spreading loose-fill insulant
Seal gaps around pipes and vents (1). Use strips of plywood to prevent insulant from blocking ventilation (2), or fit eaves vents. Use a spreader to level the insulant (3), having covered pipes with a cardboard bridge (4). Insulate and draughtproof the hatch cover (5).

QUICK-AND-EASY DOUBLE GLAZING

There are a great many different secondary glazing systems on the market, but by far the simplest and cheapest employs a sheet of thin, flexible plastic film taped across the window frame. It makes surprisingly effective double glazing and can be removed at the end of the winter. Taped film is safe because it can be cut away easily in an emergency.

Covering the window with film

Film taped to the movable sash will reduce heat loss through the glass and provide accessible ventilation, but it won't stop draughts. Film stretched right across the window frame has the advantage of cutting down heat loss and eliminating draughts at the same time.

ALLOW ONE WHOLE DAY

Stretching the film across a single window takes perhaps half an hour, but you may need most of the day to 'double-glaze' your whole house.

Essential tools

Craft knife

Hairdryer

Scissors

1 Clean the window frame and cut the plastic roughly to size, allowing an overlap all round. Apply double-sided tape to the edges of the frame, then peel off the backing paper.

2 Attach the plastic film to the top rail, then tension it onto the tape on the sides and bottom of the window frame. Apply only light pressure until you have positioned the film, and then rub it down onto the tape all round.

3 Remove all creases and wrinkles in the film, using a hair dryer set to a high temperature. Starting at an upper corner, move the dryer slowly across the film, holding it about 6mm (¼in) from the surface.

4 When the film is taut, cut off the excess plastic with a knife.

4

THE
COMPLETE
WEEKEND

Laying a small patio
84
Making a real-stone
pathway
90
Painting the living room
92
Refurbishing your kitchen
cabinets
102
Papering the spare room
104
Blocking out noisy
neighbours
114
Tiling the bathroom
117

LAYING A SMALL PATIO

Essential tools

Angle grinder

Bolster chisel

Club hammer

Face mask

Hose or watering can

Garden roller

Goggles

Handbrush or broom

Rake

Spade

Spirit level

Straightedge

Trowel

A small paved area surrounded by attractive shrubs and low planting makes a perfect suntrap for relaxing in the garden. Provided you are not too ambitious, it is also relatively easy to achieve, using cast-concrete paving slabs available from any large DIY store or garden centre. The slabs are made by hydraulic pressing or casting in moulds to create the desired surface finish. Pigments and selected aggregates added to the concrete mix create the illusion of natural stone or a range of muted colours.

Laying heavy paving slabs involves a good deal of physical labour, but in terms of technique it is no more complicated than tiling a wall. Accurate setting out and careful laying, especially during the early stages, will produce perfect results.

Shapes and sizes
There is a fairly standard range of shapes and modular sizes of paving available. Although it is possible to carry most slabs single-handed, it is advisable to have help when moving large slabs or heavy natural stones into place.

REGULAR GRID

STAGGERED SLABS

BASKET WEAVE

RANDOM PAVING

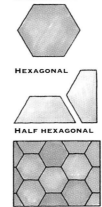

HERRINGBONE

HEXAGONAL

HALF HEXAGONAL

HONEYCOMB

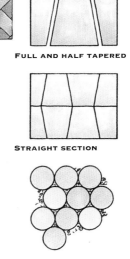

FULL AND HALF TAPERED

STRAIGHT SECTION

BUTTED CIRCULAR SLABS

PLANNING THE AREA

To eliminate the task of cutting paving slabs to fit, try to plan an area of paving to be laid with whole slabs only. If the patio is to be laid next to your house, take your measurements from a convenient wall, or allow for a 100 to 150mm (4 to 6in) margin of gravel between the paving and wall. A gravel margin not only saves time and money by using fewer slabs, but also provides an area for planting climbers and for adequate drainage to keep the wall dry. Even so, allow for a 16mm per metre (⅝in per yard) slope across the paving, so that most surface water will drain into the garden. Any paving must be 150mm (6in) below the damp-proof course to protect the building.

Allowing for the joints

As paving slabs are made to fairly precise dimensions, marking out an area simply involves accurate measurement, allowing for a 6 to 8mm (¼in) gap between slabs. Some slabs are cast with sloping edges to provide a tapered joint, and these should be butted edge to edge. Use pegs and string to mark out the perimeter of the paved area, and check your measurements before you start work.

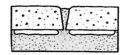

BUTT SLOPING EDGES
TOGETHER TO MAKE
A TAPERED JOINT

PREPARING A SOUND BASE FOR THE PAVING

Paving slabs must be laid upon a firm, level base, but the depth and substance of that base depends on the type of soil and the proposed use of the paving.

For small areas and light loads

For a small patio, remove grass and topsoil to allow for the thickness of the slabs, plus a 25mm (1in) layer of sharp sand and an extra 18mm (¾in) so that the paving will be below the level of surrounding turf and thus will not damage your lawn mower. Compact the soil with a garden roller, spread the sand with a rake, and level it by scraping and tamping with a length of timber.

LEVEL THE SAND BASE
WITH A STRAIGHTEDGE

FOR CLAY OR PEAT SOILS ● ● ● ● ●

To support heavier loads, or if the soil is composed of clay or peat, lay a sub-base of firmly compacted hardcore (broken bricks or crushed stone) to a depth of 75 to 100mm (3 to 4in) before spreading the sand to level the surface.

If you are planning to park vehicles on the paving, increase the depth of the hardcore to 150mm (6in).

LAYING THE PAVING SLABS

Once you have laid your base, set up the string lines again as a guide for laying the edging slabs on the sand. Work in both directions from a corner. When you are satisfied with their positions, lift the slabs one at a time and set them on a bed of mortar (1 part cement : 4 parts builder's sand). Add just enough water to make a firm mortar.

1 Lay a fist-size blob of mortar under each corner, and one more to support the centre of the slab. If you intend to drive vehicles across the slabs, lay a continuous bed of mortar about 50mm (2in) thick.

2 Lay three slabs at a time with 6mm (¼in) wooden spacers between. Level each slab by tapping with a heavy hammer, using a block of wood to protect the slab. Check the alignment with a straightedge.

3 Gauge the slope across the paving by setting up datum pegs along the high side. Drive them into the ground until the top of each corresponds to the finished surface of the paving, then use the straightedge to check the fall on the slabs. Lay the remainder of the slabs, working out from the corner each time to keep the joints square. Remove the spacers before the mortar sets.

Don't walk on the paving for two to three days, until the mortar has set. If you have to cross the area, lay planks across the slabs to spread the load.

4 To fill the gaps between the slabs, brush a dry mortar mix of 1 part cement : 3 parts builder's sand into the open joints. Remove any surplus material from the surface of the paving, then sprinkle the area with a very fine spray of water to consolidate the mortar. Avoid dry mortaring if heavy rain is imminent; it may wash the mortar out.

CUTTING SLABS TO FIT NARROW MARGINS

Sometimes it is impossible to plan an area of paving without having to use cut slabs to fill a border or to fit around immovable obstructions.

When cutting paving slabs with a chisel or an angle grinder, always protect your eyes with plastic goggles. An angle grinder throws up a great deal of dust, so wear a simple gauze face mask, too, as a safeguard.

1 Mark a line across the slab with a soft pencil or chalk. Using a bolster and hammer, chisel a groove about 3mm (⅛in) deep along the line. Continue the groove down both edges and across the underside of the slab.

2 Lay the slab on a bed of sand and place a block of wood at one end of the groove. Strike the block with a hammer while moving it along the groove until the slab splits. Clean up the edge with a bolster.

TIP
A perfect cut
For a perfect cut, hire an angle grinder fitted with a stone-cutting disc. Using the grinder, score a deep groove as before. Tap along the groove with a bolster until the slab splits.

SLAB COLOURS AND TEXTURES

THE RANDOM, REAL YORKSTONE PATH
(ABOVE), HAS OPEN, UNPOINTED
JOINTS, THIS ALLOWS FOLIAGE TO
GROW BETWEEN THE STONES.

A MORE FORMAL PATIO (RIGHT) OF
PRECAST SLABS MAKES AN IDEAL
LEVEL SEATING AREA.

CLAY PAVING BRICKS EDGED WITH
GRANITE SETS (BELOW) PROVIDE A
LABOUR-SAVING ALTERNATIVE TO
THE CONVENTIONAL GARDEN LAWN.

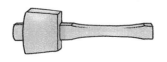

MAKING A REAL-STONE PATHWAY

Essential tools

Bolster
Broom
Club hammer
Goggles
Mallet
Old paintbrush
Spirit level
Straightedge
Trowel

The informal nature of paths or patios laid with irregular-shaped paving stones has always been popular. The random effect, which many people find more appealing than the geometric symmetry of neatly laid slabs, is also less taxing to achieve. A good eye for shape and proportion is more important than a practised technique.

Choosing your materials
Use broken concrete slabs if you can find enough of them, but in terms of appearance nothing compares with natural rock, which splits into thin layers of its own accord as it is quarried. Random broken stone is also ideal for paving and can be obtained at a very reasonable price if you can collect it yourself.

BROKEN PAVING SLABS (ABOVE) CAN MAKE ATTRACTIVE PAVING BUT NOTHING CAN BEAT THE LOOK OF NATURAL STONE AS SHOWN IN THE PATHWAY MADE OF RANDOM BROKEN LIMESTONE (RIGHT).

LAYING THE STONES

You can set out string lines to define straight edges for stone paving, although they will never be as precisely defined as those formed with regular cast-concrete slabs.

Arrange an area of stones, selecting them for a close fit but avoiding too many straight, continuous joints. Trim those that don't quite fit with a bolster and hammer. Reserve larger stones for the perimeter of the paved area, as small stones tend to break away.

2 Having bedded an area of about 1sq m (1sq yd), use a straightedge and spirit level to true up the stones. If necessary, add or remove sand beneath individual stones until the area is level.

1 Use a mallet or block of wood and a hammer to bed each stone into the sand until they are all perfectly stable and reasonably level.

3 When the main area is complete, fill in the larger gaps with small stones, tapping them into place with a mallet.

KEEP YOUR BACK STRAIGHT WHEN LIFTING HEAVY STONES

4 Fill the joints by spreading more sand across the paving and sweeping it into the joints from all directions. Alternatively, mix up a stiff, almost dry, mortar and press it into the joints with a trowel, leaving no gaps.

Use an old paintbrush to smooth the mortared joints, and wipe the stones clean with a damp sponge.

ALLOW THE COMPLETE WEEKEND

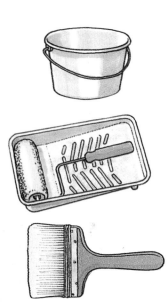

Essential tools

For painting walls:

50mm (2in) paintbrush

150mm (6in) paintbrush
or paint roller

For painting woodwork:

12, 25 and 50mm (½, 1 and
2in) paintbrushes

Paint kettle

Sharp scraping blade

See also:
Painting the ceiling, page 56
Papering the ceiling, page 54
Patching up
damaged plaster, page 74
Stripping old wallpaper, page 44

PAINTING THE LIVING ROOM

Completing even a small room in a single weekend can be difficult if you use solvent-based paints, because they must be left to dry thoroughly before you apply subsequent coats. Provided you have painted or papered the ceiling and prepared the walls the previous weekend, you should be able to apply two coats of emulsion to the walls in one day, so long as you get started reasonably early. If on the second day you are running out of time, try to leave the work at a stage where you can finish painting over a couple of evenings or the next weekend.

However, if you really need to finish the job quickly, use fast-drying acrylic paints and water-based primers, or consider using one-coat paints which eliminate the need for undercoats.

WARM COLOURS APPEAR TO ADVANCE

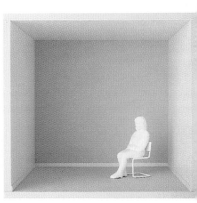

A COOL COLOUR OR PALE TONE RECEDES

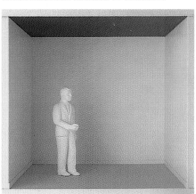

A DARK CEILING WILL APPEAR LOWER

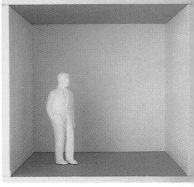

DARK SURFACES MAKE A ROOM SMALLER

STARTING WITH THE WALLS

Cover the floor with dust sheets and erect a safe work platform, so you can reach the top of a wall and cover as much of it as possible. You will complete the job in much less time and achieve better results if you don't have to keep moving a stepladder.

Choosing the paint

Emulsion paint is most people's first choice for decorating indoors: it is relatively cheap, practically odourless, and there are several qualities of paint to suit different circumstances.

Vinyl emulsions are the most popular and practical paints for walls and ceilings. They are available in liquid or thixotropic (non-drip) consistencies, with matt or satin (semi-gloss) finishes. You will need to apply two coats of standard emulsion to avoid a patchy, uneven appearance, perhaps thinning the first coat slightly when painting porous surfaces.

A one-coat, high-opacity emulsion is intended to save you time, but you will not get satisfactory results if you try to apply it too thinly, especially when overpainting strong colours.

New-plaster emulsions are specially formulated for new interior walls and ceilings, to allow moisture vapour to escape; standard vinyl emulsions are not sufficiently permeable.

The right approach

Always finish a complete wall before you take a break, otherwise a change of tone may show between two sections painted at different times.

1 Use a small brush to paint the edges, starting at a top corner of the room. If you are right-handed, work from right to left, and vice versa.

2 Using a wide brush or roller, apply emulsion paint to cover an area of about 600 to 900mm (2 to 3ft) square at a time, working in horizontal bands across the room. If you prefer to use a solvent-based paint, brush on the finish in vertical bands as shown.

PAINTING WITH BRUSHES

A brush about 200mm (8in) wide will cover an area quickly, but if you are not used to handling a large brush, your wrist will soon tire; you may find a 150mm (6in) brush more comfortable to use, even though the job will take a little longer. You will also need a 50mm (2in) brush for the edges and corners.

1 Don't overload a brush with paint; it leads to messy work, and ruins the bristles if the paint is allowed to dry in the roots. Dip no more than the first third of the brush into the paint, wiping off excess on the side of the container to prevent drips. When using thixotropic paint, load the brush and apply paint without removing excess.

2 You can hold the brush whichever way feels comfortable to you, but the 'pen' grip is the most versatile, enabling your wrist to move the brush freely in any direction. Hold the brush handle between your thumb and forefinger, with your fingers on the ferrule (metal band) and your thumb supporting it from the other side. Apply the paint in vertical strokes, then spread it at right angles to even out the coverage.

PAINTING WITH A ROLLER

A paint roller with interchangeable sleeves is an excellent tool for applying paint to large areas. Choose a roller about 225mm (9in) long for painting walls. Larger ones are available, but they become tiring to use.

There are a number of different sleeves to suit the type of paint and texture of the surface. Long-haired sheepskin and synthetic-fibre sleeves are the most practical for textured surfaces, especially when applying emulsion paint.

1 You will need a special paint tray to load a standard roller. Having dipped the sleeve lightly into the paint reservoir, roll it gently onto the ribbed part of the tray to coat the roller evenly.

2 Use zig-zag strokes with the roller, painting the surface in all directions to achieve an even coverage. Keep the roller on the surface at all times: if you let it spin at the end of a stroke, it will spatter paint onto the floor or adjacent surfaces.

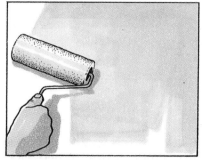

If you are using solvent-based paints, plan to decorate windows early in the day to make sure the paint will be dry enough to close the windows by nightfall. Finish with the skirting boards, in case you touch the floor with

Using solvent-based paints

The familiar solvent-based paints (oil paints) are available as high-gloss and satin finishes, with both liquid and thixotropic consistencies. Indoors, they last for years with only the occasional wash down to remove finger marks. One or two undercoats are essential.

A one-coat paint, with its creamy consistency and high-pigment content, can protect primed wood and obliterate existing colours without undercoating. Apply it liberally and allow it to flow freely, rather than brushing it out like a conventional oil paint.

Low-odour, solvent-based finishes have largely eradicated the smell and fumes associated with drying paint.

Fast-drying acrylic paints

Acrylic paints have several advantages over oil paints. Being water-based, they are non-flammable, practically odourless, and constitute less of a risk to health and the environment. They also dry very quickly.

Provided they are applied to adequately prepared wood or keyed paintwork, acrylic paints form a tough yet flexible coating. However, acrylic paints may not dry satisfactorily if they are applied on a damp or humid day. Even under perfect conditions, don't expect to achieve a high-gloss finish when using acrylic paints.

the brush and specks of dust get transferred to other areas. As a precaution, slide strips of thin card under the skirting to act as a paint shield (don't use newspaper; it will tear and remain stuck to the skirting).

APPLYING THE PAINT

Prepare and prime all new woodwork thoroughly before applying the finishing coats. Wash down old paintwork with a sugar-soap solution and key gloss paint with wet-and-dry paper.

If you are using conventional oil paint, apply one or two undercoats, depending on the covering power of the paint. As each coat hardens, rub down with fine wet-and-dry paper to remove blemishes, then wipe the surface with a cloth dampened with white spirit.

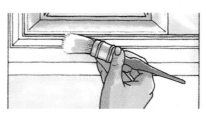

Apply the paint with vertical strokes, then spread it sideways to even out the coverage. Finish with light strokes ('laying off') in the direction of the grain.

Blend the edges of the next application while the paint is still wet. Don't go back over a painted surface that has already started to dry, or you will leave brush marks in the paintwork.

Use a different technique for spreading one-coat or acrylic paints: simply lay on the paint liberally with almost parallel strokes, then lay off lightly. Blend wet edges quickly.

PAINTING THE DOOR

Doors have a variety of faces, edges and mouldings that need to be painted separately, yet the end result must look even in colour, with no ugly brush marks or heavily painted edges. Recommended procedures for painting different types of door will help you achieve those ends.

Getting ready

Remove the door handles and wedge the door open so that it cannot be closed accidentally, locking you in the room. Keep the handle in the room with you, just in case. Aim to paint the door and its frame separately, so that there is less chance of touching wet paintwork when passing through the freshly painted doorway. Paint the door first, then when it is dry finish the framework.

If you want to use a different colour for each side of the door, paint the hinged edge the colour of the closing face (the one that comes to rest against the frame). Paint the outer edge of the door the same colour as the opening face. This means that there won't be any difference in colour when the door is viewed from either side.

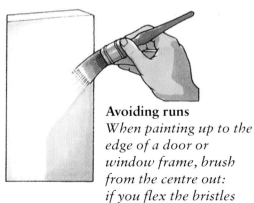

Avoiding runs

When painting up to the edge of a door or window frame, brush from the centre out: if you flex the bristles against the edge, the paint will run. Brushing across mouldings tends to flex the bristles unevenly and too much paint flows: spread the paint well, taking special care at the corners of moulded panels.

Painting a flush door

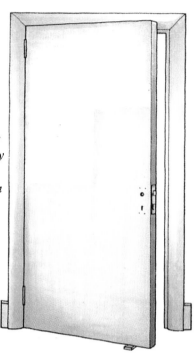

To paint a flush door, start at the top and work down in sections, blending each one into the other. Lay on the paint, then finish each section with light vertical brush strokes. Finally, paint the edges.

Painting a panelled door

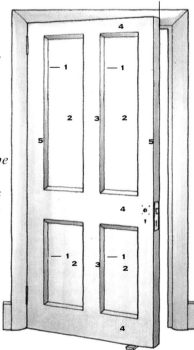

Whatever the style of panelled door you are painting, start with the mouldings (1) followed by the panels (2). Paint the muntins (3) next, then the cross rails (4). Finish the face by painting the stiles (5). Finally, paint the edge of the door (6).

PAINTING A DOOR SURROUND

PAINTING UP TO GLASS

Each side of the frame should match the corresponding face of the door. Paint the frame in the room into which the door swings, including the edge of the stop bead against which the door closes, to match the opening face. Paint the rest of the frame the colour of the closing face.

Opening side

Paint the architrave (1) and doorframe up to and including the edge of the door stop (2) one colour. Paint the face of the door and its opening edge (3) the same colour.

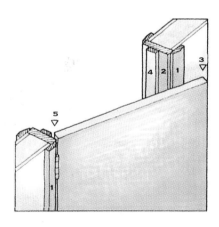

Opposite side

Paint the architrave and frame up to and over the door stop (4) the second colour. Paint the opposite face of the door and its hinged edge (5) with the second colour.

Glazed doors

Paint the glazing bars first, then the cross rails, and finish by painting the vertical stiles.

When painting the edge of glazing bars, it is usual to overlap the glass by about 2mm ($\frac{1}{16}$in) to prevent rain or condensation seeping between the glass and woodwork. However, if you find you can't make a neat job of it, try one of the following tips.

To achieve a satisfactory straight edge, use a proprietary plastic or metal paint shield, holding it against the edge of the frame to protect the glass.

Alternatively, run masking tape around the edges of the pane, leaving a slight gap so that the paint will seal the join between glass and frame. When the paint is touch-dry, carefully peel off the tape. Don't wait until the paint is completely dry, or it may peel off with the tape.

Once it has set, use a sharp blade to scrape off any paint that has accidentally dripped onto the glass. Many DIY stores sell plastic handles to hold disposable knife blades for this purpose.

GLASS SCRAPER

THE BOLD USE OF COLOUR HAS UNIFIED THIS
INTERIOR SCHEME AND DEMONSTRATES
MANY OF THE PAINTED WOODWORK
SITUATIONS THE AVERAGE HOUSEHOLDER
WILL COME ACROSS – WOOD PANELLING,
DOORS AND WINDOW FRAMES, SKIRTING
BOARDS AND STAIRS.

PAINTING A CASEMENT WINDOW

A casement window is hung on hinges and opens like a door, so if you plan to paint each side a different colour, follow a similar procedure to that described for painting doors and frames. Window frames need to be painted in strict order, so that the various components will be evenly treated, and also so you can close them at night. You also need to take care not to splash window panes with paint or apply a crooked line around the glazing bars – the mark of poor workmanship. Clean the glass in your windows before decorating to avoid picking up particles of dust in the paint.

Removing the handle and stay
Remove the stay and window catch before you paint the casement. So that you can still operate the window without touching wet paint, drive a nail into the underside of the bottom rail to act as a makeshift handle.

Temporary stay
Make a temporary stay with a length of stiff wire wrapped round the nail – hook the other end and slot it into one of the screw holes in the frame.

Applying the paint
First paint the glazing bars (1), overlapping the glass on each side (see page 98). Carry on with the top and bottom horizontal rails (2) followed by the vertical stiles (3). Finish the casement by painting the edges (4), then paint the frame (5).

PAINTING A SASH WINDOW

Sash windows are more difficult to paint than casements, as the two panes slide vertically, overlapping each other.

The following sequence describes the painting of a sash window from the inside. To paint the outside face, use a similar procedure but start with the lower sash. If you are using different colours for each side, the demarcation lines are fairly obvious: when the window is shut, all the visible surfaces from one side should be the same.

CUTTING-IN BRUSH

Following a logical sequence

Raise the bottom sash and pull down the top one. Paint the bottom meeting rail of the top sash (1) and the accessible parts of the vertical members (2). Reverse the position of the sashes, leaving a gap top and bottom, and complete the painting of the top sash (3). Paint the bottom sash (4), then the frame (5) except for the runners in which the sashes slide.

Leave the paint to dry, then paint the inner runners (6) plus a short section of the outer runners (7), pulling the cords aside to avoid splashing paint on them, as this makes them brittle. Before the paint dries, check that the window can slide.

RAISE THE BOTTOM SASH AND PULL DOWN THE TOP ONE

REVERSE THE POSITION OF THE SLIDING SASHES

LOWER BOTH SASHES IN ORDER TO PAINT THE RUNNERS

Essential tools
Paintbrush

REFURBISHING YOUR KITCHEN CABINETS

A cheap and easy way to spruce up an old wood kitchen is to revarnish all the doors and drawer fronts. You can even change the appearance of the cabinets by applying a wood-coloured varnish.

THESE EXAMPLES DEMONSTRATE HOW DIFFERENT VARNISHES AFFECT THE SAME SPECIES OF WOOD.

Varnishing serves two main purposes: to protect wood from knocks, stains and other marks, and to give it a sheen that accentuates the beautiful grain pattern. As such, it is the ideal finish for fitted furniture that has to put up with a lot of wear and tear but which must also retain its good looks with the minimum of maintenance.

Colour samples
(above)
From left to right
Untreated softwood
Clear matt varnish
Clear gloss varnish
Wood-colour varnish
Tinted satin varnish
Pure-colour varnish

CHOOSING YOUR VARNISH

BRUSHING ON THE VARNISH

Modern varnishes are waterproof, scratchproof and heat-resistant, and are available in gloss, satin or matt finishes. Conventional varnishes are thinned with white spirit, but there are also fast-drying, water-thinned, acrylic varnishes that have an opaque, milky appearance when applied, but are clear and transparent when dry.

Some varnishes are designed to provide a clear finish with a hint of colour. They are available in the normal wood shades and some strong colours. Unlike a wood dye, a coloured varnish does not sink into the timber, so there may be loss of colour in areas of heavy wear or abrasion unless you apply an additional coat of clear varnish.

When dust sticks to the varnish
Sometimes it is difficult to prevent dust particles sticking to the varnish as it sets. Let the varnish set hard, then rub it down with very fine wire wool or abrasive paper. Apply a fresh coat of varnish to restore the finish – a second coat of coloured varnish may darken the wood. Use a similar procedure to correct any unsightly runs that show after the varnish has set.

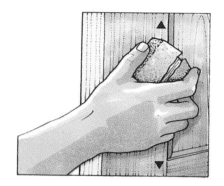

1 Lightly sand the old finish with fine wet-and-dry paper, taking care not to wear through to bare wood on the corners and edges. Make sure all surfaces are clean and grease-free.

Load a clean paintbrush by dipping the first third of the bristles into the varnish, then touch off the excess on the side of the container. Don't scrape the brush across the rim of the container as that causes bubbles in the varnish, which can spoil the finish if transferred to the woodwork.

2 Paint the varnish onto the work, brushing it in different directions to spread it evenly, then finish off by brushing lightly in the direction of the grain. Blend one section into the other before the varnish begins to set.

Essential tools

Craft knife

Paperhanger's brush

Paperhanger's scissors

Paste brush

Pasting table

Plumb line

Seam roller

Smoothing roller

Tape measure

PAPERING THE SPARE ROOM

Although most people have few qualms about picking up a paintbrush, wallpapering seems to be far more daunting – a strange reaction when you consider that so much effort has gone into making things easy for us. All but hand-printed papers are ready trimmed to width, they are colour-fast, they won't stretch or tear provided you exercise a little care, and ready-mixed or liquid pastes remove all that worry about lumpy mixes.

Described here are the skills you need for papering a small bedroom with at least one window, a fireplace and one door, but once you have mastered these basic techniques you can wallpaper a room of any size.

A weekend should give you plenty of time – an experienced decorator can usually finish papering a small room in a day – assuming you have already stripped and filled the plasterwork, and either washed down the old paintwork or applied fresh paint the weekend before. Similarly, you will have either painted the ceiling with emulsion or already have hung new ceiling paper.

See also
Painting the ceiling, page 56
Papering the ceiling, page 54
Patching up
damaged plaster, page 74
Stripping old wallpaper, page 44

THE PRETTY PAPERED BEDROOM MAKES USE OF CO-ORDINATED WALLPAPER AND FABRICS. THE DECORATIVE BORDER, AT DADO HEIGHT, CLEVERLY UNITES THE WALLPAPER AND CURTAIN MOTIFS.

WHERE TO START

You may find it easiest to paper the longest uninterrupted wall to get used to the basic techniques before tackling corners or obstructions. Hang the first length of paper near one corner, and work away from the prevailing light.

Working with bold patterns

If your wallcovering has a large regular motif, centre the first length over the fireplace for symmetry. Alternatively, centre this first length between two windows, unless you will be left with narrow strips each side, in which case it's best to butt two lengths on the centre line.

CHOOSING THE RIGHT PASTE

Most wallpaper pastes are supplied in liquid form, or as powder or flakes for mixing with water.

All-purpose paste
Standard wallpaper paste is suitable for most lightweight to medium-weight papers. If you add less water, you can use it for hanging heavyweight papers.

Heavy-duty paste
This is specially prepared for hanging embossed papers, paper-backed fabrics and other heavyweight wallcoverings.

Fungicidal paste
Most pastes contain a fungicide to prevent mould growth under impervious wallcoverings such as vinyls, washable papers and foamed-plastic coverings.

Ready-mixed paste
Tubs of ready-mixed thixotropic paste are specially made for hanging heavyweight wallcoverings.

Liquid paste
Use a liquid wallpaper paste to avoid any possibility of a lumpy mix.

Repair adhesive
This paste is sold in tubes for sticking down peeling edges and corners. It even glues vinyl to vinyl.

Ready-pasted wallcoverings
Many wallcoverings come precoated with adhesive that is activated by soaking a cut length in a trough of cold water. Mix some ordinary paste to recoat dry edges.

PASTING THE PAPER

You can use any wipe-clean table for pasting, but a narrow fold-up pasting table is a good investment if you are going to do a lot of decorating.

1 Lay several cut lengths of paper face down on the table, to keep it clean. Tuck the ends under a length of string tied loosely round the table legs to stop the paper rolling up while you are pasting. Use a large, soft wall brush or pasting brush to apply the paste. Mix the paste in a plastic bucket and tie string across the rim to support the brush, keeping its handle clean while you hang the paper.

2 Align the wallpaper with the far edge of the table, so there will be no paste on the table to be transferred to the face of the paper. Apply the paste by brushing away from the centre, pasting the edges carefully and removing any lumps. If you prefer, apply the paste with a short-pile paint roller, pouring the paste into a roller tray and rolling in one direction only towards the end of the paper.

3 Pull the wallcovering to the front edge of the table and paste the other half. Fold the pasted end over – don't press it down – and slide the length along the table in order to expose the next unpasted part.

4 Paste the other end, then fold it over to almost meet the first cut end. The second fold is invariably deeper than the first – a good way to denote the bottom of patterned wallcoverings. Fold long drops concertina-fashion.

FOLD LONG PIECES CONCERTINA-FASHION

TIP •••••••••
Leave the paper to soak Drape pasted paper over a broom handle spanning two chair backs, and leave them to soak. Some heavy coverings may need to soak for about 15 minutes. Hang vinyls and lightweight papers immediately.

Most wallcoverings are machine-trimmed to width so that you can butt adjacent lengths accurately. Some hand-printed papers are left untrimmed. These are usually expensive, so it's not worth attempting to trim them yourself: ask the wallpaper supplier to do it for you.

Cutting plain wallpaper to length
Measure the height of the wall at the point where you will hang the first 'drop'. Add an extra 100mm (4in) for trimming top and bottom. Cut several pieces from your first roll to the same length and mark the top of each one.

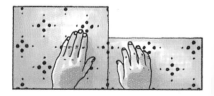

Allowing for patterned wallpaper
You may have to allow extra on alternate lengths of patterned wallpaper, in order to match the pattern.

THIS BOLDLY PATTERNED WALLPAPER HAS BEEN CENTRED BETWEEN TWO WINDOWS (SEE PAGE 106). A MATCHING DECORATIVE FRIEZE COVERS THE CUT EDGE OF THE PAPER WHERE IT MEETS THE CEILING.

STARTING WITH A STRAIGHT WALL

The walls of most rooms are rarely truly square, so use a plumb line to mark a vertical guide against which to hang the first length of wallcovering.

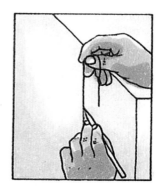

1 *Start at one end of the wall and mark the vertical line one roll width away from the corner, minus 12mm (½in) so the first length will overlap the adjacent wall.*

2 *Allowing enough wallcovering for trimming at the ceiling, unfold the top section of the pasted length and hold it against the plumbed line. Brush the paper gently onto the wall, working out from the centre in all directions to squeeze out any trapped air.*

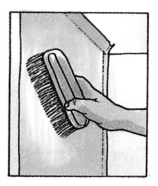

3 *When you are sure the paper is positioned accurately, lightly draw the point of your scissors along the ceiling line, peel back the top edge and cut along the crease. Smooth the paper back, and stipple it down with the brush.*

4 *Unpeel the lower fold of the paper, smooth it onto the wall with the brush, then stipple it into the corner. Crease the bottom edge against the skirting, peel away the paper, then trim and brush it back against the wall.*

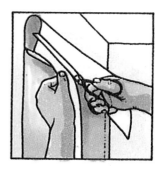

Hang the next length in the same manner. Slide it with your fingertips to align the pattern and produce a perfect butt joint. Wipe any paste from the surface with a damp cloth. Ensure that the edges of the paper adhere firmly by running a seam roller along the butt joint. Continue to the other end of the wall, allowing the last drop to overlap the adjoining wall by 12mm (½in).

HOME-MADE PLUMB LINE

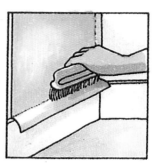

PAPERING AROUND THE CORNER

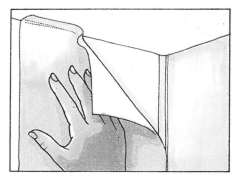

1 *Turn the corner by marking another plumbed line, so that the next length of paper covers the overlap from the first wall. If the piece you trimmed off at the corner is wide enough, use it as your first length on the new wall.*

2 *If there's an alcove on both sides of the fireplace, you will need to wrap the paper around the external corners. Trim the last length so that it wraps around the corner, lapping the next wall by about 25mm (1in). Plumb and hang the remaining strip with its edge about 12mm (½in) from the corner.*

PAPERING AROUND RADIATORS, SWITCHES AND SOCKETS

There are always small details to contend with as you paper the main areas of the room.

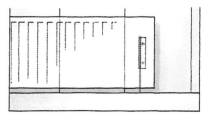

Papering behind the radiator

If you cannot remove a radiator, turn off the heating and allow it to cool. Use a steel tape to measure the positions of the brackets fixing the radiator to the wall. Transfer these measurements to a length of wallcovering and slit it from the bottom to the top of the bracket. Feed the pasted paper behind the radiator, down both sides of the brackets. Use a radiator roller to press it to the wall. Crease and trim to the skirting board.

Papering around switches and sockets

To be safe, turn off the electricity at the mains. Hang the wallcovering over the switch or socket. Make diagonal cuts from the centre of the fitting to each of its corners and tap the excess paper against the edges of the faceplate with the brush. Trim off the waste, leaving 6mm (¼in) all round. Loosen the faceplate, tuck the margin behind and retighten it.

PAPERING AROUND THE DOOR AND WINDOWS

When you get to the door, hang the length of paper beside the doorframe, brushing down the butt joint to align the pattern and allowing the other edge to loosely overlap the door.

1 Make a diagonal cut in the excess towards the top corner of the frame. Crease the waste down the side of the frame with scissors, peel it back, trim off and then brush back. Leave a 12mm (½in) strip for turning on the top of the frame.

2 Fill in with short strips above the door, then butt the next full length of paper over the door and cut the excess diagonally into the frame, pasting the rest of this strip down the side of the door. Mark and cut off the waste.

Treat a flush window frame the same way as the door. But if the window is set into a reveal, hang the length of wallcovering next to the window and allow it to overhang the opening. Make a horizontal cut just above the edge of the window reveal. Make a similar cut near the bottom, then fold the paper around to cover the side of the reveal. Crease and trim along the window frame and sill.

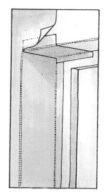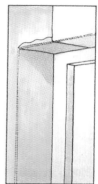

1 To fill in the window reveal, first cut a strip of paper to match the width and pattern of the overhang just above the reveal. Paste the strip, slip it under the overhang and fold it around the top of the reveal.

2 Cut through the overlap with a smooth, wavy stroke, then remove the excess paper and roll down the joint. To continue, hang short lengths on the wall below and above the window, wrapping top lengths into the reveal.

TIMESAVER TIP ● ● ● ● ● ● ● ● ● ● ● ●

Papering around the fireplace

Papering around a fireplace is similar to fitting the paper around a door. Make a diagonal cut in the waste overlapping the fireplace, cutting towards the corner of the mantel shelf. Now tuck the paper in all round for creasing and trimming to the fireplace surround.

If the surround is fairly ornate, first brush the paper onto the wall above the surround, then trim the paper to fit under the mantel shelf at each side; brush the paper around the corners of the chimney breast to hold it in place. Now gently press the wallpaper into the shape of the fire surround, then peel it away and cut round the impression with nail scissors. Smooth the paper back down with the brush.

HANGING VINYL WALLPAPER

Paste paper-backed vinyls in the normal way. Cotton-backed vinyl hangs better if you paste the wall and then leave it to become tacky before you apply the wallcovering. Use fungicidal paste.

Hang and butt-join lengths of vinyl, using a sponge, rather than a brush, to smooth them onto the wall. Crease a length top and bottom, then trim it to size with a sharp knife.

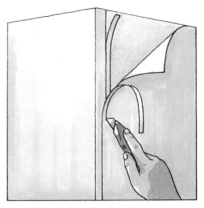

Dealing with overlaps
Vinyl will not normally stick to itself, so when you turn a corner use a knife to cut through both pieces of paper where they overlap. Peel away the excess and rub down the vinyl to produce a perfect butt joint.

Vinyls and other wallcoverings
Below (anticlockwise):
Washable papers
Vinyl wallcoverings
Paper-backed fabrics
Cork-faced paper
Grass-cloth effects
Flock papers
Foamed polyethylene

VINYL WALLCOVERINGS ARE THE IDEAL SOLUTION FOR
BATHROOMS WHERE A WATER RESISTANT, STEAMPROOF
AND EASY WIPEDOWN SURFACE IS REQUIRED.

Essential tools

Bolster chisel

Claw hammer

Craft knife

Electrician's screwdriver

Electrician's pliers

Filling knife

Mastic gun

Plumb line

Scissors

Screwdriver

Tape measure

Tenon saw

Try square

Wire strippers

Detached insulated lining
1 Head plate
2 Sole plate
3 Studs
4 Insulating blanket
5 Nogging
6 First layer of
plasterboard
7 Second layer of
plasterboard
8 Electrical fitting

BLOCKING OUT NOISY NEIGHBOURS

Noise generated by thoughtless neighbours can make life distinctly unpleasant, if not intolerable. Although it is difficult to block out unwelcome sounds completely, it is possible to reduce the amount of noise passing through a shared wall.

Sealing gaps

Sealing gaps in the shared or party wall is one obvious way to reduce airborne noise. If necessary, remove skirtings and floorboards close to the party wall so you can repoint poor mortar joints and fill any gaps around joists that are built into the masonry. After replacing the skirting and floorboards, seal any gaps between them with a flexible mastic.

It may also be worth repointing the wall in the loft, and plastering it to add mass.

LINING THE WALL

The soundproofing of a party wall can be greatly improved by building an insulated lining. However, its effectiveness will depend to some extent on the construction of the wall, whether or not there is a fireplace, the location of electrical or plumbing fittings, and the proximity of windows.

The lining – constructed in a similar way to an ordinary stud partition – is fixed to the floor, ceiling and side walls, but not to the party wall itself. The gap between the lining and the wall is filled with glass-fibre or mineral-fibre blanket insulation, and the lining is clad with two layers of plasterboard.

Adding a lining to the party wall of an older house may mean having to modify a moulded-plaster cornice; and the size of the room will be reduced, whatever the age of the house. Nevertheless, the benefits are likely to compensate for the disadvantages and effort involved.

What to do first
Switch off the electrical supply at the consumer unit, and replace any fittings attached to the party wall with junction boxes in readiness for relocating the fittings on the new lining. If your experience is limited, hire an electrician to do the electrical work for you.

Remove the skirting carefully for reuse. Mark a line on the ceiling 100mm (4in) from the party wall. Drop a plumb line and make a similar mark on the floor below.

Fixing the lining sole plate to the floor presents few problems; but if the ceiling joists run parallel to the party wall, then you may have to nail noggings (stout battens) between them to provide secure fixing points for the lining head plate.

Erecting the lining
Nail a 75 x 50mm (3 x 2in) softwood head plate and sole plate in position, with their front edges on the marked lines – this will leave a 25mm (1in) gap between them and the wall. Nail matching vertical studs between them at 600mm (2ft) intervals. Mark the position of each stud on the floor and ceiling to help you relocate them when fixing the plasterboard.

Hang floor-to-ceiling lengths of 100 x 600mm (4in x 2ft) insulating blanket between the studs, tucking the edges behind the framework. Skew-nail noggings between the studs to serve as fixing points for shelving or electrical mounting boxes.

Check that the power is still switched off at the consumer unit, then run short lengths of cable from junction boxes to the new mounting-box locations.

Cover the framework with plasterboard 12mm (½in) thick. Fill the joints and seal around the outer edges with mastic. Nail a second layer of tapered-edge boards over the first, staggering the joints and placing the nails about 150mm (6in) apart.

Fill and tape the joints between the boards, then nail the skirting board in place. Mount and wire the electrical fittings, sealing around the edges of flush-mounted electrical mounting boxes with mastic. Seal the lower edge of the skirting board, too.

TILING THE BATHROOM

Waterproof ceramic tiles are an obvious choice for lining showers or for other areas of a bathroom that will be splashed with water, and there's an almost inexhaustible range of colours, textures and patterns to choose from.

The majority of tiles are square, the dimensions varying according to use and the manufacturer's preference. Rectangular and more irregularly shaped tiles are also available, and coving tiles are sometimes used to cover the joint between the wall and a bath or basin, or for finishing the edge of a half-tiled wall.

It takes very little time to hang even a fairly large area of tiles, but the work becomes far more time-consuming when you have to cut and fit border tiles and accommodate bathroom fittings and accessories.

ALLOW THE COMPLETE WEEKEND

TILE SAW

Essential tools

Home-made gauge stick

Adhesive spreader

Tile cutter

Tile saw

Grout spreader

Tile nibblers

Tile-cutting jig

Claw hammer

Spirit level

Plumb line

TILE CUTTER

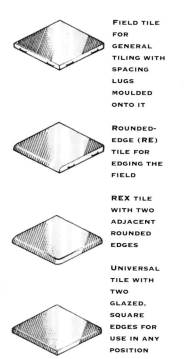

FIELD TILE FOR GENERAL TILING WITH SPACING LUGS MOULDED ONTO IT

ROUNDED-EDGE (RE) TILE FOR EDGING THE FIELD

REX TILE WITH TWO ADJACENT ROUNDED EDGES

UNIVERSAL TILE WITH TWO GLAZED, SQUARE EDGES FOR USE IN ANY POSITION

QUADRANT TILE TO FILL THE JOINT BETWEEN BATH AND WALL

MITRED TILE USED AT THE END IF YOU WANT TO TURN A CORNER

BULLNOSE TILE FOR FINISHING THE END OF A STRAIGHT RUN

See also:
Patching up
damaged plaster, page 74
Stripping old wallpaper, page 44

GETTING PREPARED

The walls of your bathroom must be clean, sound and dry. You cannot tile over wallpaper, and you need to coat flaking or powdery paint with a stabilizing primer to make a suitable base for the tiles. It is important that you make the surface as flat as possible, so the tiles will stick firmly. Setting out the prepared surface accurately is vital to hanging the tiles properly.

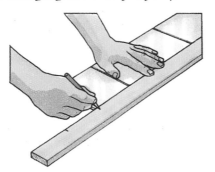

Making a gauge stick
First make a gauge stick (a tool for plotting the position of tiles on the wall) from a length of 50 x 12mm (2 x ½in) softwood. Lay several tiles beside it – butting together those with lugs, or adding spacers if the tiles are square-edged – and mark the position of each tile along the softwood batten.

Using the gauge stick
Holding the gauge stick firmly against the wall, mark the positions of the tiles on the surface.

SETTING OUT THE WALL TILES

The way you set out the walls of your bathroom depends on the scale and shape of the area you are tiling. To tile a plain uninterrupted wall, for example, use the gauge stick to plan horizontal rows starting at skirting level. If you are left with a narrow strip at the top, move the rows up half a tile width to create a wider margin.

1 *Mark the bottom of the lowest row of whole tiles. Temporarily nail a thin guide batten to the wall, aligned with the mark. Make sure it is horizontal by placing a spirit level on top.*

2 *Mark the centre of the wall, then use the gauge stick to set out the rows of tiles on each side of it. If the border tiles measure less than half a width, reposition the rows sideways by half a tile.*

3 *Use a spirit level to position a guide batten against the last vertical line, and nail it to the wall.*

4 *If you are tiling part of a wall only (up to a dado rail, for example), start by setting out a row of whole tiles at the top. This is particularly important if you plan to use RE tiles.*

5 *If you have to accommodate a window in your scheme, use it as your starting point so that the tiles surrounding it are equal in size – but not too narrow. If possible, begin a row of whole tiles at sill level.*

6 *Position cut tiles at the back of the window reveal.*

7 *Fix a guide batten over a window to position a row of tiles temporarily.*

TIP ● ● ● ● ● ● ● ● ● ● ● ● ● ● ● ● ● ●
Avoid cutting difficult shapes
Check with the gauge stick how the tiles will fit round pipes and other obstructions. Make slight adjustments to the position of the main field to avoid difficult shaping around these features.

Setting out walls for tiling
It is possible to plan different arrangements of wall tiles, using a home-made gauge stick. Try to ensure a wide margin all round.

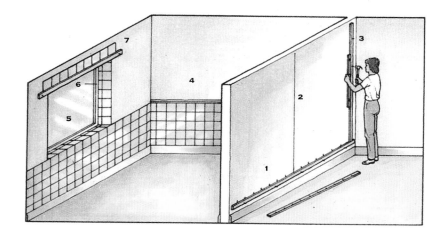

TILING THE WALLS

Most ceramic-tile adhesives are sold ready-mixed, although a few need to be mixed with water. The tubs or packets will state the coverage.

Use a waterproof tile adhesive in a bathroom or shower. Some adhesives can also be used for grouting (filling the joints between the tiles). A notched adhesive spreader is usually supplied with each tub, or you can use a special serrated trowel.

Tiling around a window
Tile up to the edges of a window, then stick RE tiles to the reveal so that they lap the edges of surrounding tiles. Fill in any space left between the edging tiles and the window with cut tiles.

SERRATED TROWEL

1 Spread enough adhesive on the wall to cover about 1 metre (3ft) square. Press the toothed edge of the spreader against the wall surface and drag it through the adhesive so that it forms horizontal ridges.

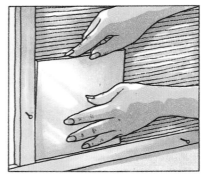

2 Press the first tile into the angle formed by the setting-out battens until it is firmly fixed, then butt up tiles on each side. Build up three or four rows at a time. If the tiles do not have lugs, place proprietary plastic spacers between them to provide space for grouting.

Wipe away adhesive from the surface of the tiles with a damp sponge. Spread more adhesive, and tile along the batten until the first rows of whole tiles are complete. From time to time, check that your tiling is accurate by holding a batten and spirit level across the faces and along the top and side edges.

When you have completed the main area, scrape adhesive from the borders and allow the rest to set before removing the setting-out battens and proceeding with marking out and cutting border tiles.

CUTTING BORDER TILES

Having finished the main field of tiles, it is necessary to cut border tiles one at a time to fit the gaps between the field tiles and the adjacent walls (since walls are hardly ever truly square, the margin is bound to be uneven). Protect your eyes with safety spectacles or goggles when snapping scored ceramic tiles.

1 Mark a border tile by placing it face down over its neighbour, with one edge against the adjacent wall. Make an allowance for normal spacing between the tiles. Transfer the marks to the edge of the tiles using a felt-tip pen.

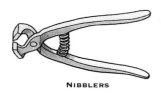

2 Use a proprietary tile cutter, held against a straightedge, to score across the face with one firm stroke to cut through the glaze. You may also have to score the edges of thick tiles.

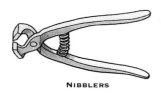

NIBBLERS

3 Stretch a length of thin wire across a panel of chipboard, place the scored line directly over the wire and press down on both sides to snap the tile. Smooth the cut edges of the tile with a tile sander or small slipstone.

1 MEASURE THE MARGIN

2 SCORE THE GLAZED SURFACE

3 SNAP THE TILE

Tile-cutting jig

If you are planning to do a lot of tiling, it is worth buying a purpose-made tile-cutting jig. Inexpensive plastic jigs are perfectly adequate for relatively thin tiles, but you can also buy more substantial jigs that will cut tiles of any thickness. These jigs enable you to score tiles accurately and snap them with ease every time.

Cutting thin strips

A cutting jig is the most accurate tool for cutting a thin strip cleanly from the edge of a tile. If you do not want to use the strip itself, chip away the waste a little at a time with tile nibblers.

CUTTING TILES TO FIT AROUND APPLIANCES

Cutting border tiles is relatively easy, but you will have to perfect different techniques to fit wall tiles around pipes and appliances.

Fitting around a pipe
Try to set out tiles so that you can cut semi-circles from the edges of two adjacent tiles.

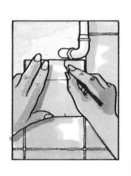

2 Make one straight cut through the centre of the circle and either nibble out the waste, having scored the curve, or clamp it in a vice, protected with softening, and cut it out with a tile saw. Stick one half of the tile on each side of the pipe.

1 If that is not possible, mark the centre of the pipe on the top and side edges of a tile and draw lines across the tile from these points. Where they cross, draw round a coin or something slightly larger than the diameter of the pipe.

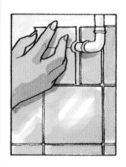

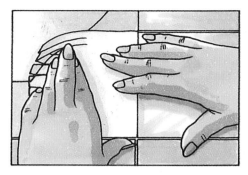

Cutting a curve
To fit a tile against a curved shape, cut a template from thin card to the exact size of a tile. Cut 'fingers' along one edge; press them against the curve to reproduce the shape. Transfer the curve onto the face of the tile and cut away the waste with a tile saw (instead of a blade, this has a thin metal rod, coated with hard abrasive particles, that will cut in any direction).

Fitting around a shaver socket
You may have to cut a square or oblong piece from one corner of a tile in order to fit around a shaver socket. Mark it from the socket, then clamp the tile in a vice, protected with softening. Score both lines, then use a saw file to make one diagonal cut from the corner of the tile to where the lines meet. Snap out both triangles.

If you have to cut a notch out of a large tile, cut down both sides with a hacksaw, then score between them and snap the piece out of the middle.

GROUTING THE TILES AND SEALING THE GAPS

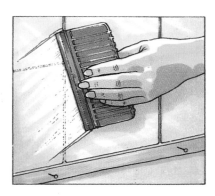

GROUT SPREADER

Use a ready-mixed paste called grout to fill the gaps between the tiles. Standard grouts are white, grey or brown, but there is also a limited range of coloured grouts to match or contrast with the tiles. If you need to match a particular colour, mix pigments into a dry powdered grout, and then add water. Waterproof grout is essential for showers and bath surrounds.

Spreading the grout
Leave the tile adhesive to harden for 24 hours, then use a rubber-bladed spreader to press grout into the joints. Spread it in all directions to make sure all the joints are well filled.

Wipe grout from the surface of the tiles with a sponge before it sets. Smooth the joints with a blunt-ended stick – use a knife and abrasive paper to shape one end of a dowel. When the grout has dried, polish the tiles with a dry cloth.

Leave the grout to harden for about a week before using a tiled shower.

SEALING AROUND BATHROOM FITTINGS

It's best not to use grout to seal the gap between a tiled wall and shower tray, bath or basin – the fittings can flex sufficiently to crack a rigid seal, and allow water to seep in. Instead, use a silicone-rubber caulking compound to fill the gaps. The compound, which is packed in cartridges with pointed nozzles, remains flexible enough to accommodate any movement. These sealants are available in a choice of colours to match tiles and bathroom fittings, and can cope with gaps up to 3mm (⅛in) wide.

Using a sealant
Trim the end off the plastic nozzle (the amount you cut off dictates the thickness of the bead) and press the tip into the joint at an angle of 45 degrees. Push forward at a steady rate while squeezing the applicator's trigger or the base of the cartridge itself to apply a bead of sealant. Smooth any ripples with the handle of a wetted teaspoon.

OUTDOORS

1

A
COUPLE
OF HOURS

Tips for planning
your garden
128

Quick fix for a
rotting fence
134

Stopping your pond
overflowing
135

Camouflaging an
ugly wall
136

Levelling a loose
paving slab
138

Lopping branches
139

Saving rainwater
140

Plant protection
142

Making a garden
incinerator
144

ALLOW A COUPLE OF HOURS

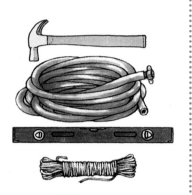

Essential tools

Hammer

Hosepipe

Long straightedge

Short wooden stakes

Spirit level

Strong twine

Tape measure

See also:
Building a cascade, page 108
Building a flight of strong steps,
page 94
Constructing a rockery, page 100
Laying out a parking space, page 96
Laying stepping stones across your
lawn, page 30
Making a gravel garden, page 74
Making a small pond, page 102
Screening off a patio, page 82
Terracing a steep garden, page 90

TIPS FOR PLANNING YOUR GARDEN

Designing a garden is not an exact science. Plants and shrubs may not thrive even when you select species recommended for your particular soil conditions and for the amount of sunlight your garden receives; and trees may never reach the size specified in a catalogue. Nevertheless, forward planning produces a more satisfactory result than a haphazard approach, which may cause expensive mistakes – like laying a patio where it will be in shade for most of the day, or digging a fish pond that is too small to create the required conditions for the fish. It is these permanent features you should concentrate on planning first, at the same time keeping in mind how they will fit with planted and turfed areas of the garden.

There's no rush

Designing a complete garden can take a long time. When you move into a new home, it may well pay to delay major decisions about the garden for at least twelve months, so you can make notes on how the conditions change from season to season. This also gives you the opportunity to experiment with different garden arrangements and to sketch your ideas on paper – pleasant and useful ways to spend your time, if only for a couple of hours at a stretch.

DECIDING ON THE APPROACH

Before you put pencil to paper, think about the type of garden you want and ask yourself whether it will sit happily with your house and its immediate surroundings. Is it to be a formal garden, laid out in straight lines or geometric patterns – a style that often marries successfully with modern architecture? Or do you prefer the more relaxed style of a rambling cottage garden? If you opt for the latter, remember that natural informality may not be as easy to achieve as you think, and your planting scheme will probably take several years to mature into the romantic garden that you have in mind. Or maybe you are attracted by the idea of a Japanese-style garden – a blend of both styles, with every plant, stone and pool of water carefully positioned, so that it bears all the hallmarks of a man-made landscape yet conveys a sense of natural harmony.

A garden for all tastes
Good garden design does not rely on having a large plot of land. Here, curvilinear shapes draw the eye through a delightful array of foliage and flowers planted around a beautifully manicured lawn and a small but perfectly balanced fish pond.

Getting inspired

There is no shortage of material from which to draw inspiration – there are countless books and magazines devoted to designing and planning gardens. Since no two gardens are completely alike, you probably won't find a plan that fits your plot exactly, but you may well be able to adapt a particular approach or develop a small detail into your own design.

Visiting other gardens is an even better way of getting ideas. Although large country estates and city parks are designed on a much grander scale, they at least enable you to see how mature shrubs look or how plants, stone and water have been used in a rockery or water garden. Don't forget that friends may also have had to tackle problems similar to yours – if nothing else, you may be able to learn from their mistakes!

MEASURING UP

In order to make the best use of your particular plot of land, you need to take fairly accurate measurements and check the prevailing conditions.

Taking overall measurements
Note down the overall dimensions of your garden. At the same time, check the diagonal measurements, because a garden that appears to be exactly rectangular or square may not in fact be so. The diagonals are especially important when plotting irregular shapes.

Keep any useful features
Plot the position of features you want to retain in your plan, such as existing pathways, areas of lawn, established trees, and so on.

TIP ● ● ● ● ● ● ● ● ● ● ● ● ●
Soil conditions
The type of soil you have in your garden will of course influence your choice of plants, although you can easily adjust soil content by adding peat or fertilizers. Clay soil, which is greyish in colour, is heavy when wet and tends to crack when dry. A sandy soil feels gritty and loose in dry conditions. Acidic peat soil is dark brown and flaky. Pale-coloured chalky soil, which often contains flints, will not support acid-loving plants. Any soil that contains too many small stones or gravel is unsuitable as topsoil.

Making a note of slopes and gradients
Check how much the ground slopes. An accurate survey is not necessary, but at least jot down the direction of the slope and plot the points where it begins and ends. You can get some idea of the differences in level by using a long straightedge and a spirit level. Place one end of the straightedge on the top of a bank, for example, and measure the vertical distance from the other end to the foot of the slope.

Using a steep gradient to advantage
Some of the most dramatic gardens have resulted from having to contend with a sloping site. The photograph above shows how retaining walls can be used to terrace a steep bank of colourful shrubs.

How about the weather?
Check the passage of the sun and the direction of prevailing winds. Don't forget that the angle of the sun will be higher in summer, and a screen of deciduous trees will be less effective as a windbreak when they drop their leaves.

Armed with all the measurements you have taken, make a simple drawing to try out your ideas. Then mark out the shapes and plot the positions of the important features in your garden, to make sure that your plan will work in reality.

Drawing a plan

Draw a plan of your garden on paper. It must be a properly scaled plan or you are sure to make some gross errors, but it need not be professionally perfect. Use squared graph paper to plot the dimensions – but do the actual drawing on tracing paper laid over the graph paper, so you can try out several ideas and adapt your plan without having to redraw it every time.

TIP ● ● ● ● ● ● ● ● ● ● ●

Common-sense safety

Don't make your garden an obstacle course. For example, a narrow path alongside a pond may be intimidating to an elderly relative, and low walls or planters near the edge of a patio could cause someone to trip.

Plotting your design

Planning on paper is only the first stage. Gardens are rarely seen from above – it is therefore essential to plot the design on the ground, so you can check your dimensions and view the features from different angles.

A pond or patio that seems enormous on paper may look pathetically small in reality. Other shortcomings, such as the way a tree will block the view from your proposed patio, become obvious once you lay out the plan full size.

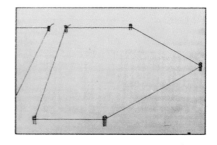

1 *Plot individual features by driving pegs into the ground and stretching string lines between them.*

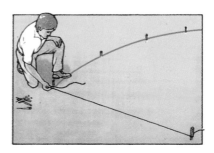

2 *Scribe arcs on the ground with a rope tied to a peg, and mark the curved lines with stakes or a row of bricks.*

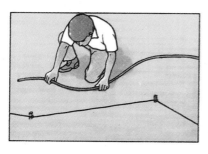

3 Use a garden hose to mark out less regular curves and ponds. If you can scrape areas clear of weeds, that will define the shapes still further.

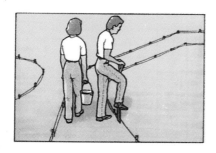

4 When you have marked out your design, carry out a few experiments to check that it is practicable. Will it be possible, for instance, for two people to pass each other on a path without having to step into the flowerbeds?

TIP ● ● ● ● ● ● ● ● ● ● ● ●
Siting a pond
Site a pond away from overhanging trees and in an area where it will catch at least half the day's sunlight. Check that you can reach it with a hose, and that you can run electrical cables to power a pump or night-time lighting.

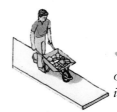

5 Can you set down a wheelbarrow on the path without one of the legs slipping into a flowerbed?

6 Try placing some furniture on the area you have marked out for a patio, to make sure there is enough room to relax comfortably or sit down to a meal with visitors.

7 Allow a minimum width of 3m (9ft 9in) for a driveway, making sure there is enough room to open the doors of cars parked alongside a wall. If possible, allow room for the turning circle of your car. And make sure that when you pull out into the road you will have a clear view of the traffic.

8 Bear in mind that vehicles larger than your own may need to use the drive or parking space.

ALLOW A COUPLE OF HOURS

A CORDLESS DRILL IS
IDEAL FOR OUTDOOR WORK

Essential tools
Electric drill and bits
Garden spade
Spanner
Spirit level
Trowel

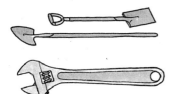

See also:
Replacing a fence post, page 34

QUICK FIX FOR A ROTTING FENCE

Buried timber fence posts often rot below ground level, leaving a perfectly sound section above. Eventually a strong wind snaps the weakened wood – and before you know it the whole fence begins to sway, putting additional strain on the remaining posts.

The best option is to replace the damaged fence post, but you can make a passable repair by bracing the upper section with a short concrete post known as a spur, which comes ready-made with holes for bolting it to the sound section of the fence post using coach screws (woodscrews with square heads).

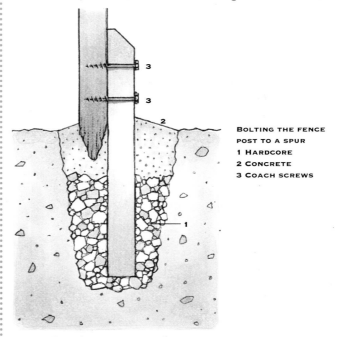

BOLTING THE FENCE
POST TO A SPUR
1 HARDCORE
2 CONCRETE
3 COACH SCREWS

Erecting the spur
Dig the soil from around the rotted stump and remove it. Insert the concrete spur in the hole and pack hardcore around it. Make sure the spur is upright, then fill the hole with concrete.

Drill pilot holes in the wooden post for the coach screws and, using a spanner, draw the post tightly against the spur. Smooth the concrete around the spur with a trowel.

STOPPING YOUR POND OVERFLOWING

Every garden pond needs topping up from time to time – and as many gardeners know to their cost, it is all too easy to forget to turn off the water and flood the garden when the pond overflows. As a precaution, build a simple drain beneath the pond's edging stones to allow excess water to escape. This also provides a means of running electric flex into the pond to power a pump or lighting.

ALLOW A COUPLE OF HOURS

Essential tools

Hacksaw or tenon saw

Pop riveter

1 *Cut corrugated-plastic sheet into two strips about 150mm (6in) wide and long enough to run under the edging stones. Pop-rivet the strips together to make a channel about 25mm (1in) deep.*

2 *Scrape earth and sand from beneath the pond liner in order to accommodate the channel, then lay edging stones on top to hold it in place.*

Dig a small soakaway behind the channel and fill it with rubble topped with fine gravel or turf up to the level of the stones.

ALLOW A COUPLE OF HOURS

Essential tools

Electric drill

Hammer

Masonry bit

Pliers

Fixing a trellis to a wall
You can buy trellis panels made from treated timber or from polystyrene that come in a range of sizes and shapes. There are also expanding trellises, which you open out to a width that is suitable for your particular location. Attach the trellis to the masonry, using rust-proof screws driven into wall plugs. A plastic trellis spacer or short strip of wood slipped around each screw will hold the trellis away from the wall, to provide a clear path for the climbing plants.

See also:
Brightening up a dull wall, page 118
Refurbishing an old wall, page 64

CAMOUFLAGING AN UGLY WALL

Since brick and stone are attractive building materials, they rarely require any form of embellishment to make them acceptable. Indeed, unless painting walls is the tradition in your part of the country, masonry is generally best left unfinished. But if you look out onto the end of a terrace of houses or the back wall of an extension, you may want to disguise the expanse of featureless masonry with climbing plants such as ivy, clematis or Virginia creeper.

PROVIDING SUPPORT FOR CLIMBERS

Because the adventitious roots of ivy grip the surface of a wall, a mature plant does not need further support. Similarly, Virginia creeper has sticky tendrils that will adhere to the masonry. However, both plants require training wires or a supporting trellis to get them started and to help them climb in the required direction. Both clematis and passion flowers need wires or a trellis as anchor points for their clinging tendrils.

PUTTING UP TRAINING WIRES

Run lengths of galvanized or plastic-covered training wire up or across the wall. Place the wires about 450mm (1ft 6in) apart.

1 At each end of each run of wire, drill and plug a hole for a long screw eye.

2 Twist one end of the training wire through one of the screw eyes.

3 At about 2m (6ft) intervals, thread the wire through a stamped-metal vine eye driven into the pointing. Twist the wire onto another screw eye at the far end.

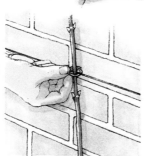

4 Attach the plant stem to the wire using plastic split rings or garden ties, or tie it loosely with garden twine.

Will ivy harm masonry?

There is a widely held belief that climbing plants, especially ivy, will damage any masonry wall. If exterior rendering or the mortar between bricks or stonework is in a poor condition, then a vigorous ivy plant will undoubtedly weaken the structure as its aerial roots attempt to extract moisture from the masonry. The roots will invade broken joints or rendering and, on finding a source of nourishment for the plant, will expand and burst the weakened material, thus encouraging damp to penetrate.

However, with sound bricks and mortar ivy can do no more than climb with the aid of training wires and its own suckerlike roots, which do not provide nourishment but are for support only.

So long as the structure is sound and free from damp, there is even some benefit in allowing a plant to clothe a wall, since its close-growing mat of leaves, mostly with their drip tips pointing downwards, acts as insulation and provides protection against the elements.

TIP ● ● ● ● ● ● ● ● ● ● ● ● ●
Keeping climbers under control
Climbers must be pruned regularly, so that they do not penetrate between roof tiles or slates or clog drainpipes and gutters.

If a robust climber is allowed to grow unchecked, the weight of the mature plant may eventually topple a weakened wall.

LEVELLING A LOOSE PAVING SLAB

Unless paving is firmly bedded on a layer of concrete, the long-term effects of rainwater, ants or tree roots can cause one or more slabs to become unstable. If you discover that a paving slab rocks every time you step on it, level the slab without delay – before it causes someone to trip.

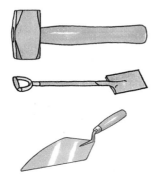

Essential tools
Club hammer

Garden spade

Small trowel

1 Insert the tip of a spade into the joint on one side of the loose slab, and lever it carefully out of its recess.

2 Level the exposed area, adding hardcore or sharp sand to fill hollows and tamping it flush with a stout piece of wood.

3 Make a stiff mortar, using 1 part cement to 4 parts builder's sand. Put a fist-size blob of mortar in each corner of the recess, and one more in the middle.

4 Lower the slab into place and position it centrally, using the tip of the spade. Lay a stout wooden batten across the slab and tap it down with a club hammer until the slab is flush with the ones surrounding it.

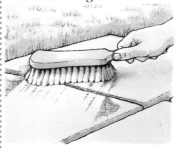

5 Brush a dry mortar mix (1 part cement to 3 parts sand) into the joints and sprinkle it lightly with water. Don't step on the slab for at least 24 hours.

LOPPING BRANCHES

Most trees require no more than light pruning to keep them in shape and prevent them casting too much shadow over your garden. If you want to reduce the height of a large tree or remove a tree that appears to be damaging neighbouring property, always seek the advice of a professional tree surgeon and contact your local authority to check whether the tree is protected. Obtaining official permission to fell trees is especially relevant if you live in a conservation area. Consult your neighbours, and think carefully before you do anything to a mature tree that might harm it or spoil the local environment.

1 Partially cut through the underside of the branch, about 300mm (1ft) from the main stem or trunk.

2 Make a second partial cut, this time through the upper side of the branch about 25mm (1in) further away from the trunk.

3 As the second cut comes near to the first, the branch will fall away, without stripping the bark of the tree back to the trunk.

4 Remove the remaining stump with a single saw cut, almost flush with the stem or trunk, then trim the rough edges with a pruning knife. Paint the cut end with a proprietary pruning sealant to protect the tree from disease, frost damage and excessive damp.

ALLOW A COUPLE OF HOURS

Essential tools

Pruning knife

Pruning saw or log saw

Old paintbrush

Removing damaged or diseased branches

You can safely remove small diseased branches or trim back the remains of broken tree limbs, so long as you take adequate precautions to ensure that severed wood can fall harmlessly to the ground. Don't climb trees in order to reach damaged branches unless you can construct a secure working platform or harness yourself safely to the tree trunk.

The technique shown here is designed to remove a branch without the wood tearing back to the main stem or tree trunk.

Unless urgent treatment is required, it is usually best to wait until late winter or early spring before removing branches. However, some fruit trees (such as damson, plum and cherry) should only be pruned in midsummer.

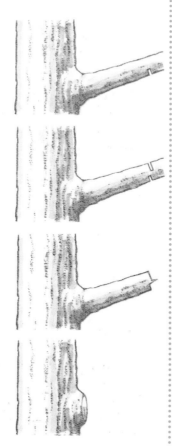

Essential tools
Hacksaw

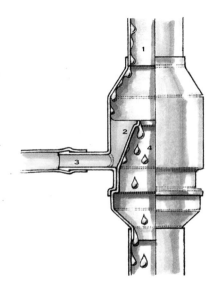

Inside a diverter
*Water running down the
inside wall of the downpipe
(1) is collected in a circular
channel (2) and diverted
into the filler tube (3) that
runs to the butt. When
the butt is filled to
capacity, the channel
overflows into the
lower section of the
downpipe (4).*

SAVING RAINWATER

Long dry summers often create temporary
water shortages that lead to a ban on using
hosepipes for watering gardens. Conserving
rainwater for your own use is good for the
environment – and if you do not have an
outside tap, it may be more convenient to fill
watering cans from a water butt in the garden
rather than use a tap in the house.

Rainwater diverters and butts

By inserting a plastic diverter into a guttering downpipe, you can deliver rainwater via a flexible filler tube
into a storage butt standing alongside.

For a large garden, it is possible to couple two butts
together, using another flexible tube. Alternatively, it
may be convenient to fill one butt from a downpipe on
the house and a second one from a garage or shed at
the far end of the garden. Place each butt on a ready-
made stand or build a plinth from concrete blocks, so
you can place a watering can beneath the tap

There are a number of rainwater
diverters on the market. Many of
them will fit downpipes of various
diameters; some can be adapted
to take square pipes.

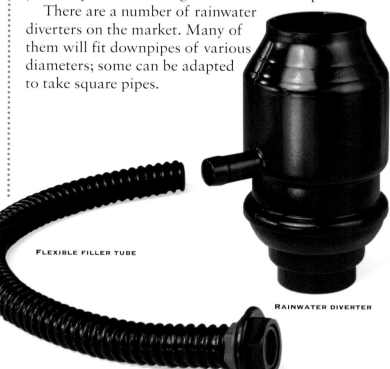

FLEXIBLE FILLER TUBE

RAINWATER DIVERTER

FITTING A RAINWATER DIVERTER

Since each brand of diverter is slightly different, you will need to follow the manufacturer's detailed instructions.

The following describes the general principles for fitting a diverter into a circular downpipe.

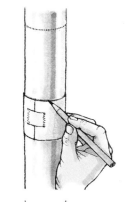

1 Mark a line round the pipe, level with the top of the water butt, remembering to include the height of the stand or plinth.

Mark a similar line below the first. The exact location of this line will depend on the size of your diverter (see manufacturer's instructions).

2 Cut out the section of pipe between the two lines, using a hacksaw.

3 Locate the diverter on the end of the top section of downpipe, then slide it up the pipe until you can insert it into the lower section of the downpipe.

Swivel the diverter to direct its outlet towards the water butt.

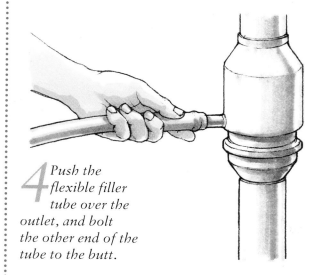

4 Push the flexible filler tube over the outlet, and bolt the other end of the tube to the butt.

TO MAXIMIZE STORAGE, COUPLE TWO BUTTS TOGETHER

TIP ● ● ● ● ● ● ● ● ● ● ● ● ●

Fitting a safe lid

Make sure a water butt is sealed with a lid fitted with a child-proof catch. You may be able to buy a replacement if your water butt is not already fitted with this type of lid.

PLANT PROTECTION

Newly planted shrubs and trees, especially conifers, are particularly vulnerable to the cold drying winds often prevalent from late autumn to early spring. The same seasons bring damaging frosts. As autumn approaches, take a few simple precautions to protect exposed plants.

PROTECTING PLANTS FROM WIND

Permanent protection can be provided by planting hedges or screens of hardy trees and shrubs on the windward side of the garden (this is normally to the north or northeast). If permanent screening is impractical, there are a number of ways to provide temporary protection.

Supporting bushy plants
To help bushy plants withstand the punishing effects of wind, push twiggy sticks into the ground around them. Alternatively, insert garden canes and tie the plants to them loosely with twine.

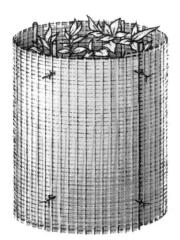

Reducing the impact of icy winds
Effective protection can be achieved by screening plants with a material that will reduce the strength of the wind while allowing air to circulate. One way is to wire purpose-made reed or thatch screening to existing chain-link fencing or an open ranch-style fence. Alternatively, make a temporary cage from plastic windbreak netting or old sacking, wired or stapled to strong garden canes or wooden stakes.

See also:
Providing support for climbers, page 19

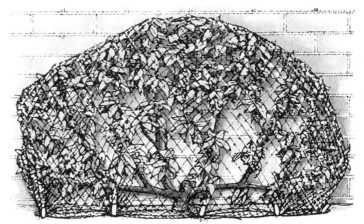

Protecting climbers and fruit trees
Tie a blanket of windbreak netting over vulnerable climbers or fruit trees growing against a wall. Wire the netting to wall-mounted training wires or vine eyes and stake it to the ground.

FROST PROTECTORS

When planning your garden, give some thought to where frost is most likely to occur, and plant accordingly. Don't place susceptible plants in the lower parts of a site, because these are where cold air tends to collect.

As a matter of course, prudent gardeners lay a mulch of straw or peat around plants to prevent frost attacking at soil level. Hold straw in place with wire or canes.

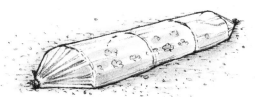

Protecting low-growing plants
Buy a plastic-tunnel cloche kit to protect a row of plants from frost. Each kit consists of a polyethylene cover that is stretched over polypropylene hoops driven into the soil. You can make a similar cloche from a sheet of plastic supported by a row of bent canes.

Screening taller plants
Cover small individual plants with clear-plastic bottles. Cut off the bottom of each bottle and press the cut edge into the soil. Stick short twigs into the soil around the plant to support the bottle cover from inside.

Wrap sheets of plastic or sacking around canes to protect larger plants; or make a cane-and-wire tent stuffed with bracken, which will provide both wind and frost protection.

Staking freestanding trees
Young trees must be staked to provide them with support until they are strong enough to withstand strong winds. Dig a hole for the rootball of the tree and drive in a strong stake on the windward side of the hole.

Plant the tree and heel it in, then secure the stem to the stake just beneath the lower branches, using a tree tie – a plastic or rubber strap available from garden centres. Place the tie's buckle between the tree and the stake. If necessary, carefully saw the top off the stake so that it is the same height as the tree stem.

Essential tools

Club hammer

Cold chisel

Alternative tools

Hole saw

Power drill

See also:
Making a compost bin, page 50

MAKING A GARDEN INCINERATOR

Vegetable matter and, to some extent, paper can be converted into compost for spreading on the garden. Some waste, however, will not break down readily and is best disposed of by burning in an efficient incinerator. Instead of buying a ready-made incinerator, you can make your own from an old metal dustbin or a pile of second-hand bricks. First, check that the burning of garden waste is not prohibited in your area.

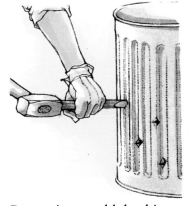

Converting an old dustbin
An old galvanized dustbin can be turned into a useful incinerator – although it will eventually rust through, once the heat has removed the protective plating.

Half-fill the dustbin with sand and, using a cold chisel and club hammer, drive a series of randomly spaced holes all round the lower part of the bin. Wear protective leather gloves and goggles for this work.

Alternatively, for a neater appearance, drill round holes, using a 25mm (1in) diameter high-speed-steel hole saw fitted in an electric drill.

After emptying out the sand, make a few rainwater-drainage holes in the bottom, working from inside.

Stand the bin on old bricks or concrete blocks.

YOU CAN FIT A METAL-CUTTING, HIGH-SPEED-STEEL HOLE SAW WITH A 25MM (1IN) DIAMETER INTO THE CHUCK OF AN ELECTRIC DRILL

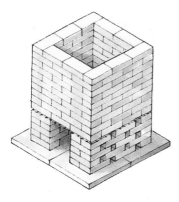

Making a brick incinerator

Choose a level site, away from the house and where there is no overhanging foliage. The incinerator is made from a total of 140 dry-laid bricks, to build a chamber 15 courses high.

Lay a square base, using four paving slabs, though this is not essential if the ground is well compacted.

For the bottom course, lay eight bricks to form a square, spacing the bricks 50mm (2in) apart. Make an ash hole by laying the middle brick end on, or use a half brick. Lay the next four courses in a similar manner, but work in alternate directions so the spaces are staggered. After building the first five courses, lay on a square of heavy-gauge wire mesh.

For the remaining 10 courses, use 10 bricks per course, butting their ends together and staggering the vertical joints.

When you are loading the incinerator, cut up branches into manageable sizes – don't ram in large pieces, as that can dislodge the bricks.

BUILDING A BRICK INCINERATOR
1 PAVING-SLAB BASE
2 SPACES PROVIDE UPDRAUGHT
3 ASH HOLE
4 WIRE MESH
5 BRICK CHIMNEY

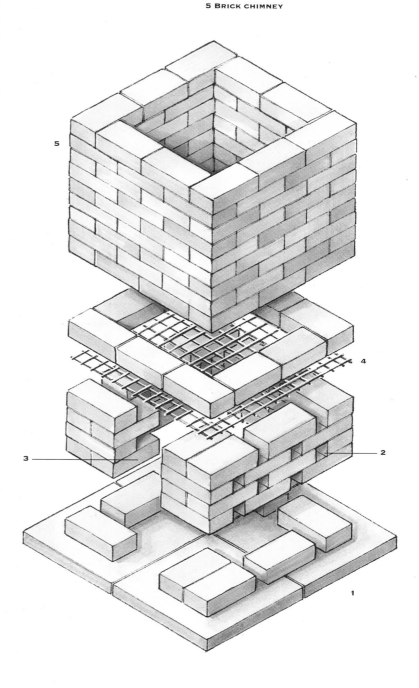

145

2

A
MORNING'S
WORK

**Laying stepping stones
across your lawn
148**

**Laying decorative
cobblestones
149**

**Maintaining garden steps
150**

**Replacing a fence post
152**

**Making a hanging
bird table
156**

**A nesting box for
garden birds
158**

**Window boxes and
planters
160**

**Storing your garden tools
163**

ALLOW A WHOLE MORNING

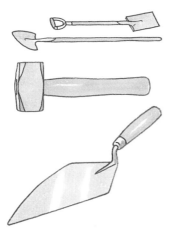

Essential tools

Spade or trowel

Club hammer

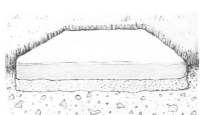

MERGE STEPPING STONES
WITH CRAZY PAVING

LAYING STEPPING STONES ACROSS YOUR LAWN

It makes sense to pave regularly used routes (for example, from your back door to the garage or to a greenhouse at the bottom of the garden), especially if the toing and froing is wearing bald patches across the grass. If a continuous pathway would look too formal, lay a row of cast-concrete flagstones to serve as stepping stones – or, better still, use flat slabs of real stone.

1 Cut around the edge of each stone with a spade or trowel, and remove the area of turf directly beneath.

2 Scoop out the earth to allow for a 25mm (1in) bed of sharp sand plus the stone, which needs to be about 18mm (¾in) below the level of the surrounding turf to avoid damaging the cutters of your lawn mower.

3 Tap the stone into the sand until it no longer rocks when you step on it.

TIP ●
Merging with a patio
You could combine a stepping-stone pathway with a patio laid with crazy paving. Create a broken edge to the patio, so the path merges naturally.

LAYING DECORATIVE COBBLESTONES

Cobbles, the large flint pebbles found on many beaches, can be laid loose, perhaps mingled with larger rocks and plants. Setting them in mortar or concrete creates a more permanent paved area. You can buy cobbles from large garden centres and some DIY stores.

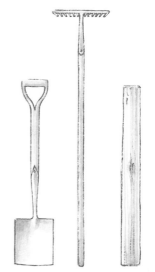

Bedding cobbles in concrete
Consolidate a layer of hard-core and cover it with a levelled layer of dry concrete mix about 50mm (2in) deep.

Press the cobbles into the dry mix, packing them tightly together and leaving them projecting above the surface.

Using a stout batten, tamp the cobblestones level, then lightly sprinkle the whole area with water, both to initiate the concrete-hardening process and to clean the surfaces of the cobbles.

Essential tools

Heavy tamping batten

Rake

Spade

Lay wet or dry
You can bed cobbles into concrete, leaving pockets here and there for plants (above). Or you can lay them loose to create a natural beach effect – attractive and labour-saving (left).

See also:
Mixing concrete, page 111

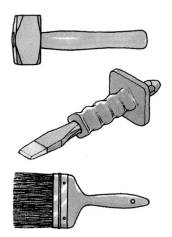

Essential tools

Club hammer

Cold chisel

Edging trowel

Metal trowel
or wooden float

Paintbrush

Safety goggles

See also:
Building a flight of strong steps,
page 94
Levelling a loose paving slab,
page 20
Repointing masonry, page 67

MAINTAINING GARDEN STEPS

Inspect garden steps regularly to make sure they are not deteriorating beyond a safe condition. Replace cracked paving slabs, and secure any slabs that are loose or rocking. Repoint brickwork supports before the mortar starts to fall out, and replace rotting timber steps and risers.

TIP ● ● ● ● ● ● ● ● ● ● ● ● ● ● ● ● ● ● ●
Don't let steps become slippery
Algae tends to develop in damp conditions (especially under trees), and steps can become slippery if it is allowed to build up on the surfaces. Brush them with a solution of 1 part household bleach to 4 parts water. After 48 hours, wash with clean water and repeat if the fungal growth is heavy. Alternatively, use a proprietary fungicidal solution, following the manufacturer's instructions carefully.

As part of your routine maintenance, sweep wet leaves off steps and pathways.

REPAIRING CONCRETE STEPS

Like other forms of masonry, concrete suffers from spalling: frost breaks down the surface and flakes off fragments of material. Spalling frequently occurs along the front edges of steps, where foot traffic adds to the problem. Repair broken edges without delay. Besides being ugly, with uneven edges the steps are not as safe as they might be.

1 Wearing safety goggles, chip away concrete around the damaged area in order to provide a good grip for fresh concrete. Cut a board to the height of the riser and prop it against the step with bricks. Dilute some PVA bonding agent with water – say 3 parts water to 1 part bonding agent – and brush it onto the damaged area, taking care to stipple it into the crevices.

2 Mix a small batch of general-purpose concrete (1 part cement, 2 parts sharp sand and 3 parts aggregate), adding a little PVA bonding agent to help it stick to the step. When the surface becomes tacky, fill the hole with concrete mix, flush with the edge of the board.

3 Radius the front edge slightly with a home-made edging trowel, running it against the board.

Making an edging trowel
Bend a piece of sheet metal over a rod or tube that has a diameter of 18mm (¾ in), then screw a handle in the centre.

As you finish the surface of the concrete, run the radiused edge of the trowel against the board to keep the tool on a straight path.

ALLOW A WHOLE MORNING

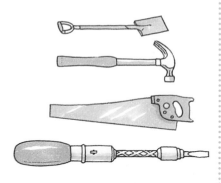

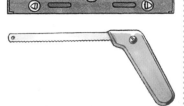

Essential tools

Garden spade

Hacksaw

Hammer

Panel saw

Screwdriver

Spirit level

For post spikes

Sledgehammer

Spanner

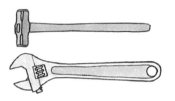

See also:
A quick fix for a rotting fence, page 16

REPLACING A FENCE POST

Strong winds play havoc with old fences, especially as it used to be the practice to bury the ends of the posts in nothing more than rammed hardcore. This, coupled with the fact the posts were not pressure-treated with preserver, as they are today, means that one or more posts can easily work loose or become seriously weakened by wet rot.

You can get away with quick fixes for a while, but eventually you are better off replacing suspect posts, if for no other reason than to preserve the appearance of a well-maintained fence.

It shouldn't take longer than half a day to replace a single post – although if you have set it in concrete, you will have to wait for the concrete to set before you can complete the job.

Choose a post that matches the size of the original, but remember to allow extra on the length – at least one quarter of the post should be buried to provide a firm foundation, and you need a bit extra so you can cut the post down to match the height of the fence after it is in place.

PRESERVING FENCE POSTS

A new pressure-treated post will carry a substantial guarantee against rot – but if you can't get one that matches the colour of your fence, it pays to treat the new post yourself by soaking it in chemical preserver.

CLEAR   **COLOURED**   **GREEN**

Types of preserver

There are clear solvent-based preservers that protect timber from wet rot only. Alternatively, use an all-purpose fluid that also provides protection against wood-boring insects. Most modern solvent-based products are harmless to plants when dry, but it makes sense to check this before you buy. Water-based preservers are odourless, and safe to use on horticultural timbers.

Tinted preservers have the advantage of colouring the post while protecting the wood against rot. Various brown shades are available, intended to simulate the most common hardwoods. Solvent-based preservers are made with light-fast pigments that inhibit fading. They do not penetrate as well as a clear preserver, but generally offer slightly better protection than the coloured water-based preservers.

SOAKING THE POST IN PRESERVER

Any wood in contact with the ground benefits from prolonged immersion in preserver. You should at least stand the fence post on end in a bucket of fluid overnight.

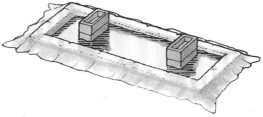

1 For better protection, make a shallow bath from loose bricks and line it with thick polyethylene sheet. Fill the trough with preserver and immerse one or more of the posts, weighing them down with bricks to prevent them from floating.

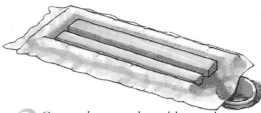

2 Cover the trough and leave the wood to soak overnight. To empty the bath, sink a bucket at one end of the trough, then remove the bricks at that end so the fluid will pour out. Let the post dry out for 24 hours.

TIP ● ● ● ● ● ● ● ● ● ● ● ● ●
Safety with preservers
Solvent-based preservers are flammable – so do not smoke while using them, and extinguish any naked lights. Wear protective gloves and goggles when applying preservers. Wash spilt preserver from your skin and eyes with water immediately, and get medical advice if irritation persists.

REMOVING THE OLD POST

Support the panel on each side of the fence, using long strips of wood wedged firmly under the top strip or the arris rail.

1 Cut the old post free, using a hack-saw blade to sever nail fixings.

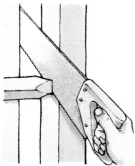

2 If the post is attached to a closeboard fence, remove the first vertical board on each side of the post and then saw through the arris rails.

3 Removing the topsoil from around the post may loosen it sufficiently for you to pull it out. If the post is bedded firmly, or sunk into concrete, lever it out with a stout batten. First, drive large nails into two opposite faces of the post, about 300mm (1ft) from the ground. Then bind a length of rope around the post just below the nails and tie the ends to the tip of the batten. Build a pile of bricks close to the post and use it as a fulcrum to lever the post out of the ground.

ERECTING THE NEW POST

Dig out the hole. If you experience difficulty in digging the hole to the required depth or want to use a post-hole auger, remove one or both of the fence panels to give you more room to manoeuvre.

1 Pack the bottom of the hole with hardcore (broken bricks or small stones) to a depth of about 150mm (6in).

2 Put the post in the hole, using the panels as a guide to its position. Ram some more hardcore around the post to keep it upright, then fill the hole with concrete.

3 Nail the panels to the post or attach the severed arris rails, using end brackets made for the purpose. Check that the post is upright, and support the fence while the concrete sets.

4 Next day, cut the post to length. Cut it square and nail on a post cap, or simply cut a bevel and paint the end with preserver.

USING METAL SPIKES

If you don't want to go to the trouble of anchoring a fence post in concrete, you can plug it into the square socket of a metal fence-post spike driven into firm ground. Use a 600mm (2ft) spike for fences up to 1.2m (4ft) high, and a 750mm (2ft 6in) spike for a 1.8m (6ft) fence.

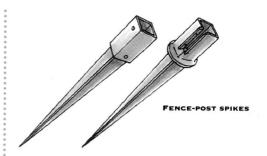

FENCE-POST SPIKES

1 Place a scrap of hardwood post into the socket to protect the metal, then using the edge of the panel to position the spike, drive it partly into the ground with a sledgehammer.

2 Hold a spirit level against the socket to make certain the spike is upright, then hammer the spike into the ground until only the socket is visible.

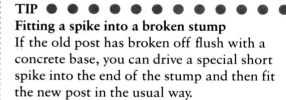

3 Insert the new post and secure it by screwing through the side of the socket or by tightening clamping bolts, depending on the type of spike. Refix the panels and cut the post to length.

TIP ● ● ● ● ● ● ● ● ● ● ● ● ●
Fitting a spike into a broken stump
If the old post has broken off flush with a concrete base, you can drive a special short spike into the end of the stump and then fit the new post in the usual way.

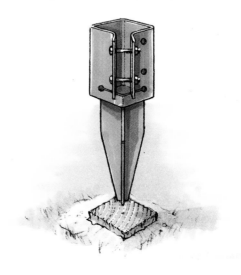

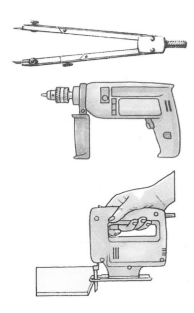

Essential tools

Pair of compasses

Power drill and bits

Power jigsaw

Ruler

MAKING A HANGING BIRD TABLE

A well-stocked bird table will encourage birds to visit your garden, particularly in winter when food sources are scarce. Basically all you need is a simple platform hung from a tree or set on a post – but with only a little more effort you can make an attractive hanging table with feeding and drinking cups, and a woven fence that prevents food scraps being blown over the edge.

TIP
A bird-feeder anchor

As an additional food source, hang a proprietary wire-cage bird feeder from a screw hook driven into the underside of the table. A feeder hanging from the centre acts as an anchor that helps to keep the table on an even keel.

156

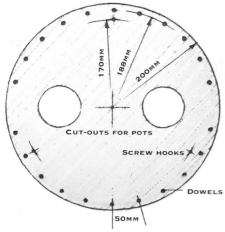

170MM
188MM
200MM

CUT-OUTS FOR POTS

SCREW HOOKS

DOWELS

50MM

Marking out the table

Cut a 425mm (1ft 5in) square from 12mm (½in) exterior-grade plywood, and draw diagonals from each corner to find the centre of the square.

1 *Using a pair of compasses, mark out a circle with a radius of 200mm (8in), then mark a 188mm (7½in) circle inside the first.*

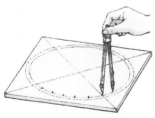

2 *Set the compasses to 50mm (2in) and, starting where one of the diagonals bisects the inner circle, mark off five equally spaced dowel centres on each side of the line for the fence posts.*

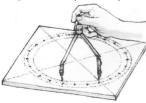

3 *To establish the positions for three brass screw hooks from which to suspend the table, mark another circle, with a radius of 170mm (6¾in), from the same centre. With the compasses set to the same radius, mark off six equally spaced points around the circle. Mark alternate points for positioning the three screw hooks.*

4 *Choose a pair of clean, shallow round plastic pots, such as used for food packaging, to use as feeder cups. Drill drainage holes in one of them. Mark out equally spaced holes in the table to receive the pots so they can be suspended from their rims.*

CUTTING AND ASSEMBLING THE BIRD TABLE

Cut out the plywood disc with a power jigsaw, following the outer line. Sand the edge smooth. Also cut out the holes for the feeder cups.

On the marked centres, drill holes with a diameter of 6mm (¼in) to a depth of 9mm (⅜in) for the fence posts. Also drill pilot holes for the screw hooks. Sand the surface of the board ready for finishing.

For the fence posts, cut pieces of dowelling 38mm (1½in) long. Sand their ends, then glue them into place with a waterproof adhesive.

Finish the board with an acrylic exterior wood stain, and leave it to dry. Rub down and apply a second coat.

Weaving the fence

Weave straight hazel, willow or wisteria twigs between the posts to create a fence on each side. Add a dab of glue to the top twig where it touches each post.

Hanging the table

Insert the brass screw hooks into their pilot holes and hang the table from three lightweight chains cut to an appropriate length. Link the three ends of the chains with a shackle or S-hook. Suspend the table from a convenient support and drop the feeder cups into place.

A NESTING BOX FOR GARDEN BIRDS

A nesting box hung from a tree or screwed to a wall in a quiet corner of the garden will encourage small birds to set up residence.

You can make a box from an offcut of softwood floorboard, measuring 600 x 25mm (2ft x 1in). The size of the entrance hole will determine the species of bird that can use the box. Drill a 25mm (1in) hole for blue tits, or a 32mm (1¼in) hole for larger species of tit. For robins, which need a larger aperture still, make a shorter front panel, with a triangular opening above.

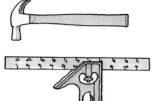

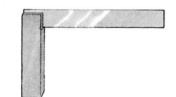

Essential tools

Hammer

Mitre square

Panel saw

Power drill and bits

Screwdriver

Try square

USING A NAIL SET

TREAT THE WOOD WITH AN ACRYLIC EXTERIOR WOOD STAIN. ALLOW IT TO DRY, THEN HANG THE BOX AT LEAST 2.5M (8FT) ABOVE THE GROUND.

NESTING-BOX COMPONENTS
1 RIDGE COVER
2 ROOF
3 BACK PANEL
4 SIDE PANEL
5 BOTTOM
6 FRONT PANEL

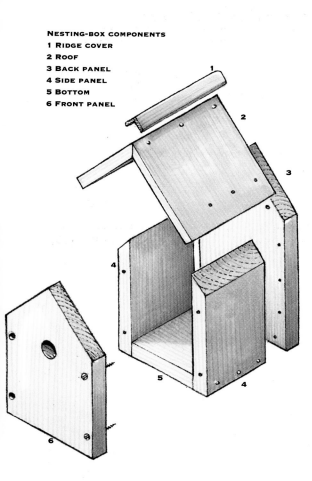

ASSEMBLING THE PARTS

Fix the mitred ends of the roof pieces together, using galvanized nails. Pin a length of wooden corner moulding along the ridge of the roof.

Nail the side panels to the ends of the bottom piece, with their ends flush. Nail the back panel to the sides and bottom.

Fix the front panel to the sides with countersunk brass screws. This will allow you to remove the front of the box at the end of the nesting season, so you can clean out contaminated nesting material.

Nail the roof in place through the back panel, then remove the front panel to fix the roof with nails from inside the box.

Cutting the boards to size

1 *Start by cutting a 260mm (10¼ in) length off a floorboard. Then mark and saw it into two equal parts, cutting a 45-degree bevel through its thickness.*

This single saw cut produces both halves of the pitched roof.

2 *Cut a piece of board 384mm (15in) long, and reduce its width to 100mm (4in).*

For the bottom of the box, cut a piece 100mm (4in) long from one end of the reduced board.

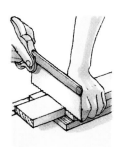

3 *To make the side panels, saw the remainder into two equal parts, cutting a 45-degree bevel across the board.*

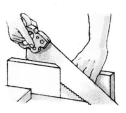

4 *For the back panel, cut a 260mm (10¼ in) length of board. Mark and cut off the top corners at 45 degrees, to form a point at the centre. Drill a fixing hole 90mm (3½ in) below the apex.*

5 *Make the front panel, 200mm (7⅞ in) long, in a similar way. Drill an entrance hole through the panel about 80mm (3in) below the apex.*

ALLOW A WHOLE MORNING

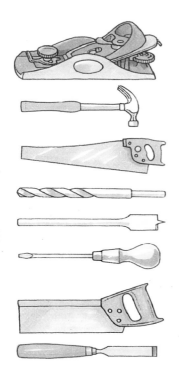

Essential tools

Block plane

Fast-action clamps

Hammer

Jigsaw or panel saw

Masonry bit

Nail set

Paintbrush

Power drill

Screwdriver

Spade bit

Tape measure

Tenon saw

Try square

Twist drills

Wood chisel

WINDOW BOXES AND PLANTERS

A window box allows selected plants to be placed in full view of a window – providing an ideal way for people without gardens to cultivate and enjoy plants. In older houses with recessed windows, boxes can sit on the wide sills. But if the frames of your windows are more or less flush with the outside wall, then window boxes will need to be supported on metal brackets.

Planters are attractive containers for creating a display of garden plants on a patio or balcony. You can either make a planter to accommodate a large plastic tub or pot, or line the inside so the planter can contain soil.

160

MAKING A WINDOW BOX

You can make a simple window box using 150 x 25mm (6 x 1in) softwood board, then paint or varnish it – but prior to finishing, it is essential to treat the wood with preserver.

Measure the width of the window opening for a box that is to sit on the sill; for one that will be hung from the wall on brackets, you need to measure the length of the sill itself. Cut three lengths of board slightly less than this dimension, and two end pieces to the appropriate size. Bore some drainage holes in the bottom panel.

Decorating the front panel

You can leave the boards plain or decorate the front panel. To create the cloverleaf pattern shown here, set out a line of 25mm (1in) equilateral triangles spaced 150mm (6in) apart. Drill out the cloverleaf shape, using a 25mm (1in) spade bit centred on the points of each triangle. Use a chisel to trim off the points left by the drilling.

Attaching the box with brackets

To mount the box on a wall, buy strong metal brackets to fit the depth of the box and fix them securely, using masonry wall plugs. Fix the box to the brackets with screws.

1 BACK PANEL
2 FRONT PANEL
3 BOTTOM PANEL
4 END PANEL
5 FILLET
6 SUPPORT

ASSEMBLING THE BOX

1 Glue and nail the bottom, back and front panels to the ends. Pin and glue triangular or quadrant fillets into the angle at the front and back.

2 Make three supports from 25 x 25mm (1 x 1in) softwood. Each support should be as long as the width of the bottom panel. Glue them to the underside of the box.

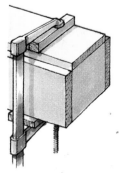

3 Plane the supports to accommodate the slope of the sill, so the bottom of the box is level. Fill the nail holes and finish the box with a polyurethane paint or varnish. Make a fitted liner from polyethylene sheet and pierce the material to make drainage holes. Place the box on the sill and fasten it to the window frame with wire ties.

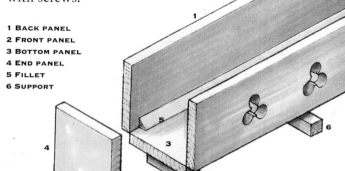

See also:
Types of preserver,
page 35

MAKING A PLANTER

Cut 24 equal lengths of 50 x 25mm (2 x 1in) softwood. Plane chamfers along all their edges. Drill a clearance hole for a screw in the side of each piece, 12mm (½in) from one end and level with the centre line. Soak the wood in preserver.

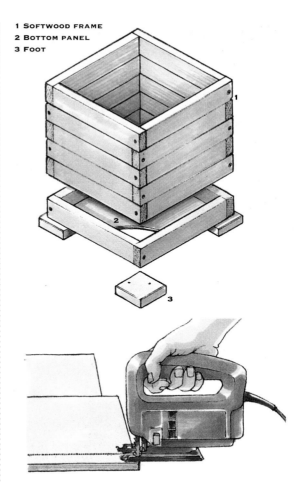

1 SOFTWOOD FRAME
2 BOTTOM PANEL
3 FOOT

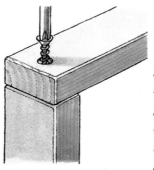

1 Make six identical frames by gluing and screwing a butt joint at each corner. Check that the frames are square.

2 Glue the frames one on top of the other, alternating the direction of the corner joints to create a decorative effect with the end grain.

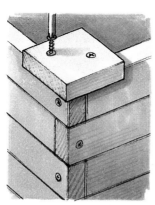

3 Make four feet, each 75mm (3in) square, from wood 25mm (1in) thick, and chamfer their top edges. Glue and screw a foot under each of the corners, with only 12mm (½in) projecting on the two sides.

4 Cut a piece of exterior-grade plywood to fit inside the box and rest on the feet. Finish the planter with exterior wood stain or polyurethane varnish.

Line the box with plastic sheeting or fit a suitable pot.

See also:
Types of preserver, page 35

162

STORING YOUR GARDEN TOOLS

Unless you are very disciplined, your shed or garage is likely to get cluttered with garden tools and other equipment. With careful planning and a few home-made gadgets, you can store your tools neatly so they are easy to find – and at the same time create space in which to move. It should take no longer than about half a day to complete any one project.

ALLOW A WHOLE MORNING

LADDER STORAGE

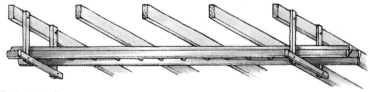

RAFTER BRACKET

Long ladders
Long extending ladders, used primarily for house maintenance, can be stored on suspended wooden frames bolted to the rafters of a garage. Alternatively, hang your ladders on wood or metal brackets fixed along a wall.

Hanging step ladders
Step ladders, used for pruning or harvesting fruit, can be suspended vertically or horizontally on wood or metal brackets screwed to the garage wall.

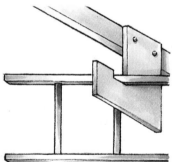

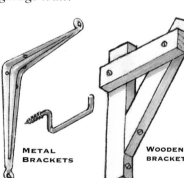

METAL BRACKETS　　**WOODEN BRACKET**

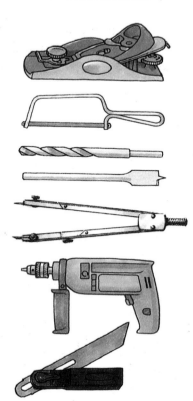

Essential tools
Block plane

Hacksaw

Masonry bits

Pair of compasses

Panel saw

Power drill and bits

Screwdriver

Sliding bevel

Spade bit

Tenon saw

Wood and metal files

Wood chisel

See also:
Laying a firm base for a tool shed, page 110

MAKING A PEGGED HANGING RAIL

A simple line of 12mm (½in) dowel pegs fixed, at a slight angle, into a wooden rail provides convenient storage for a wide range of garden tools. Set in pairs, they will hold garden forks and spades, rakes and brooms. You can tie a loop of string through the handle of other tools and hang them from individual pegs. Use similar pegs to hang up your work clothes.

Hooks and eyes
Screw-in metal hooks and eyes provide a convenient means of hanging small handtools. Fit a screw eye in the end of each handle and hang them on a row of hooks screwed into a rail fixed to the shed or garage wall.

STORING A WHEELBARROW
Tipping a wheelbarrow on end and fastening it to a wall saves space and prevents the barrow collecting rainwater. Screw a bevelled batten about 300mm (12in) from the ground to take the lip of the barrow. Screw a second batten, higher up, to fit between the handles when the barrow is resting on the lower batten. Fit wooden turn buttons to secure the handles.

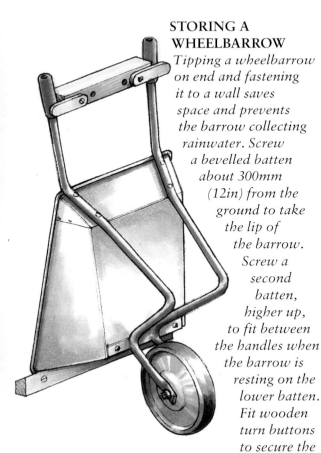

STOWING A LAWN MOWER

Relatively small cylinder and hover mowers that have fold-flat handles can be usefully hung from a wall, but may be awkward to handle and heavy to lift.

To help make storage easier, make a pulley-operated pivoting frame that will lift and hold the mower against the wall. Make the width of the frame to fit inside the machine's handlebar.

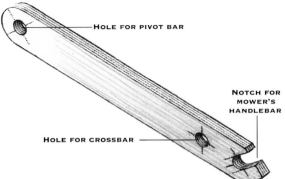

HOLE FOR PIVOT BAR

NOTCH FOR MOWER'S HANDLEBAR

HOLE FOR CROSSBAR

Making the side arms of the frame
Cut two 600 x 60mm (2ft x 2⅜in) side arms from plywood 18mm (¾in) thick. On each side arm, draw a diagonal line from both corners of one end, marking the centre for a 25mm (1in) diameter metal-tube pivot bar. Set a pair of compasses on this centre and mark a semicircle on the end. Mark the centre for a 25mm (1in) metal-tube crossbar, 120mm (5in) from the other end. Mark a 45-degree angled notch to suit the size of the mower's handlebar.

Drill the holes for the metal tubes, shape the end curves, then drill and saw out the notches at the ends.

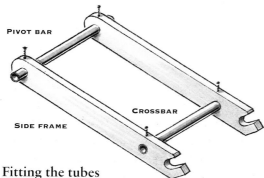

PIVOT BAR

CROSSBAR

SIDE FRAME

Fitting the tubes

Cut the crossbar tube to the required length; and cut the pivot-bar tube 50mm (2in) longer. Glue both tubes into the holes in the side arms with epoxy-resin adhesive. Set the crossbar flush with the outside faces of the arms, so that the pivot bar projects 25mm (1in) from each side. Drill pilot holes and reinforce the glued joints with self-tapping screws.

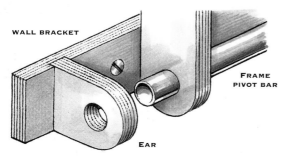

WALL BRACKET

FRAME PIVOT BAR

EAR

Making the wall bracket

Make a wall bracket from sections of 18mm (¾in) plywood 75mm (3in) wide to accommodate the pivoting frame. Mark, drill and shape the projecting 'ears' of the bracket as described for the pivoted ends of the side arms.

Cut 6mm (¼in) housing joints in the back rail for the ears. Assemble the bracket around the pivot bar of the frame, and screw and glue the ears into their housings.

Once the glue has set, screw the bracket to the wall at the required height to enable the mower to be lifted clear of the floor.

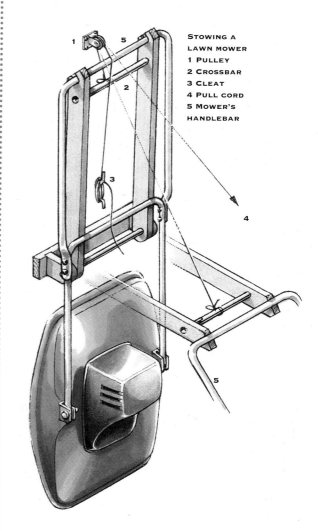

STOWING A
LAWN MOWER
1 PULLEY
2 CROSSBAR
3 CLEAT
4 PULL CORD
5 MOWER'S
HANDLEBAR

Fixing the pulley

Fix a pulley wheel to the wall above the frame's crossbar when it is in the raised position. Tie a length of cord to the crossbar and pass it through the pulley. Screw a cleat to the wall below the pulley for securing the pull cord.

Using the lifting frame

Release the pull cord and let the frame tip forward. Locate the handlebar of the folded mower into the notches and, using the cord, pull the frame into the vertical position. Tie off the cord to stow the mower securely.

3

A WHOLE DAY

Making a compost bin
168
Hanging a garden gate
172
Creating a water feature
for your patio
177
Laying on a water supply
180
Protecting your fish
from cats
181
Refurbishing an old wall
182
Smartening up a
tarmac drive
189
Making a gravel garden
192

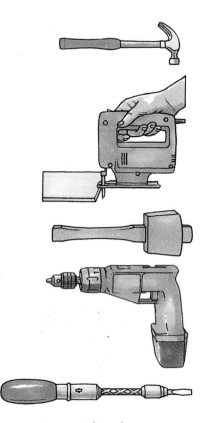

ALLOW ONE WHOLE DAY

MAKING A COMPOST BIN

A wide range of ready-mixed composts is available for the cultivation of plants, either for potting seeds or cuttings, or use in plant containers, or to enrich your garden soil.

Both farm manure and well-rotted home-made organic-matter compost make ideal soil improvers. As well as being good for the garden, the latter provides a useful way to recycle kitchen and garden waste.

You can make garden compost from soft vegetative materials, including leaves, grass clippings, flowers and kitchen waste such as vegetable peelings. It should not contain woody branch material or roots, nor tough vegetable stems, such as cabbage, unless they have been shredded. Badly diseased or insect-ridden material and perennial weeds should always be rejected.

Essential tools

Hammer

Jigsaw

Mallet

Panel saw

Power drill and bits

Screwdriver

Tenon saw

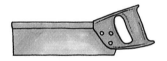

See also:
Types of preserver, page 35

Starting a compost heap
Begin with vegetable matter from the kitchen or garden.

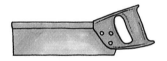

DESIGNING A COMPOST BIN

A good compost bin needs to contain waste in a tidy manner, have an easy-to-load top and some means of extracting well-rotted matter at the bottom, and enclose the waste effectively enough to help generate heat and therefore speed up the rotting process. Ideally, two bins are better than one – so you are able to replenish one bin while continuing to extract rotted material from the other. There is a range of ready-made units on the market, but you can make your own from second-hand floorboards and wooden battens. A bin in the form of a 1m (3ft 3in) cube makes a useful single container. Double this for a twin unit.

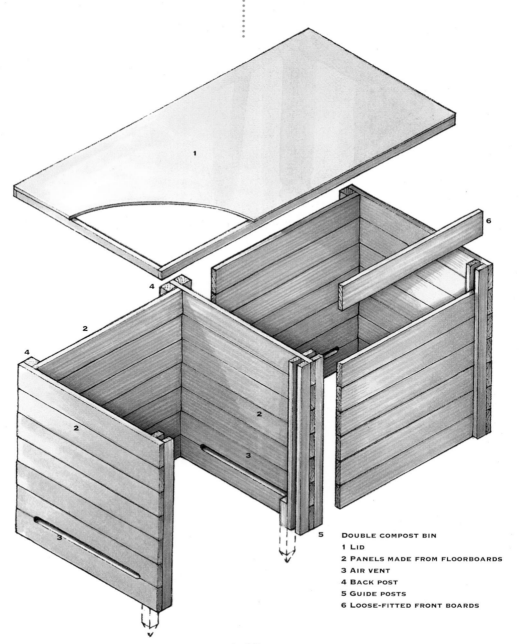

DOUBLE COMPOST BIN
1 LID
2 PANELS MADE FROM FLOORBOARDS
3 AIR VENT
4 BACK POST
5 GUIDE POSTS
6 LOOSE-FITTED FRONT BOARDS

MAKING A SINGLE CONTAINER

Make the front, back and sides from second-hand 150 x 25mm (6 x 1in) floorboards. Saw them into 1m (3ft 3in) lengths. Cut sufficient boards to make up panels about 1m (3ft 3in) high when placed edge to edge.

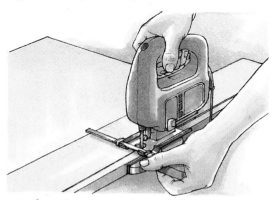

1 Take the two bottom boards on each side and at the back, and cut away 12mm (½in) on their meeting edges, stopping about 150mm (6in) from each end. This will create air vents 25mm (1in) wide at the bottom.

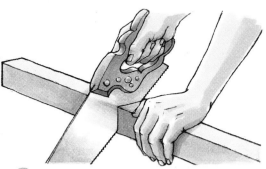

2 Cut two back posts from 50 x 50mm (2 x 2in) softwood to match the height of the side panels. Then cut four front guide posts from 50 x 25mm (2 x 1in) softwood to the same length. Treat all the parts with a wood preserver.

ASSEMBLING THE PARTS
Make up the sides first.

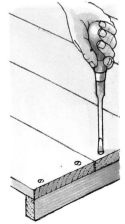

1 With their edges butted together, screw the boards to a back post and to one of the front guide posts. Set their ends flush with the outside faces of the posts.

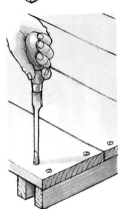

2 Screw a second front guide post parallel to the first, leaving a space between them which is slightly wider than the thickness of the front boards. This forms a track to retain the loose-fitted front boards. Assemble the opposite side in the same way.

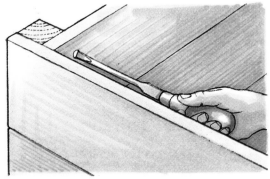

3 Screw the back boards to the inside of the back posts. Set the assembly square and level on flat ground. Drive 50 x 50mm (2 x 2in) pretreated wooden stakes into the ground just inside the front posts. Screw the bottom side boards to the stakes. Drop the front boards into place between the guide posts.

Making an extension unit

To make a twin compost bin, simply extend the first unit. Cut sufficient boards to make up another side panel and another back. Fix a back post and a pair of guide posts to the side of the first bin, then attach the back boards and additional side panel as described above.

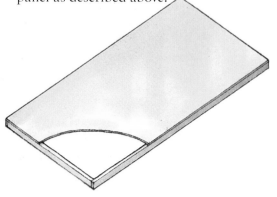

Making the lid

Make a lid to fit over the top of the bin, to prevent rainwater from washing out nutrients and slowing down the rotting process by reducing the heat.

1 Using 50 x 25 (2 x 1in) soft-wood, make up a simple butt-jointed glued-and-screwed frame to fit over the top of the bin.

2 Cut a sheet of thin exterior-grade plywood to fit the frame. Pin and glue it all round. Cover the lid with roofing felt, or water-proof it with paint or preserver. Also, to help retain heat, cover the compost heap with a piece of old carpet.

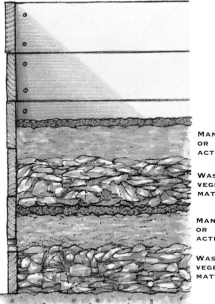

MANURE OR ACTIVATOR

WASTE VEGETABLE MATTER

MANURE OR ACTIVATOR

WASTE VEGETABLE MATTER

TIP ● ● ● ● ● ● ● ● ● ● ● ● ● ● ● ●
Making compost

Begin by building up a layer of mixed vegetable matter about 150mm (6in) deep. Sprinkle it with water.

Add a layer of farm manure or compost activator, available from garden centres. The latter is produced in granular form and as a liquid. Follow the manufacturer's instructions for quantities.

A thin layer of soil, about 12mm (½in) thick, is often recommended for the next layer, to introduce microbes and nutrients and to retain heat. However, if an activator is used, soil is not always essential.

Add another layer of vegetable matter, and repeat the layering process until the bin is filled.

After about 4 to 6 weeks, turn the heap over with a fork. Then leave to rot down for about 3 months.

ALLOW ONE WHOLE DAY

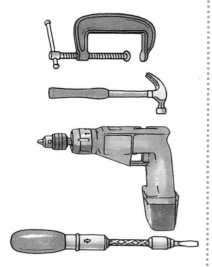

Essential tools
G-cramps
Hammer
Power drill and bits
Screwdriver
Spade
Spirit level
Trowel

HANGING A GARDEN GATE

Although a well-made gate will last for years, eventually the ravages of wet rot and rust take their toll. When faced with replacing a gate, it pays to look for an exact replica, as you know it will fit between the posts and you can probably reuse the existing fittings. However, since manufacturers update their catalogues from time to time, trying to track down an identical gate may prove to be a fruitless task.

With luck, you may find a different style of gate that is an exact fit. Or a replacement only slightly wider than the original, so you can skim a little wood off the stiles until it fits well. A narrower gate may be accommodated by screwing a batten to each post, though that probably won't be a very elegant solution. Yet another option is to have a new gate made to measure – but that is likely to be relatively expensive, so you may be better off erecting a new pair of posts for a ready-made gate.

You can hang any gate in a day, but allow the complete weekend if you also have to set posts in concrete.

ABOVE:
DOUBLE GATES FOR
A DRIVE OR GARAGE
CENTRE:
WROUGHT-IRON SIDE
GATE TO A GARDEN
RIGHT:
SMALL-SCALE WOODEN
ENTRANCE GATE

CHOOSING A NEW GATE

There are several points to consider when choosing a gate, not the least the cost. All gates are relatively expensive – but don't be tempted to buy one solely because it is cheaper than another. A gate must be sturdy if it is to be durable, and it must also be mounted on strong posts.

Entrance gates

An entrance gate tends to be designed as much for its appearance as its function. But it will be in constant use, so it pays to buy one that is properly braced, for example with a diagonal strut running from the top of the latch stile down to the bottom of the hanging or hinge stile. If you hang a gate with the diagonal strut running the other way, the bracing will have no effect whatsoever.

The most common fence structures are reflected in the style of entrance gates. Picket, closeboard and ranch-style gates are all available, as well as simple and attractive frame-and-panel gates. With the latter style of gate, the solid timber or exterior-grade plywood panels keep the frame rigid. If the tops of the stiles are cut at an angle or rounded over, they shed rainwater, reducing the likelihood of wet rot – a small but important point to bear in mind when you are buying a wooden gate.

Decorative iron gates are a frequent choice for entrances. When buying one, make sure the style is not too grandiose for the building or its location.

Side gates

A side gate is designed to protect a pathway next to a house from intruders. Side gates are invariably 2m (6ft 6in) high, and are made from wrought iron or stout sections of timber. Wooden gates are heavy and are therefore braced with strong diagonal members to keep them rigid. With security in mind, choose a closeboard or tongue-and-groove gate, since vertical boards are difficult to climb – and when you hang the gate, fit strong security bolts top and bottom.

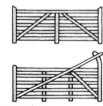

Drive gates

First, decide whether hanging a gate across a driveway to a garage is a good idea. For example, where will you park your car in order to open the gate? This can be a difficult and sometimes dangerous manoeuvre unless you have enough room to pull the car off the road with the gate closed.

Drive gates invariably open into the property, so check whether there is sufficient ground clearance for a wide gate if your drive slopes up from the entrance. An alternative is to hang two smaller gates that meet in the centre. If you decide on a wide gate, consider a traditional five-bar gate both for strength and for appearance.

Materials for gates

Many wooden gates are made from relatively cheap softwood – but a more durable wood, such as cedar or oak, is a better investment.

Most so-called wrought-iron gates are made from mild-steel bar, which must be primed and painted if it is to last any time at all.

HANGING A GATE

The way a gate is hung on its post will vary, depending on the style of gate and type of fittings you choose to hang it from, but the principles are generally basically the same.

The method described here is for hanging a wooden entrance gate with strap hinges and an automatic latch.

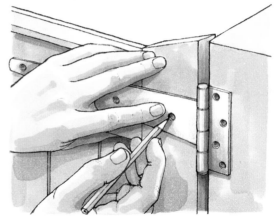

2 Use a spirit level to check that the top rail is horizontal, then hold each hinge in place and mark the screw holes. Drill pilot holes and drive in two screws for each flap on both hinges. Before inserting the rest of the screws, check that the gate can swing properly.

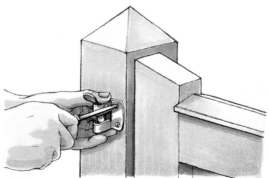

3 Fit the two parts of the catch in a similar way. Check that it operates easily before securing the fitting with all the screws.

1 Stand the gate between the posts, and prop it up on a pair of bricks or wooden blocks to hold it the required height off the ground. Tap in pairs of wedges on each side of the gate until it is held securely with sufficient gaps between it and the posts to accommodate the hinges and catch. When fitting strap hinges, the back faces of the gate and the posts should be flush.

See also:
Replacing a fence post, page 34
Erecting new posts, page 58

TIP ● ● ● ● ● ● ● ● ● ● ● ● ●
Fitting double gates
When hanging a pair of gates between posts, clamp the two latch stiles together, with a suitable spacer sandwiched between them. Wedge the clamped gates between the posts and fit the hinges as described above.

You need specialized hinges and catches to take
the considerable strain that garden gates impose.

Strap hinges
*Side gates and most wooden entrance gates are
hung on strap hinges or T-hinges. Screw the
long horizontal flaps to the gate rails; and the
vertical flaps to the face of the post. Heavier
gates need a stronger version bolted through
the top rail.*

*Wide drive gates need a double strap hinge
with a long flap bolted on each side of the top
rail. These heavy-duty hinges are supported by
bolts that pass through the gatepost.*

Hinge pins
*On metal gates, metal collars welded to the
hinge side drop over hinge pins attached to
gateposts in a variety of ways. They may be
screw-fixed to timber posts; bolted through
concrete; built into the mortar joints of
masonry piers; or welded to metal posts.
Unless you either reverse the top pin or drill
a hole and fit a split pin and washer, the gate
can be lifted off its hinges at any time.*

Automatic latches
*Simple wooden gates are fitted with a latch
that operates automatically as the gate is
closed. Screw the latch bar to the latch stile
of the gate and use it to position the latch on
the post.*

Thumb latches
*Cut a slot through a closeboard side gate for
the latch lifter of a thumb latch. Pass the sneck
(lifter bar) through the slot and screw the
handle to the front of the gate. Screw the latch
beam to the inner face so that the sneck
releases the beam from the hooked keeper.*

Ring latches
*A ring latch works in much the same way as
a thumb latch, but is operated by twisting the
ring handle to lift the latch beam.*

Chelsea catches
*Bolt a Chelsea catch through a drive gate. The
latch pivots on the bolt to drop into a slot in
the catch plate screwed to the post.*

Loop-over catches
*When a pair of gates are used for a drive
entrance, one gate is fixed with a drop bolt
located in a socket concreted into the ground.
A simple U-shaped metal bar, bolted through
the latch stile of the other gate, drops over the
stile of the fixed gate.*

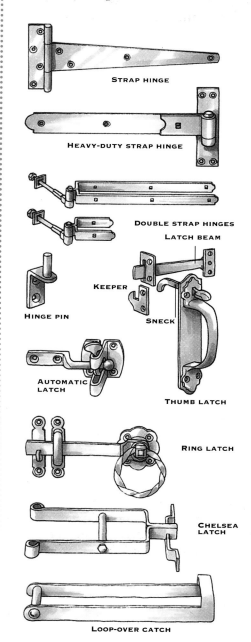

STRAP HINGE

HEAVY-DUTY STRAP HINGE

DOUBLE STRAP HINGES

LATCH BEAM

KEEPER

HINGE PIN

SNECK

AUTOMATIC LATCH

THUMB LATCH

RING LATCH

CHELSEA LATCH

LOOP-OVER CATCH

ERECTING NEW POSTS

Gateposts and masonry piers have to take a great deal of strain, so they must be both strong and anchored securely in the ground. Use hardwood for wooden posts whenever possible, and select the section according to the weight of the gate. Posts 100mm (4in) square are adequate for most entrance gates, but use 125mm (5in) posts for gates 2m (6ft 6in) high. For a gate across a drive, choose posts 150mm (6in) or even 200mm (8in) square.

Concrete posts are a possibility – but unless you find a post predrilled to accept hinges and catch, you will have to screw them to a strip of timber bolted securely to the post.

Square or cylindrical tubular-steel metal posts are available with hinge pins, gatestop and catch welded in place. Like metal gates, they need to be painted to protect them from rust, unless they have been coated with plastic at the factory.

Brick piers
A pair of masonry piers is another possibility. Each of the piers should be a minimum of 328mm (1ft 1½ in) square and built on a firm concrete footing. For large, heavy gates, the hinge pier at least should be reinforced with a strong metal rod, buried in the footing and running centrally through the pier.

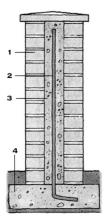

REINFORCED BRICK PIER
1 BRICK PIER
2 METAL ROD
3 CONCRETE INFILL
4 FOOTING

ERECTING WOODEN GATEPOSTS

Gateposts are set in concrete like ordinary fence posts, but the post holes are linked by a concrete bridge to provide extra support.

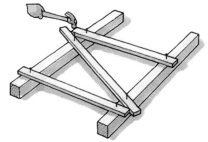

1 Lay the gate on the ground, with a post on each side. Check that the posts are parallel and the required distance apart to accommodate hinges and catch. Nail two horizontal battens from post to post, and another diagonally to keep the posts in line while you erect them.

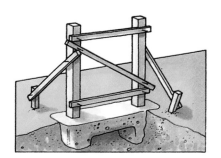

2 Dig a trench 300mm (1ft) wide across the entrance. Make it long enough to accept both posts. It need not be deeper than 300mm (1ft) in the centre, but dig an adequate post hole at each end: 450mm (1ft 6in) deep for a low entrance gate, and 600mm (2ft) deep for a taller side gate.

Set the battened gateposts in the post holes with hardcore and concrete, using temporary battens to hold them upright until the concrete sets.

At the same time, fill the trench with concrete and either level it flush with the pathway or allow for the thickness of paving slabs or blocks.

Having hung the new gate, fill nail holes with coloured putty.

CREATING A WATER FEATURE FOR YOUR PATIO

One of the pleasures of a secluded garden is to be able to appreciate the natural sounds of rustling trees, bird song and, if you are particularly fortunate, the rippling tones of running water. As a rule, nature will provide the wind and the birds, but most of us have to supply the sound of running water ourselves.

Given sufficient space, most people opt for a fountain or a small cascade trickling into a garden pond. But what if you only have a small garden or patio? A space-saving water feature is the ideal solution. This need not involve more than a submersible recirculating pump placed in a miniature moulded-plastic pool set in the ground and covered with decorative pebbles. This type of water feature can be situated close to the house – within earshot of the windows and also conveniently placed for wiring into your power supply.

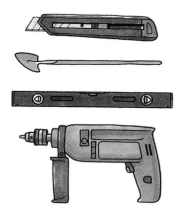

Essential tools

Craft knife

Garden fork

Garden spade

Power drill and bits

Spirit level

Trowel

Types of pump

Submersible pumps are made to provide a fountain, cascade or combination of both, and are produced in a range of sizes and performance. The manufacturers specify the performance of a pump in litres or gallons per hour, related to the height of the fountain spray or cascade volume. Pumps are powered by an electric motor, which is operated either by mains electricity or a low-voltage mains-powered transformer or, in some cases, by a solar-powered panel. They are fully insulated and supplied as ready-wired kits for connecting to your power supply. All the necessary fittings are generally provided, including a length of flexible hose.

For a patio water feature, choose a small cascade-type pump. If you are in doubt about the performance of a particular unit, check the manufacturer's literature or consult your supplier.

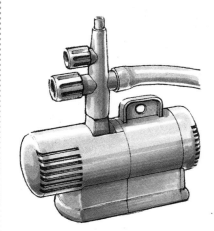

SUBMERSIBLE PUMP FOR A PATIO WATER FEATURE

INSTALLING A MOULDED POOL

Moulded-plastic pools take the form of shallow round or square trays with a deep bucket-like centre section or sump. A perforated or moulded lid is provided to cover the sump, and to support the layer of pebbles used to disguise the feature once it has been installed.

Excavating the pond

Start by digging a hole slightly larger than the size of the tray. Make the hole deep enough to set the edge of the tray level with or just below the surface of the patio. You also need to allow for a layer of sand – to be placed on the compacted base of the excavated hole – on which to bed the sump. Set the sump in place and partially fill it with water to help keep it steady. Carefully back-fill the sides with earth or sand; build up the infill until the sump and tray are well supported and level.

Fitting the pump

Following the manufacturer's instructions, connect the pump's cable to your power supply, which must include a residual-current device (RCD) to protect the circuit.

Drill a discreet hole in a convenient door or window frame for the pump's cable, and seal the gap around the cable with silicone sealant. If you are in any doubt about the installation, consult an electrician.

Connect a length of hose to the pump's water outlet and place the pump in the sump, which you can now fill with water. Test the pump is working.

Lead the hose to one side and fit the lid in place. It may be necessary to trim the edge of the lid to accommodate the hose.

Making the cascade

Two ceramic plant pots make an attractive cascade. Balance one of the pots at an angle on the rim of the other, and stand them on the tray. Feed the end of the hose into the drain hole in the bottom of the angled pot, then seal the hole with silicone sealant. This may be easier to do if you disconnect the hose from the pump once the hose has been cut to length.

With the pots in position, place some random-size decorative pebbles around them to cover the pond tray. Put a few pebbles inside the angled pot to weigh it down and to conceal the end of the hose.

Arrange potted plants to help disguise the hose at the rear. Run the pump, and place pebbles in and around the pots so as to create an attractive cascade.

Routine maintenance

Top up the buried pond occasionally to make up for natural evaporation. At the end of the season, remove the pump and clean the filter. This will mean rearranging the pebbles, which provides an opportunity to remove leaf litter and clean up generally.

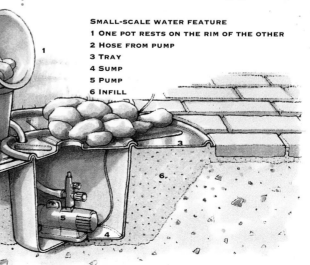

SMALL-SCALE WATER FEATURE
1 ONE POT RESTS ON THE RIM OF THE OTHER
2 HOSE FROM PUMP
3 TRAY
4 SUMP
5 PUMP
6 INFILL

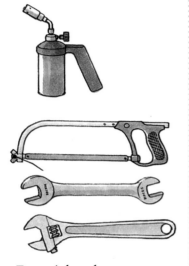

Essential tools

Blowtorch

Hacksaw/pipe cutter

Masonry bits

Power drill

Spanners

LAYING ON A WATER SUPPLY

A bib tap situated on an outside wall is handy for attaching a hose for a lawn sprinkler, topping up a pond or washing the car.

To comply with bylaws, a double-seal non-return check valve must be incorporated in the plumbing to prevent contaminated water being drawn back into the system.

Also, it is advisable to incorporate a means of shutting off the water supply and draining the pipework during winter.

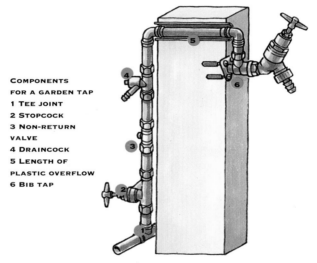

COMPONENTS
FOR A GARDEN TAP
1 TEE JOINT
2 STOPCOCK
3 NON-RETURN
VALVE
4 DRAINCOCK
5 LENGTH OF
PLASTIC OVERFLOW
6 BIB TAP

Pipes and fittings to supply a garden tap
Turn off the main stopcock and drain the rising main. Fit a tee joint (1) in the rising main to run the supply to the tap. Run a short length of pipe to a convenient position for another stopcock (2) and the non-return valve (3), making sure the arrows marked on both fittings point in the direction of flow. Fit a draincock (4) after this point. Run a pipe through the wall inside a length of plastic overflow (5), so that any leaks will be detected quickly and will not soak the masonry. Wrap PTFE tape around the bib-tap thread before screwing it into a wallplate attached to the masonry outside (6).

PROTECTING YOUR FISH FROM CATS

Cats are attracted to fish swimming near the surface of a garden pond, although they often seem merely to be mesmerized by the movements of the fish rather than actively intent on poaching. However, a predatory cat can harm fish basking near the surface, even if it can't manage to scoop them out of the water.

The floating leaves of water lilies provide some shelter, but the fact that you want to enjoy a clear view of the fish precludes having a large expanse of overlapping leaves. Instead, create an edging of trailing plants to your pond – without a firm foothold, no cat will attempt to reach into the water.

ALLOW ONE WHOLE DAY

Essential tools

Pointing trowel

Tinsnips

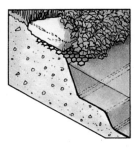

Making a soft edge
Bed a strip of soft wire netting in mortar below flat edging stones. Cut the strip to overhang the water by about 150mm (6in), as a support for trailing plants. Once the plants are established, they will disguise both the wire strip and the exposed edge of a pool liner.

See also:
Making a small pond, page 102

ALLOW ONE WHOLE DAY

Essential tools

Mould growth

Bristle brush

Face mask

Goggles

Large paintbrush

Spatula

Cleaning

Face mask

Garden hose

Goggles

Old paintbrush

Repointing

Bristle brush

Club hammer

Cold chisel

Face mask

Frenchman

Goggles

Hawk

Pointing trowel

Spalled brick

Club hammer

Cold chisel

Electric drill

Masonry bit

See also:

Brightening up a dull wall, page 118
Patching up rendered walls,
page 116

REFURBISHING AN OLD WALL

Older brickwork has a quality that cannot be matched by new materials. It's not that new brickwork is inferior in any way, nor does it means that current builders are any less skilful than their predecessors. It is simply that over the years weathering tends to create colours and textures that are difficult to reproduce by artificial means.

However, along with these advantages, weathering can cause all manner of problems that need to be tackled in order to preserve old walls. It is unlikely that your particular wall is suffering from every problem listed here – if it is, then you will certainly be faced with more than a weekend's work to fix them. Unless the area of brickwork is very large, you should be able to complete the bulk of any single task in a day, or at most a weekend. Many of these techniques can be adapted for stonework.

SHIFTING UNSIGHTLY MOULD GROWTH

Colourful lichens growing on garden walls can be very attractive. Indeed, some people actively encourage their growth by painting masonry with liquid manure. However, since the spread of moulds and lichens depend on moist conditions, it is not a good sign when they occur naturally on the walls of your house.

Try to identify the source of the problem before treating the growth. For example, if one side of your house never receives any sun, it will have little chance of drying out. However, you can relieve the problem by cutting back overhanging trees or adjacent shrubs to increase ventilation to the wall.

Make sure the damp-proof course (DPC) is working adequately and is not being bridged by piled earth or debris.

Cracked or corroded rainwater pipes leaking onto walls are a common cause of organic growth. Feel behind the pipe with your fingers, or slip a hand mirror behind it to see if there's a leak.

HEALTH AND SAFETY

Cleaning brickwork or stone can be an unpleasant, dusty job – so wear old clothes, a face mask, goggles and gloves, particularly when working with fungicides and cleaning agents.

Removing and neutralizing the mould growth

This is one of those jobs that involves about a day's work in total, but it has to be spread over several days in order to kill off the spores.

First remove heavy organic growth, by scraping it from the bricks with a non-metallic spatula. Then, starting at the top of the wall, paint on a solution of 1 part household bleach and 4 parts water to kill the remaining spores.

Leave the wall to dry out for a couple of days, then wearing protective clothing (see bottom left), brush the masonry vigorously with a stiff-bristle brush. Don't use a wire brush, as that can damage the masonry. Brush away from you to avoid debris being flicked into your face. Apply a second wash of bleach solution, then leave the wall to dry out.

Using a fungicide

If the wall continues to suffer from persistent fungal growth, use a proprietary fungicide (available from most DIY stores).

Dilute the fungicide with water, following the manufacturer's instructions, and apply it liberally with an old paintbrush. Leave it for 24 hours, then rinse the wall with clean water.

In extreme cases, give the wall two washes of fungicide, allowing 24 hours between applications and a further 24 hours before washing it down with water.

CLEANING DIRTY BRICKWORK

Part of the charm of old masonry is the way it has mellowed, an effect that is due in part to discoloration caused by airborne dirt and pollution. However, if you are bothered by the appearance of your brickwork, you can often spruce it up by washing off surface grime with water. One alternative is to rent high-pressure spraying equipment, which is very efficient for cleaning masonry, but the jet of water is so powerful that it can dislodge loose or cracked mortar and break up spalled masonry. It is therefore safer to use gentler methods on old walls. Even then, avoid soaking brick or stone if a frost is forecast. Strong solvents will harm certain types of stone – so, before applying anything other than water, seek the advice of an experienced local builder who is used to working on the stonework indigenous to your area.

Washing the wall
You can improve the appearance of brick and stone by washing it with clean water. Starting at the top of the wall, play a hose gently onto the masonry while you scrub it with a stiff-bristle brush. Scrub heavy deposits with half a cup of ammonia added to a bucketful of water, then rinse again.

Removing stains
Soften tar, grease and oil stains by applying a poultice made from fuller's earth or sawdust soaked in white spirit or paraffin or in a proprietary grease solvent. If you are using a proprietary solvent, follow the manufacturer's instructions.

Wearing protective gloves, dampen the stain with solvent then spread on a layer of poultice 12mm (½in) thick. Tape a sheet of plastic over the poultice, and leave it to dry out and absorb the stain. Scrape off the dry poultice with a wooden or plastic spatula, then scrub the wall with water.

Stripping spilled paint
To remove a patch of spilled paint from brickwork, use a proprietary paint stripper. Follow the manufacturer's recommendations, and wear old clothes, protective gloves and goggles.

Stipple the stripper onto the rough texture. Leave it for about 10 minutes, then remove the softened paint with a scraper and gently scrub the residue out of the deeper crevices with a stiff-bristle brush and water. After removing the residue of the paint, rinse the wall with clean water.

EFFLORESCENCE

Removing efflorescence from masonry
Soluble salts within building materials such as cement, brick and stone gradually migrate to the surface, along with the moisture, as a wall dries out. The result is a white crystalline deposit known as 'efflorescence'.

The same condition can occur on old masonry that is subjected to more than average moisture. Efflorescence itself is not harmful, but the source of the damp causing it must be identified and cured.

Regularly brush the deposit from the wall with a dry stiff-bristle brush or coarse sacking until the crystals cease to form. Do not attempt to wash off the crystals – they will merely dissolve in the water and soak back into the wall.

REPOINTING MASONRY

A combination of frost action and erosion tends to break down the mortar pointing of bricks and stonework. As a result, the mortar eventually falls out, exposing the open joints to wind and rain, which drive dampness through the wall to the inside. Cracked joints may also be caused by using a hard, inflexible mortar.

Replacing defective pointing is a straightforward but time-consuming task. Tackle a small manageable area at a time, using either a ready-mixed mortar or your own mix, consisting of 1 part cement, 1 part lime and 6 parts builder's sand. All the ingredients are available from builders' merchants.

MIXING MORTAR

Thoroughly mix the dry ingredients on a flat board, then scoop a well in the centre of the mound. Pour some clean water into the hollow, then shovel the dry materials from around the edges into the centre until the water has been absorbed. Blend the ingredients, then once again make a well and add more water until the mortar has the consistency of soft butter.

Mortar containing cement sets in a couple of hours, so don't mix too much at a time. Always wear gloves, goggles and a face mask when handling hydrated lime.

Preparation

Rake out the old pointing with a thin wooden lath, to a depth of about 12mm (½in). Use a cold chisel and a club hammer to dislodge short sections that are firmly embedded, then brush out the joints with a stiff-bristle brush.

Spray the wall with water so that the bricks or stones will not absorb too much moisture from the fresh mortar.

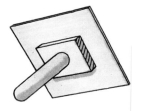

TIP ● ● ● ● ● ● ● ● ● ● ● ● ●
Making a small hawk
You will need a small lightweight hawk for carrying pointing mortar to the wall. Nail a block of wood to the underside of a plywood board, then drill a hole in the block and plug a handle into it.

PICK UP A LITTLE SAUSAGE OF MORTAR ON THE BACK OF A SMALL POINTING TROWEL

Filling the joints with mortar

Transfer some mortar to your hawk. Pick up a little sausage of mortar on the back of a small pointing trowel and push it firmly into the upright joints. This can be difficult to do without the mortar dropping off, so hold the hawk under each joint to catch it. Try not to smear the face of the bricks with mortar, as it will stain. Use the same method for the horizontal joints. The actual shape of the pointing is not vital at this stage.

Once the mortar is firm enough to retain a thumbprint, it is ready for shaping. Because it is so important that you shape the joints at exactly the right moment, you may have to point the work in stages in order to complete the wall. Shape the joints to match existing brickwork, or choose a profile suitable for the prevailing weather conditions in your area.

SHAPING THE MORTAR JOINTS

The joints shown here are all commonly used for brickwork. Flush or rubbed joints are best for most stonework. Leave the pointing of dressed-stone ashlar blocks to an expert.

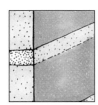

Flush joint
This is the easiest profile to produce. Scrape the mortar flush, using the edge of your trowel, then stipple the joints with a stiff-bristle brush to expose the sand aggregate.

Rubbed (concave) joint
This is a utilitarian joint that is ideal for an old wall built with bricks that are not of a sufficiently good quality to take a crisp joint. Bricklayers make a rubbed joint using a jointer, a tool shaped like a sled runner with a handle – the semicircular blade is run along the joints. Improvise by bending a length of metal tube or rod (use the curved section only to shape the joint, or you will gouge the mortar). Flush the mortar first, then drag the tool along the joints. Finish the vertical joints, then shape the horizontal ones. Having shaped the joints, stipple them with a brush so that they look like weathered pointing.

USING A JOINTER

Raked joint
A raked joint is used in order to emphasize the bonding pattern of a brick wall. It does not shed water, so it is not suitable for an exposed site. Use a piece of wood or metal to rake out the joints to a depth of about 6mm (¼in), and then compress the mortar by smoothing it lightly with a lath or a piece of rounded dowel rod.

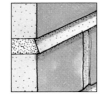

Weatherstruck joint
Designed to shed rainwater from the wall, the sloping profile of this joint is ideal for harsh conditions.

(SEE RIGHT-HAND COLUMN)

1 *Use a small pointing trowel to shape the joints. Start with the vertical ones. These can slope to the left or right, but be consistent throughout the same section of brickwork. Then shape the horizontal joints, allowing the mortar to spill out slightly at the base of each joint.*

2 *Finish the joint by cutting off excess mortar with a Frenchman, a tool that looks like a table knife with the tip bent at 90 degrees (see below). You will find it easiest to use a wooden batten to guide the blade of the Frenchman along the joints. Nail scraps of wood at each end of the batten to hold it off the wall. Align the batten with the bottom of the horizontal joints, then draw the tool along it to trim off the mortar.*

Brushing the face of the wall
Whatever type of joint you choose, let the pointing harden a little before you clean scraps of mortar from the face of the wall. Use a medium-soft banister brush to do this, sweeping it lightly across the joints so as not to damage them.

TIP ● ● ● ● ● ● ● ● ● ● ● ●
Making a Frenchman
You can make a Frenchman to finish off weatherstruck joints from a thin metal strip, binding it with insulating tape to form a handle. Alternatively, bend the tip of an old kitchen knife, after heating it in the flame of a blowtorch or cooker burner.

REPLACING A SPALLED BRICK

In freezing conditions the expansion of water trapped just below the surface of the masonry can cause bricks to spall (flake). If spalling is widespread, the only practical solution is to accept its less-than-perfect appearance, repoint the masonry, and apply a clear water repellent that will help protect the wall from any further damage, while at the same time allowing it to breathe.

More often, spalling affects only a small area of a wall, so individual bricks can be cut out and replaced. Cracked bricks can be replaced in a similar way. However, there is a limit to the number of bricks you can take out without a wall collapsing – so if more than two or three bricks have to be removed, ask a builder for advice before proceeding with the repair.

Cutting out the spalled brick
Use a cold chisel and club hammer to rake out the pointing surrounding the brick, then prise out the brick itself. If the brick is difficult to remove, drill numerous holes in it, using a large-diameter masonry bit, then slice up the brick with the cold chisel and hammer; it should crumble, enabling you to remove the pieces easily.

Inserting the replacement
First dampen the opening and spread mortar on the base and one side. Then dampen the replacement brick, butter the top and one end with mortar, and slot the brick into the hole. Shape the pointing to match the surrounding brickwork.

TIP ● ● ● ● ● ● ● ● ● ● ● ● ● ● ●
Turning a spalled brick
If you can't find a replacement brick of a suitable colour, remove the spalled brick carefully, then turn it round to reveal its undamaged face and reinsert it.

SMARTENING UP A TARMAC DRIVE

You can smarten up an old tarmac path or drive, or any sound but unsightly paved area, by resurfacing with cold-cure tarmac.

It makes a serviceable surface, and is ready to lay straight from the sack.

ALLOW ONE WHOLE DAY

Cold-cure tarmac

Cold-cure tarmac is available in 25kg (55lb) sacks that will cover an area of about 0.9sq m (10sq ft) with a thickness of 12mm (½in). You can buy both red and black. Each sack contains a separate bag of decorative stone chippings for embedding in the soft tarmac as an alternative finish. The tarmac can be laid in any weather, but it is much easier to level and roll it flat on a dry, warm day. If you have to work in cold weather, store the materials in a warm place the night before laying. Although it is not essential, edging the tarmac with bricks, concrete kerbs or wooden boards will improve the appearance of the finished surface.

Essential tools

Garden roller

Rake

Shovel

Spade

Stiff-bristle broom

Removing weeds

Pull up all weeds and grass growing between cracks in the old paving, then apply a strong weedkiller to the surface two days before laying the tarmac.

Filling potholes

Sweep the area clean, and level any potholes. Cut the sides of potholes vertical, remove dust and debris from the hole, then paint the cavity with the bitumen emulsion supplied by the tarmac manufacturer. Wait until the bitumen has turned black before filling the hole with 18mm (¾in) layers of tarmac, compacting each layer until the surface is level.

TIP ● ● ● ● ● ● ● ● ●

Surface treatment

If you have an old tarmac path or drive that is in sound condition, you can improve its appearance and extend its life with a protective acrylic coating applied with a brush or paint roller. Such coatings provide an attractive, non-slip surface.

See also:
Laying out a parking space, page 96

PREPARING THE SURFACE

Apply a tack coat of bitumen emulsion to the entire surface, to make a firm bond between the new tarmac and the old paving. Mask surrounding walls, kerb stones and manhole covers. Stir the emulsion with a stick before pouring it from its container, then spread it thinly with a stiff-bristle broom. Try not to splash; and avoid leaving puddles, especially at the foot of a slope. Leave the tack coat to set for about 20 minutes; in the meantime, wash the broom in hot soapy water. Don't apply the tack coat when there is a possibility of rain.

APPLYING THE TARMAC

1 Rake the tarmac to make a layer about 18mm (¾ in) thick, using a straightedge to scrape the surface flat. Press down any stubborn lumps with your foot. Spread the contents of no more than three sacks before rolling.

2 Keep the roller wet to avoid picking up specks of tarmac. Don't run the roller onto grass or gravel, or you may roll particles into the tarmac. Spread and roll tarmac over the whole area, then compact it by rolling thoroughly in several directions.

3 Lightly scatter the chippings before making your final pass with the roller.

You can walk on the tarmac immediately, but avoid wearing high-heeled shoes. Don't drive on it for a day or two; and if you have to erect a ladder on it, spread the load by placing a board under the ladder. You should always protect tarmac from oil and petrol spillage, but take special care while the surface is fresh.

TIP ● ● ● ● ● ● ● ● ● ● ● ● ● ● ● ● ● ●
Laying a new path
Although cold-cure tarmac is primarily a resurfacing material, it can be applied to a new hardcore base that has been firmly compacted, levelled and sealed with a slightly more generous coat of bitumen emulsion.

DRESSING WITH STONE CHIPPINGS

As an alternative to tarmac, completely resurface a path or drive with natural-stone chippings embedded in fresh bitumen emulsion. The emulsion is available in 5, 25 and 200kg (11, 55 and 440lb) drums. A 5kg (11lb) drum will cover about 7sq m (8sq yd), provided that the surface is dense macadam or concrete; an open-textured surface will absorb considerably more emulsion. Chippings in various colours come in 25kg (55lb) sacks, which cover about 2.5sq m (3sq yd).

Applying emulsion

It takes about 12 hours for bitumen emulsion to become completely waterproof, so check the weather forecast to avoid wet conditions. You can lay emulsion on a damp surface, but not on an icy one. Apply weedkiller and fill potholes, as for laying tarmac.

Decant the emulsion into a bucket, so it is easier to pour onto the surface. Brush it out, not too thinly, with a stiff broom.

Scattering the chippings

Having brushed out one bucket of emulsion, spread the stone chippings evenly with a shovel. Hold the shovel horizontally just above the surface, and gently shake the chippings off the edge of the blade. Don't pile chippings too thickly, but make sure the emulsion is covered completely.

Cover an area of about 5sq m (6sq yd), then roll the chippings to press them down. When the entire area is covered, roll it once more. If traces of bitumen show between the chippings, mask them with a little sharp sand and roll again.

You can walk or drive on the dressed surface immediately. One week later, gently sweep away the surplus chippings. Patch any bare areas by re-treating them with emulsion and chippings.

TIP ● ● ● ● ● ● ● ● ● ● ● ● ● ● ● ●

Double dressing

If the surface you are dressing is in a very poor condition or exceptionally loose, apply a first coat of bitumen emulsion, then cover the surface with chippings and roll thoroughly. Two days later sweep away loose chippings, then apply a second coat of emulsion and finish with chippings.

Essential tools

Brick trowel

Rake

Garden roller

Shovel

Spade

Spirit level

See also:
Designing steps, page 94

MAKING A GRAVEL GARDEN

Low-maintenance gravel drives and pathways feature in many gardens, but you can make more creative use of the colour and texture of gravel – as an attractive contrast to the softer shapes of spreading plants and as a sympathetic background for larger rocks and stones. Areas of gravel for planting are particularly easy to construct and, unless you are planning a large or complex gravel garden, you can complete the work easily in a day.

Laying out gravel for planting
To lay an area of gravel for planting, simply excavate the soil to accept a bed of fine gravel 25mm (1in) deep. You can either set the gravel 18mm (¾in) below the level of the lawn or edge the gravel garden with bricks or flat stones. Scrape away a small area of gravel to allow for planting, then sprinkle the gravel back again to cover the soil right up to the plant.

LAYING A GRAVEL PATHWAY OR DRIVE

If an area of gravel is to be used as a pathway or for motor vehicles, first construct retaining edges, consisting of bricks, concrete kerbs or treated wooden boards. This will stop gravel being spread outside its allotted area.

Building pathways takes longer than laying gravel planting areas – because you need to allow extra time for laying and compacting a 50mm (2in) bed of hardcore and for constructing the retaining edges.

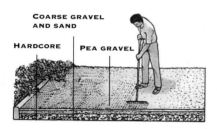

To lay a gravel drive, the sub-base and the gravel itself must be compacted and levelled, to prevent cars skidding and churning up the material. Lay a 150mm (6in) bed of firmed hardcore topped with 50mm (2in) of very coarse gravel mixed with sand. Roll it flat, then rake an 18 to 25mm (¾in to 1in) layer of fine 'pea' gravel across the sub-base and roll it to make it firm.

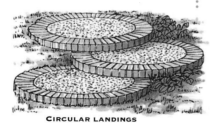

CIRCULAR LANDINGS

INCORPORATING STEPS

Because gravel is so versatile, you have much greater freedom to incorporate curved or flowing shapes into your garden design. Terracing a sloping site with curved gravel-covered steps or landings is as easy as building regular steps from more conventional paving materials. However, building even a short flight of steps will take up most of a weekend.

Constructing curved steps

To build a series of curved steps, choose materials that will make the job as easy as possible. You can use tapered concrete slabs for the treads, designing the circumference of the steps to suit the proportions of the slabs. Alternatively, use bricks laid flat or on edge. Set the bricks to radiate from the centre of the curve, and fill the slightly tapered joints with mortar.

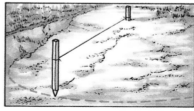

Use a length of string attached to a peg driven into the ground as an improvised compass to mark out the curve of each step. Terrace the slope by cutting into the soil, and lay concrete-strip or hardcore foundations for the risers. As you construct each step, fill in behind the brick tread with compacted hardcore, allowing for a 25mm (1in) bed of gravel.

Building circular landings

To construct a series of wide landings, build the front edges with bricks, as for curved steps. When the mortar has set, fill the area of the landing with compacted hardcore and lay gravel up to the level of the tread.

4

THE COMPLETE WEEKEND

Erecting a panel fence
196
Screening off a patio
200
Building a dry-stone wall
204
Terracing a steep garden
208
Laying a log path
210
Making steps from logs
211
Building a flight of
strong steps
212
Laying out a parking space
214
Constructing a rockery
218
Making a small pond
220
Building a cascade
226
Laying a firm base for a tool
shed
228
A new life for the
garage floor
232
Patching up rendered walls
234
Brightening up a dull wall
236

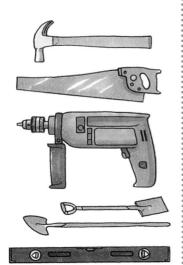

ERECTING A PANEL FENCE

Fences made from prefabricated panels nailed between timber posts are very common, perhaps because they are particularly easy to erect. Standard panels are 1.8m (6ft) wide and range in height from approximately 600mm (2ft) to 1.8m (6ft); they are supplied in 300m (1ft) gradations. Most panels are made from interwoven or overlapping strips of larch sandwiched between a frame of sawn timber. Overlapping-strip panels are usually designated 'larchlap'; or if the strips have a natural wavy edge, 'rustic larchlap'. You may also see them described as 'waney-edged', referring to where the thin strips of bark were, or maybe still are, attached to the planks.

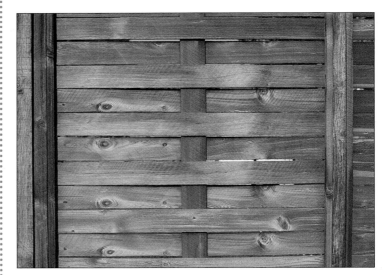

Essential tools

Claw hammer

Panel saw

Power drill and bits

Screwdriver

Spade or post-hole auger

Spirit level

Trowel

Post-hole auger
A post-hole auger is a special tool for boring holes in the ground.

Interwoven panel
An interwoven-panel fence offers good value for money and makes a reasonably durable screen, but if privacy is important, choose the lapped type – since interwoven strips shrink to some extent in the summer, leaving gaps.

PUTTING UP FENCE POSTS

Drive a peg into the ground at each end of the fence run and stretch a line between the pegs. If one or more posts have to be inserted across a paved patio, lift enough slabs to dig the necessary holes. You may have to break up a section of concrete beneath the slabs, using a cold chisel and hammer.

Digging holes

Bury one quarter of each post to provide a firm foundation. For a fence 1.8m (6ft) high, dig a 600mm (2ft) hole to take a 2.4m (8ft) post. You can hire a post-hole auger to remove the central core of earth. Twist the tool to drive it into the ground, and pull it out after every 150mm (6in) to remove the soil. When you have reached a sufficient depth, taper the sides of the hole slightly, so that you can pack hardcore and concrete around the post.

Anchoring the first post

Ram a layer of hardcore (broken bricks or small stones) into the bottom of the hole to provide drainage and to support the base of the first post. Ask someone to hold the post upright while you brace it with battens nailed to the post and to stakes driven into the ground. (Use guy ropes to support a concrete post.) Check with a spirit level that the post is vertical.

Packing with concrete

Ram more hardcore around the post, leaving a hole about 300mm (1ft) deep for filling with concrete. Mix some concrete to a firm consistency, using 1 part cement, 2 parts sharp sand and 3 parts aggregate. Use a trowel to drop concrete into the hole, all round the post, and tamp it down with the end of a batten.

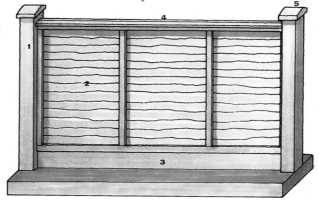

PREFABRICATED PANEL FENCE
1 FENCE POST
2 RUSTIC LARCHLAP PANEL
3 GRAVEL BOARD
4 CAPPING STRIP
5 POST CAP

FIXING PANELS

Support the first panel on bricks and get someone to hold it upright and push it against the post while you fix it with nails or brackets.

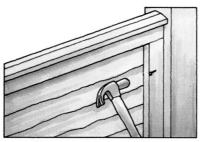

Skew-nailing
Skew-nail through the panel's framework into the post. If you can work from both sides, drive three nails from each side of the fence. If the wood used for the frame is likely to split, blunt the nails by tapping their points with a hammer.

Erecting the fence
Construct the entire fence erecting panels and posts alternately. To fill the gaps at ground level, fit pressure-treated gravel boards, using metal angle brackets. Nail capping strips across the panels, if not already fitted by the manufacturer. Finally, cut each post to length and cap it.

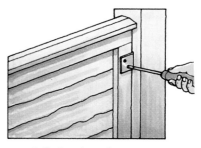

Using panel-fixing brackets
As an alternative to nails, use rustproofed metal angle brackets to secure the panels. Drill pilot holes before screwing the brackets to the panels and posts.

Topping up with concrete
Wedge struts made from scrap timber against each post to keep it vertical, then top up the holes with concrete to just above the level of the soil and smooth the concrete to slope away from the post. This will help shed water and prevent rot. If you are unable to work from both sides, you will have to fill each hole as you build the fence. Leave the concrete to harden for about a week before removing the struts.

ERECTING A PANEL FENCE
1 DIG HOLES FOR POSTS
2 SUPPORT EACH PANEL ON BRICKS
3 HOLD PANEL UPRIGHT
4 NAIL PANEL TO POST
5 FIT GRAVEL BOARDS
6 NAIL ON CAPPING STRIPS
7 CAP POSTS
8 TOP UP HOLES WITH CONCRETE

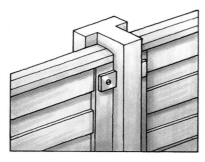

GROOVED CONCRETE POST

ERECTING FENCES ON SLOPING GROUND

If you intend to erect panel fencing on a sloping site, you will need to order longer posts.

Crossways slope
If a slope runs across your garden so that a neighbour's garden is higher than yours, either build brick retaining walls between the posts or set paving stones in concrete to hold back the soil.

RECESSED CONCRETE POST

TIP ● ● ● ● ● ● ● ● ● ● ●
Using concrete posts
Grooved concrete posts will support panels without the need for additional fixings. Recessed concrete posts are supplied with metal brackets for screw-fixing the panels.

Downhill slope
The posts need to be set vertically, even when you are erecting a fence on a sloping site. The fence panels should be stepped, and the triangular gaps beneath them filled with gravel boards or retaining walls.

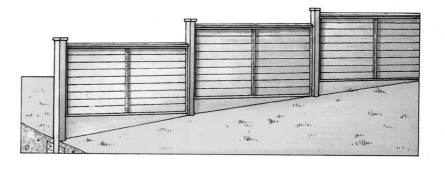

ALLOW THE COMPLETE WEEKEND

Essential tools

Brick trowel

Builder's line

Hammer

Jointer

Mallet

Mattock

Shovel

Spade

Spirit level

PIERCED CONCRETE-BLOCK SCREEN

See also:
Repointing masonry, page 67

SCREENING OFF A PATIO

A pierced screen provides a degree of privacy without completely cutting off your view or throwing dense shade onto the patio. It is also relatively easy to build, using cast-concrete screen blocks about 300mm (1ft) square and 100mm (4in) wide. Since screen blocks are not bonded together like brickwork or structural concrete blocks, they require supporting piers. These are made from pilasters 200mm (8in) square, with locating channels to take the pierced blocks. Use coping slabs to finish the top of the screen and piers.

PIERCED CONCRETE BLOCK

Designing the screen wall

Building a pierced screen is one of those projects that you cannot complete in a single weekend, mainly because at various stages concrete and mortar have to be left to set hard before you can continue. How much time it takes will also depend on the size and extent of the wall.

Because the blocks are stacked with continuous vertical joints, the piers must be reinforced vertically with 16mm ($\frac{5}{8}$in) steel rods or 50mm (2in) angle iron. If the screen is going to be higher than 600mm (2ft), the blocks will need to be reinforced horizontally too, with galvanized mesh. Position the supporting piers no more than 3m (9ft 9in) apart.

Like all garden walls, a concrete-block screen must be supported on a firm concrete base or footing. If the patio does not already have one, then you will need to allow extra time for laying a footing 400mm (1ft 4in) wide and 500mm (1ft 8in) deep.

LAYING THE FOOTING

A non-loadbearing garden screen can be built upon a concrete footing laid in a straight-sided trench. The soil must be firm and well-drained, to avoid possible subsidence. It is unwise to set footings in ground that has been filled recently, such as a new building site. Take care also to avoid tree roots and drainpipes. If the trench begins to fill with water as you are digging, seek professional advice before proceeding. If the soil is not firmly packed when you reach the required depth, dig deeper until you reach a firm level, then fill the bottom of the trench with compacted hardcore up to the lowest level of the proposed footing.

PROFILE BOARD

Setting out the footing

For a straight footing, set up two profile boards made from timber 25mm (1in) thick nailed to stakes driven into the ground at each end of the proposed trench but well outside the work area.

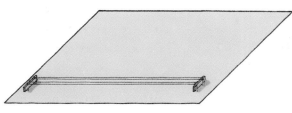

1 Drive nails into the top edge of each board, and stretch lines between them to mark the front and back edges of the screen. Then drive nails into the boards on each side of the wall line, to indicate the width of the footing, and stretch more lines between them. When you are satisfied that the setting out is accurate, remove the lines marking the screen.

2 Place a spirit level against the remaining lines to mark the edge of the footing on the ground. Mark the ends of the footing: these need to extend beyond the line of the screen by 600mm (8in). Mark the edge of the trench on the ground with a spade and remove the lines. Leave the profile boards in place.

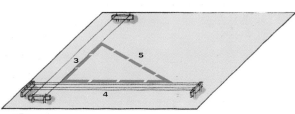

3 If your screen is to have a right-angled corner, set up two sets of profile boards, as before, checking carefully that the lines form a true right angle, using the 3 : 4 : 5 principle.

Digging the trench

Excavate the trench, keeping the sides vertical, and check that the bottom is level, using a long, straight piece of wood and a spirit level.

Drive a stake into the bottom of the trench, near one end, till the top of the stake represents the upper surface of the footing. Drive in more stakes at about 1m (3ft) intervals, checking that the tops are level.

Inserting reinforcing rods

Drive the reinforcing rods into the bottom of the trench at the required intervals. Check with a spirit level that each rod is upright, then support it with guy ropes until the concrete is poured and set.

Filling the trench

Mix the concrete (1 part cement : 2.5 parts sharp sand : 3.5 parts aggregate). Pour the concrete into the trench, and tamp it down firmly with a stout piece of timber until it is exactly level with the top of the stakes. Check that the reinforcing rods have not moved, and then leave the footing to harden thoroughly. As this is going to take at least three days, wait until the concrete is surface hard then cover it with polyethylene sheet, weighted down with bricks along the edges, until the following weekend.

CONSTRUCTING THE SCREEN

To help you mark the position of the screen blocks, restretch the lines between the profile boards. Hold a plumb line or spirit level lightly against each line and mark the concrete with chalk.

1 Lower a pilaster block over the first rod, setting it onto a bed of mortar laid around the base of the rod. Check that the block is perfectly vertical and level, and that its locating channel faces the next pier. Pack mortar or concrete into its core, then add two more pilaster blocks on top, packing the core of each with mortar or concrete, so that the pier will correspond to the height of two mortared screen blocks. Check that the pier is plumb and level.

Continue with erecting the piers, constructing each in the same way – except that intermediate piers will have a locating channel on each side.

Point the piers (concave joints are the most suitable for decorative screening) and allow the mortar to harden overnight.

2 Lay a mortar bed for two screen blocks next to the first pier. Butter the vertical edge of a screen block and press it into the pier's locating channel. Tap it into the mortar bed and check that it is level.

3 Mortar the next block and place it alongside the first. When buttering screen blocks, take special care to keep the faces clean by making a neat chamfered bed of mortar on each pierced block.

4 Lay two more blocks against the next pier. Then stretch a builder's line to gauge the top edge of the first course and lay the rest of the blocks towards the centre, making sure the vertical joints are aligned perfectly. Before building any higher, embed a galvanized wire-mesh reinforcing strip, running from pier to pier, in the next mortar bed.

5 Continue to build the piers and blocks up to a maximum height of four courses. Embed another reinforcing strip, then lay coping slabs along the top of the screen and on top of each pier. Finish by pointing the joints.

Don't build it too high

You can construct a screen up to 2m (6ft 6in) high, but do not build more than four courses of blocks at a time without allowing the mortar to harden overnight.

TIP ● ● ● ● ● ● ● ● ● ● ● ● ● ●
Pale-coloured mortar
If you don't like the appearance of ordinary mortar joints, rake out some of the mortar and repoint with mortar made with silver sand.

ALLOW THE COMPLETE WEEKEND

BUILDING A DRY-STONE WALL

Constructing garden walling with natural stone requires a different approach to that needed for bricklaying or building with concrete blocks. A dry-stone wall must be as stable as one built with conventional methods, but its visual appeal relies on the coursing being less regular; indeed, there is no real coursing when a wall is built with undressed stone or rubble.

Essential tools

Builder's line

Club hammer

Mallet

Mattock

Spade

Spirit level

Stiff-bristle brush

DESIGNING THE WALL

A well-built stone wall does not require mortar to hold the stones together, although it is often used to provide additional stability. As a result, many stone walls taper, having a wide base of heavy flat stones and gradually decreasing in width as the wall rises. This traditional form of construction was developed to prevent walls of unmortared stones toppling over when subjected to high winds or the weight of farm animals. Far from being intrusive or detracting from the garden's appearance, this informal construction suits a country-style garden perfectly.

See also:
Laying the footing, page 83

CONSTRUCTING THE WALL

A true dry-stone wall is built without mortar, relying instead on a selective choice of stones and careful placement to provide stability. Experience is needed for perfect results – but there is no reason why you cannot introduce mortar, particularly within the core of the wall, and still retain the appearance of dry-stone walling.

You can also bed the stones in soil, packing it firmly into the crevices as you lay each course. This enables you to plant alpines or other suitable rockery plants in the wall, even during construction.

When you select the masonry, look out for flat stones in a variety of sizes and make sure you have some large enough to run the full width of the wall, especially at the base of the structure. These 'bonding' stones, placed at regular intervals, are important components, as they tie the loose rubble into a cohesive structure.

Even a low wall will inevitably include some heavy stones. When you lift them, keep your back straight and your feet together, using the strong muscles of your legs to take the strain.

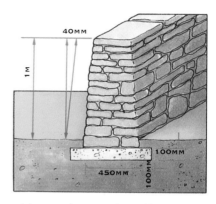

Building a 'battered' wall
A dry-stone wall has to be 'battered' – in other words, it must have a wide base and the sides need to slope inwards. For a wall about 1m (3ft 3in) in height – it is risky to build a dry-stone wall any higher – the base should be not less than 450mm (1ft 6in) wide. You should aim to provide a minimum slope of 25mm (1in) for every 600mm (2ft) of height.

Traditionally, the base of this type of wall rests on a 100mm (4in) bed of sand laid on compacted soil at the bottom of a shallow trench. For a more reliable foundation, lay a concrete footing 100 to 150mm (4 to 6in) thick. Make the footing approximately 100mm (4in) wider than the wall on each side.

1 Assuming you are using soil as a jointing material, spread a 25mm (1in) layer over the footing and place a substantial bonding stone across the width to form the bed of the first course.

2 Lay other stones that are about the same height as the bonding stone along each side of the wall, pressing them down into the soil to make a firm base. It is worth stretching a builder's line along each side of the wall to help you make a reasonably straight base. Lay smaller stones between to fill out the base of the wall, and then pack more soil into all the crevices.

3 Spread another layer of soil on top of the base and lay a second course of stones, bridging the joints between the stones below. Press them down so that they angle inwards towards the centre of the wall. Check by eye that the coursing is about level as you build the wall, and remember to include bonding stones at regular intervals.

4 Introduce plants into the larger crevices or, alternatively, hammer smaller stones into the chinks to lock the larger stones in place. At the top of the wall, either fill the core with soil for plants or lay large flat coping stones, firming them with packed soil. Finally, brush loose soil from the faces of the wall.

OPPOSITE:
TERRACE A SLOPING SITE WITH LOW
RETAINING WALLS (SEE PAGE 90)

Essential tools

Brick trowel

Builder's line

Hammer

Jointer

Mallet

Mattock

Shovel

Spade

Spirit level

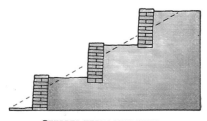

**STEPPED TERRACING WITH
RETAINING WALLS**

See also:
Building a dry-stone wall, page 86
Laying the footing, page 83

TERRACING A STEEP GARDEN

Terracing a sloping site by building a series of low retaining walls is an attractive solution that offers opportunities for imaginative planting. This project may well take a number of weekends to complete, depending on the number and size of the walls, and also because you will need to allow the concrete footings to set hard before you can begin building.

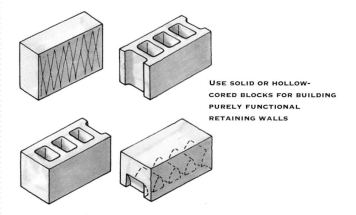

**USE SOLID OR HOLLOW-
CORED BLOCKS FOR BUILDING
PURELY FUNCTIONAL
RETAINING WALLS**

Choosing your materials

Both bricks and concrete blocks are suitable materials to choose for constructing a retaining wall, so long as it is sturdily built. It is best to support walls of this kind with reinforcing bars buried in the concrete footing. Either run the bars through hollow-core blocks or build a double skin of solid blocks or bricks, rather like a miniature cavity wall, using wall ties to bind each skin together. If you are unfamiliar with standard bricklaying techniques, it may be wisest to get a builder to construct the walls for you.

The mass and weight of natural stone make it ideal for retaining walls. The wall should be 'battered' to an angle of 50mm (2in) to every 300mm (1ft) of height, so that it virtually leans into the bank. For safety, keep the height below 1m (3ft 3in). A skilful builder may be able to construct a dry-stone retaining wall perfectly safely, but it pays to use mortar for additional rigidity.

TYPES OF RETAINING-WALL CONSTRUCTION

A RETAINING WALL OF HOLLOW CONCRETE BLOCKS

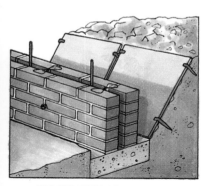

USE TWO SKINS OF BRICK TIED TOGETHER

LEAN A STONE WALL AGAINST THE BANK OF EARTH

CONSTRUCTING THE WALL

Laying the footings

Excavate the soil to provide enough room to dig the footings and construct the walls. If the soil is loosely packed, restrain it temporarily with sheets of scrap plywood or corrugated iron, or similar sheeting. Drive long metal pegs into the bank to hold the sheets in place. Lay the footing at the base of each bank, and allow it to set before you begin building the wall.

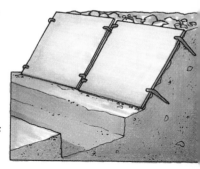

Laying stones

Lay uncut stones as if you were building a dry-stone wall, but set each course on mortar. If you use regular stone blocks, select stones of different proportions to add interest to the wall, and stagger the joints. Bed the stones in mortar. It is essential to allow for drainage behind the wall, to prevent

the soil becoming waterlogged. When you lay the second course of stones, embed 22mm (¾ in) plastic pipes in the mortar bed, allowing them to slope slightly towards the front of the wall. The pipes should be placed at about 1m (3ft) intervals and pass right through the wall, projecting a little from the face.

Finishing stone walls

When the wall is complete, rake out the joints to give a dry-stone wall appearance. An old paintbrush is a useful tool for smoothing the mortar in deep crevices, to make firm watertight joints. Alternatively, you can point regular stones with flush or rubbed joints.

Allow the mortar to set for a day or two before filling behind the wall. Lay hardcore at the base to cover the drainage pipes and pack shingle against the wall as you replace the soil. Finally, provide a generous layer of topsoil, so you can plant up to the wall.

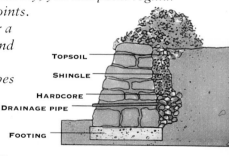

TOPSOIL
SHINGLE
HARDCORE
DRAINAGE PIPE
FOOTING

STONE RETAINING WALL

Essential tools

Broom

Club hammer

Log saw or chain saw

Mattock

Rake

Shovel

Spade

TIP ● ● ● ● ● ●

Planting between logs
If you want to plant
between the logs, scrape
out some of the sand
and gravel and replace it
with topsoil.

LAYING A LOG PATH

If a large tree has been felled in your garden, or you live in a rural district where sizable logs are readily available, you can make a practical and charming footpath, using 150mm (6in) lengths of sawn timber, set on end.

Lay the logs together like crazy paving, or use large pieces of wood as stepping stones. To hold wood rot at bay, soak the sawn timber in chemical preserver.

Excavating the pathway
Dig a trench along the line of the pathway to a depth of 200mm (8in). Spread a layer of gravel-and-sand mix 50mm (2in) deep across the bottom – either use ready-mixed concreting ballast or make up the mix yourself. Level the bed by scraping and tamping with a straightedge.

1 Place the logs on end on the bed of gravel and sand, arranging them to create a pleasing combination of shapes and sizes.

2 Work the logs into the bed until they stand firmly and evenly, then pour some more gravel and sand between them.

3 Brush the material across the pathway in all directions until the gaps between the logs are filled flush with the surface. If any logs stand proud, which could cause someone to trip, tap them down with a heavy hammer, until level.

MAKING STEPS FROM LOGS

If you are able to get sawn lengths of timber from a felled tree, you can use them to build attractive steps that suit an informal or country-style garden. Try to construct risers of a fairly regular height – otherwise someone may stumble, if they are forced to break step. As it is not always possible to obtain uniform logs, you may have to make up the height of the riser with two or more slimmer logs. Alternatively, buy purpose-made pressure-treated logs, machined with a flat surface on two faces. Soak your own timber in chemical preserver overnight.

ALLOW THE COMPLETE WEEKEND

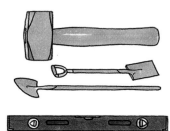

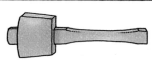

Essential tools

Club hammer

Hatchet

Log saw

Mallet

Shovel

Spade

Spirit level

1 Cut a regular slope in the earth bank and compact the soil by treading it down.

Drive stakes, cut from logs 75mm (3in) diameter, into the ground, placing one at each end of a step.

2 Place a heavy log behind the stakes, bedding it down in the soil.

3 Pack hardcore behind the log to make the tread of the step. Shovel a layer of gravel on top of the hardcore to finish the step.

4 If large logs are in short supply, you can build a step from two or three slim logs instead, holding them against the stakes with hardcore as you construct the riser.

LOG STEPS
1 RETAINING STAKE
2 LOG RISER
3 HARDCORE INFILL
4 GRAVEL

See also:
Types of preserver, page 35

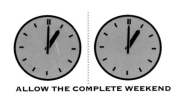

Essential tools

Club hammer

Pointing trowel

Shovel

Spade

Spirit level

Trowel

BUILDING A FLIGHT OF STRONG STEPS

Designing a garden for a sloping site offers many possibilities for creating attractive changes of level by making terraced areas or holding plant beds in place with retaining walls. It will probably also involve building at least one short flight of steps, so it is possible to get from one level to another safely.

DESIGNING STEPS

For steps to be comfortable and safe to use, the ratio between the tread (the part you stand on) and the riser (the vertical part of the step) is crucial.

As a rough guide, construct your steps so that the depth of the tread (measured from front to back) plus twice the height of the riser equals 650mm (2ft 2in). For example, match 300mm (1ft) treads with 175mm (7in) risers; 350mm (1ft 2in) treads with 150mm (6in) risers; and so on. Never make treads less than 300mm (1ft) deep, or risers higher than 175mm (7in).

STEPS BUILT FROM PAVING SLABS
1 CONCRETE FOOTING
2 BRICK-BUILT RISER
3 HARDCORE INFILL
4 PAVING-SLAB TREAD

See also:
Repointing masonry, page 67

USING PAVING SLABS

Concrete paving slabs in their various forms are ideal for making firm flat treads for garden steps.

Construct the risers from concrete facing blocks or bricks, allowing the treads to overhang by 25 to 50mm (1 to 2in) – so they will cast an attractive shadow line which also defines the edge of the step.

1 Measure the difference in height from the top of the slope to the bottom to gauge the number of steps required. Mark the position of the risers with pegs and roughly shape the steps in the soil as confirmation.

2 Either lay concrete paving slabs, bedded in sand, flush with the ground at the foot of the slope or dig a trench for hardcore and a 100 to 150mm (4 to 6in) concrete base to support the first riser.

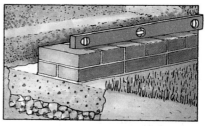

3 When the concrete has set, construct the riser from two courses of mortared bricks, each course set at right angles to the other. Check the alignment with a spirit level.

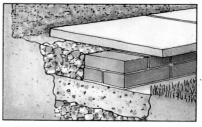

4 Fill behind the riser with compacted hardcore until it is level, then lay the tread on a bed of mortar. Using a spirit level as a guide, tap down the tread until it slopes very slightly towards its front edge – in order to shed rainwater and so prevent ice forming in cold weather.

5 Measure from the front edge of the tread to mark the position of the next riser on the slabs, then construct the next step in the same way. Set the final tread flush with the paved area or lawn at the top of the flight of steps.

TIP ● ● ● ● ● ● ● ● ● ● ● ● ● ● ●

Landscaping each side

It is usually possible to landscape the slope at each side of the flight of steps, and to turf or plant it to prevent the soil washing down onto the steps. Another solution is to retain the soil with large stones, perhaps extending into a rockery on one or both sides.

Essential tools

Bolster/brick guillotine

Broom

Club hammer

Mattock

Plate vibrator

Rake

Shovel

Spade

Trowel

Spirit level

See also:
Types of preserver, page 35

LAYING OUT A PARKING SPACE

There is no reason why the parking space for a car, or other vehicles, has to be an unattractive expanse of flat concrete. Brick pavers come in a range of subtle colours and shapes, and with care and patience it is easy enough to lay them in an almost infinite variety of patterns.

Ordinary housebricks are often used for paths and small patios, but they are not suitable if the paved area is to be a parking space or driveway, especially if it is to be used by heavy vehicles. For a surface that is more durable, even under severe conditions, use special pavers. These are slightly smaller than standard housebricks, measuring 200 x 100 x 65mm (8 x 4 x 2½in). Red and grey pavers are widely available, and you can obtain other colours by special order.

Brick pavers
Brick pavers are made in a wide variety of colours and textures. Rectangular pavers are the easiest to lay, but other shapes are also available.

BRICK PATTERNS

Concrete bricks have one surface face with chamfered edges all round, and spacers moulded into the sides to form accurate joints. Unlike brick walls, which must be bonded in a certain way for stability, brick paving can be laid to any pattern that appeals to you.

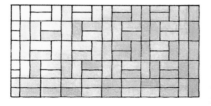

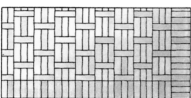

EXTEND A PARKING AREA TO INCLUDE A LABOUR-SAVING FRONT YARD

DEFINE EDGES WITH STONE SETS AND PAVING SLABS

FROM TOP TO BOTTOM:
HERRINGBONE PATTERN WITH STRAIGHT EDGING
ANGLED HERRINGBONE WITH STRAIGHT EDGING

WHOLE BRICKS SURROUNDING COLOURED SQUARES
STAGGERED BASKET-WEAVE PATTERN
STRETCHER-BONDED BRICKWORK
CANE-WEAVE PATTERN

LAYING A FIRM BASE

Lay down a 150mm (6in) hardcore base covered with a 50mm (2in) layer of sharp sand. Fully compact the hardcore and fill all voids, so that sand from the bedding course is not lost to the sub-base.

Provide a slight cross-fall to shed rainwater and, to protect the building, make sure the surface of the paving is at least 150mm (6in) below a damp-proof course.

RETAINING EDGES

Unless the brick paving is laid against a wall or some similar structure, the edges of the paving will need to be contained by a permanent restraint.

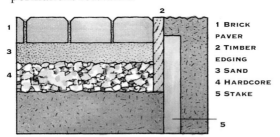

1 BRICK PAVER
2 TIMBER EDGING
3 SAND
4 HARDCORE
5 STAKE

1 Timber edging boards nailed to 50 x 50mm (2 x 2in) stakes are one solution. The edging boards should be flush with the surface of the paving – but drive the stakes below ground, so they can be covered with soil or turf. Treat all timber with a chemical preserver.

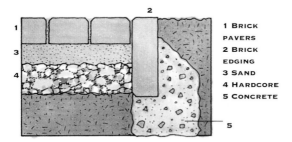

1 BRICK PAVERS
2 BRICK EDGING
3 SAND
4 HARDCORE
5 CONCRETE

2 A better alternative for a parking space is to set an edging of bricks in concrete. Dig a trench deep and wide enough to accommodate a row of bricks on end plus a 100mm (4in) concrete 'foundation'. Lay the bricks while the concrete is still wet, holding them in place temporarily with a staked

board while you pack more concrete behind the edging. When the concrete has set, remove the board and lay hardcore and sand in the excavation.

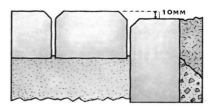

10MM

3 When bricks are first laid upon the sand they should project 10mm (⅜in) above the edging restraints, to allow for bedding them in at a later stage.

4 To level the sand accurately, lay levelling battens on the hardcore base and scrape the sand to the required depth, using a straightedge. Remove the battens and fill the voids carefully with sand. Keep the sand bed dry at all times. If it rains before you can lay the bricks, either let the sand dry out thoroughly or replace it with dry sand.

LAYING THE BRICKS

Having chosen your bricks, prepared the ground and set the retaining edges, you can start laying your paving.

1 Lay an area of bricks on the sand to your chosen pattern. Work from one end of the site, kneeling on a board placed across the bricks. Never stand on the bed of sand. Lay whole bricks only, leaving any gaps at the edges to be filled with cut bricks after you've laid an area of approximately 1 to 2 sq m (1 to 2½ sq yd). Concrete bricks have fixed spacers, so butt them together tightly.

2 Fill any remaining spaces with bricks cut with a bolster chisel. If you're paving a large area, you can hire a hydraulic guillotine.

3 When the area of paving is complete, tamp the bricks into the sand bed, using a hired plate vibrator. Pass the vibrator over the paved area two or three times, until it has worked the bricks down into the sand and flush with the outer edging. Vibrating the bricks will work some sand up between them; complete the job by brushing more sand across the finished paving and vibrating it into the open joints.

INTERLOCKING CONCRETE PAVERS

CONSTRUCTING A ROCKERY

A rockery makes an attractive feature for any garden – and as a bonus, building one gives you an opportunity to use up waste rubble from building projects and soil excavated for a pond. Constructing a rockery can be hard work, especially when moving heavy rocks into place, but the process of creating a unique and thoroughly convincing feature from rock and soil is also a highly enjoyable challenge.

Essential tools
Bristle brush
Garden trowel
Shovel

A convincing rockery
Once plants become established, a rockery should blend into a garden without any hint of artificiality. A 'natural' effect relies on the careful positioning of stones during its construction.

Small-scale rockeries
Don't be put off just because you don't have the room for a large rockery. A successful combination of natural forms can be no less rewarding on a small scale.

AN ADEQUATE SUPPLY OF ROCKS

Buying a sufficient number of natural stones to give the impression of a real rocky outcrop can work out extremely expensive if you order them from a garden centre. A cheaper way is to use hollow-cast reproduction rocks, which will eventually weather in quite well. However, your best option is to purchase natural stone direct from a local quarry.

Rocks can be extremely heavy, so get the quarry to deliver them as close to the site as possible, and hire a strong trolley to facilitate moving individual stones about the garden. Take care not to strain yourself when lifting rocks. Keep your feet together and use your leg muscles to do the work, keeping your back as straight as possible. To move a very heavy rock, slip a rope around it and get an assistant to help you lift it.

Select and place each stone in the rockery carefully, to create an illusion of layers of rock. Stones placed haphazardly at odd angles tend to resemble a spoil heap rather than a natural outcrop.

1 Lay large flat rocks to form the front edge of the rockery, placing soil behind and between them to form a flat, level platform. Compact the soil to make sure there are no air pockets, which can damage the roots of the plants.

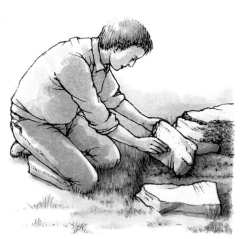

2 Lay subsequent layers of rock set back from the first, but not in a regular pattern. Place some to create steep embankments, others to form a gradual slope of wide steps. Brush soil off the rocks as the work progresses.

TIP ● ● ● ● ● ● ● ● ● ● ● ● ● ● ● ●

Planting spaces

Pockets of soil for planting alpines or other small rockery plants will be formed naturally as you lay the stones, but plan larger areas of soil for specimen shrubs or dwarf trees.

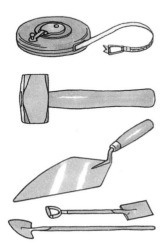

Essential tools

Bolster chisel

Club hammer

Mallet

Mattock

Paintbrush

Scissors

Shovel

Spade

Spirit level

Tape measure

Trowel

Wheelbarrow

See also:
Building a cascade, page 108
Constructing a rockery, page 100
Protecting your fish from cats,
page 63
Stopping your pond overflowing,
page 17

MAKING A SMALL POND

There is nothing like still or running water to enliven a garden. Waterfalls and fountains have an almost mesmerizing fascination, and the sound of trickling water has a delightfully soothing effect. Even a small area of still water will support all manner of interesting pond life and plants – with the additional bonus of images of trees, rocks and sky reflected on the placid surface.

EASY-TO-INSTALL POND LINERS

It is not by chance that the number of garden ponds has increased enormously over recent years – their popularity is largely due to the availability of easily installed rigid and flexible pond liners, which have made it possible to create a complete water garden by putting in just a few days' work. Depending on the size and type of liner, it may take longer than a single weekend to complete the installation, but the bulk of the work can be undertaken in the first two days. You can introduce plants into a pool lined with plastic or rubber as soon as the water itself has matured, which takes no more than a few days.

Pond under construction
This relatively ambitious landscaping project utilizes a flexible liner in the construction of a water garden.

CHOOSING A POND LINER

There are a number of options to choose from, depending on the size and shape of the pond you wish to create and how much you propose to spend.

Rigid liners

Regular garden-centre visitors will be familiar with the range of preformed plastic pond liners. A rigid liner is in effect a one-piece pond, including planting shelves and, in some cases, recessed troughs for marsh or bog gardens.

The best liners are those made from rigid glass-reinforced plastic (fibreglass), which is very strong and resistant to the effects of frost or ice. Almost as good, and more economical, are liners made from vacuum-formed plastic.

Provided they are handled with a reasonable degree of care and installed correctly, rigid plastic pond liners are practically leak-proof. A very acceptable water garden can be created with a carefully selected series of pond liners, linked together by watercourses.

Flexible liners

For complete freedom of design, choose a flexible-sheet liner designed to hug the contours of a pond of virtually any shape and size. Flexible plastic liners range from inexpensive polyvinyl acetate (PVC) and polyethylene sheet to better-quality low-density polyethylene and nylon-reinforced

PVC. Plastic liners, especially those reinforced with nylon, are guaranteed for many years of normal use – but if you want your pond to last for 50 years or more, choose a thicker membrane made from synthetic butyl rubber. Black and stone-coloured butyl liners are made in a wide range of stock sizes up to 6.5 x 10.75m (22 x 35ft), and larger liners can be supplied to order.

Ordering a flexible liner

Use the following simple formula to calculate the size of liner you will need. Disregard the design, planting shelves and so on that you have planned. Simply take the overall length and width of the pond, and add twice the maximum depth to each dimension in order to arrive at the size of the liner. To save money, adapt your design to fall within the nearest stock liner size.

DESIGNING YOUR POND

A pond must be sited correctly if it is to have any chance of maturing into an attractive clear expanse of water. Never place a pond under deciduous trees – falling leaves will pollute the water as they decay, causing fish to become ill and even die. Laburnum trees are especially poisonous.

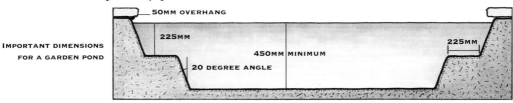

IMPORTANT DIMENSIONS
FOR A GARDEN POND

50MM OVERHANG
225MM
450MM MINIMUM
20 DEGREE ANGLE
225MM

The need for sunlight

Although sunlight promotes the growth of algae, which cause ponds to turn a pea-green colour, it is also necessary to encourage the growth of other water plants. An abundance of oxygenating plants will compete with the algae for mineral salts and, aided by the shade cast by floating and marginal plants, will help keep the pond clear.

Volume of water

The dimensions of the pond are important in creating harmony between plants and fish. It is difficult to maintain the right conditions for clear water in a pond that is less than 3.75sq m (40sq ft) in surface area, but the volume of water is even more vital. A pond up to 9sq m (100sq ft) in area needs to be 450mm (1ft 6in) deep. As the area increases you will have to dig deeper, to about 600mm (2ft) or more, although it's hardly ever necessary to dig deeper than 750mm (2ft 6in).

Designing the shape of your pond

Although there is a huge variety of rigid-plastic liners available, you are limited to the shapes selected by the manufacturers. There are no such limitations when using flexible liners, although curved shapes take up the slack better than straight-sided pools.

The profile of the pond must be designed to fulfil certain requirements. To grow marginal plants, you will need a shelf 225mm (9in) wide around the edge of the pond, 225mm (9in) below the surface of the water. This will take a standard 150mm (6in) planting crate with ample water above, and you can always raise the crate on pieces of paving or bricks. The sides of the pond should slope at about 20 degrees, to prevent soil collapse during construction and to allow the liner to stretch without promoting too many creases. It will also allow a sheet of ice to float upwards without damaging the liner. Judge the angle by measuring 75mm (3in) inwards for every 225mm (9in) of depth. If the soil is very sandy, increase the angle of slope slightly for extra stability.

A SLOPING SITE

BANKED-UP EARTH
LINE OF ORIGINAL SLOPE
RETAINING WALL

Accommodating a sloping site

On a sloping site build up the low side with earth, turfing up to the paving surround. Cut back the higher side and build a low retaining wall, or bed stones against the earth to create a rockery.

222

INSTALLING A RIGID LINER

Stand a rigid liner in position and prop it up with cardboard boxes, both to check its orientation and to mark its perimeter on the ground.

1 *Use a spirit level to plot key points on the ground and mark them with small pegs. You will need to dig outside this line, so absolute accuracy is not required. As you remove the soil, either take it away in a wheelbarrow or pile it close by, ready to incorporate into a rockery or cascade.*

2 *Lay a straightedge across the top and measure the depth of the excavation, including marginal shelves. Keep the excavation as close as possible to the shape of the liner, but extend it by about 150mm (6in) on all sides.*

3 *Compact the base and cover it with a layer of sharp sand 25mm (1in) deep. Lower the liner and bed it firmly into the sand. Check that it is sitting level, and wedge it temporarily with wooden battens until the back-fill of soil or sand can hold it firmly in place.*

4 *Start to fill the liner with water from a hose. At the same time, pour sifted soil or sand behind the liner. There is no need to hurry, as it will take some time to fill, but keep pace with the rising level of the water. Reach into the excavation and pack soil under the marginal shelves with your hands.*

Finishing the edges
When the liner is firmly bedded in the soil, either finish the edge with stones or re-lay turf to cover the rim of the liner.

CONSTRUCTING A POND WITH A FLEXIBLE LINER

Mark out the shape of the pond on the ground. A garden hose is useful for trying out curvilinear shapes.

1 Excavate the pond to the level of the planting shelf, then mark and dig out the deeper sections. Remove sharp stones and roots from the bottom and sides of the excavation, in case they puncture the liner.

2 The top of the pond must be level, and the surrounding stone or concrete slabs needs to be 18mm (¾ in) below the turf. For both reasons, cut back the turf to accommodate the edging stones or slabs and then drive wooden datum pegs, every metre (3 to 4 ft) or so, into the exposed surround. Level the tops of all the pegs, using a straightedge, and check the level across the pond as well. Remove or pack earth around the pegs until the compacted soil is level below their tops.

3 When the surround is level, remove the pegs and, to cushion the liner, spread a 12mm (½ in) layer of slightly damp sand over the base and sides of the excavation. Alternatively, cover the excavation with a proprietary pond-liner underlay.

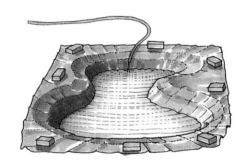

4 Drape the liner across the excavation with an even overlap all round, and hold it in place with bricks while you introduce water from a hose. It will probably take several hours to fill the pond, but check it regularly, moving the bricks as the liner stretches. A few creases are inevitable around sharp curves, but you will lose most of them by keeping the liner fairly taut and easing it into shape as the water rises.

FINISHING THE EDGES OF THE POND

Lay flat stones dry at first, selecting ones that follow the shape of the pond with a reasonably close fit between them. Let the stones project over the water by about 50mm (2in) to cast a deep shadow line and reflection. Wearing goggles, use a bolster chisel to cut stones to fit the gaps behind the larger edging stones.

Cut off surplus liner
Turn off the water when the level reaches 50mm (2in) below the edge of the pond. Cut off surplus liner with scissors, leaving a 150mm (6in) overlap all round. Push 100mm (4in) nails through the overlap into the soil, so the liner cannot slip while you place the edging stones.

Bedding stones on mortar
Lift the stones one or two at a time and bed them on two or three strategically placed mounds of mortar, mixed with 1 part cement to 3 parts soft sand. Tap the stones level with a mallet and fill the joints with a trowel. Use an old paintbrush to smooth the joints flush. Take care not to drop mortar into the water, or you will have to empty and refill the pond before introducing fish or plants.

Bringing rocks down into the water
Edging a pond with flat stones provides a safe and attractive footpath for tending water plants and fish – but a more natural setting is often required, particularly for a small header pool in a rockery.

Incorporate a shelf around the pond – as for marginal plants, but this time to accommodate an edging of rocks. If you place them carefully, there is no need to mortar them. Arrange more rocks behind the edging to cover the liner.

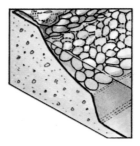

Creating a pebble beach
If you want to create a shallow beach-like edging, slope the soil at a very shallow angle and lay large pebbles or flat rocks upon the liner. You can either merge them with a rockery or let them form a natural water line.

Essential tools

Mattock

Scissors

Shovel

Spade

Wheelbarrow

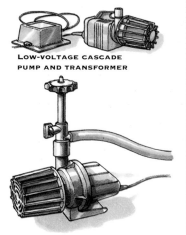

LOW-VOLTAGE CASCADE
PUMP AND TRANSFORMER

COMBINATION FOUNTAIN-
AND-CASCADE PUMP

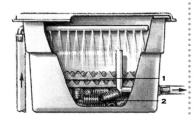

FILTER TANK
1 FOAM FILTER
2 BIOLOGICAL MEDIUM

See also:
Constructing a rockery, page 100
Creating a water feature for your
patio, page 59
Making a small pond, page 102

BUILDING A CASCADE

A cascade complemented by a rockery planted with alpines or graceful shrubs and trees, such as Japanese maples or dwarf conifers, adds a further dimension to a water garden. The technique for building a series of watercourses is not as complicated as one might expect, and at the same time you can cover much of the groundwork needed for creating the rockery. Providing running water is also an ideal way of filtering your pond.

You will be surprised at the amount of soil produced by excavating a pond. To avoid waste and the chore of transporting it to a local dump, use it to create your poolside rockery. If you include a filter and a small reservoir liner on the higher ground, you can pump water from the main pond through the filter into the reservoir and return it via the trickling cascade.

Pumps and filters

Small submersible pumps for fountains and cascades are operated either directly from the mains electrical supply or through a transformer that reduces the voltage to 24 volts. Mains electricity and water can be lethal, so get a qualified electrician to help you install the necessary equipment.

Place a submersible cascade pump close to the edge of the pond, so you can reach it to disconnect the hose running to the cascade when you need to service the pump. Stand combined cascade-and-fountain units on a flat stone or securely propped up on bricks, so the jet is vertical.

Pumps usually have built-in foam filters, but these are not sufficient to keep the water in a sizable pond clear and healthy for fish. It is preferable to install a plastic tank containing a combination of foam filters that will remove debris, plus a layer of a biological filter medium to take out pollutants created by rotting vegetation and fish excreta. Conceal the filter tank behind rocks and plants at the back of the rockery, where it can discharge filtered water into the top reservoir.

TERRACING WITH FLEXIBLE LINER

Rigid-liner manufacturers make moulded cascade kits for embedding into rockeries; you simply cover the edges with stones, soil and trailing plants. Alternatively, create a custom-made watercourse yourself, using offcuts of flexible liner.

Installing the liner

So that the waterfall can discharge directly into the main pond, form a small inlet at the side of the pond by leaving a large flap of flexible liner (1). Build shallow banks at each side of the inlet and line it with stones. Create a stepped watercourse, ascending in stages to the reservoir. Line the watercourse with flexible liner, overlapping the offcuts on the face of each cascade. Tuck the edge of each lower piece of liner under the edge of the piece above and hold the pieces in place with stones. To retain water in small pools along the watercourse, cut each step with a slope towards the rear (2) and place stones along the lip to achieve the desired effect (3); a flat stone will produce a sheet of water, a layer of pebbles a rippling cascade.

As the construction work progresses, test the watercourse by running water from a garden hose, as it is difficult to adjust the angle of stones once the watercourse has been completed.

Bury the flexible hose from the cascade pump in the rockery, making sure there are no sharp bends, which would restrict the flow of water. Attach the hose to the filter tank at the top of the rockery (4).

A rigid-plastic reservoir will have a lip moulded in one edge, which allows water to escape down the watercourse. If you construct a reservoir with flexible liner (5), however, you will need to shape the edge to form a low point (6) and support a flat stone over the opening to hide the liner.

Terraced watercourse

This cross section shows a series of cascades running from reservoir to pond.

**WATERCOURSE
CONSTRUCTED FROM
FLEXIBLE LINER
1 INLET
2 SLOPED STEP
3 EDGING STONES
4 HOSE RUNS TO
FILTER TANK
5 RESERVOIR
6 RESERVOIR OUTLET**

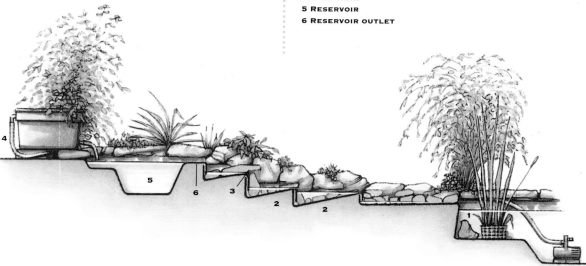

ALLOW THE COMPLETE WEEKEND

Essential tools

Edging float

Garden roller

Hammer

Hosepipe

Mallet

Rake

Shovel

Spade

Spirit level

Tamper

Wheelbarrow

See also:
Maintaining garden steps, page 32

LAYING A FIRM BASE FOR A TOOL SHED

Even a small garden shed needs to be erected on a firm, flat base – which will also help to prevent the timber rotting by shedding rainwater. Unless the ground is very uneven or boggy, you can simply lay a pad of concrete paving slabs on a bed of soft sand.

However, a simple rectangular pad of solid concrete makes a more stable and durable base, especially for larger sheds or similar structures. It is not a difficult task, so long as your initial setting out is accurate and you take care with the construction of the necessary formwork. Provided that the base is less than 2m (6ft 6in) square, there is no need to include control joints to prevent the pad cracking.

LAYING A PAVING-SLAB BASE

Choose simple flat slabs that, when butted together, will make a pad not less than 50 to 75mm (2 to 3in) larger than the shed on all sides. If possible, construct the pad using whole paving slabs, in order to avoid the tedious task of cutting them.

Laying and levelling

Clear and scrape the site level, then spread a layer of soft sand, 25mm (1in) thick, over the area to be paved. Lay the slabs on the sand, butting them together and tamping them down to form a flat, level surface. There's no need to point the slabs, as minor gaps will help to drain away water.

LAYING A CONCRETE BASE

Mixing concrete

For a small shed base, mix 1 part Portland cement, 2 parts sharp sand and 3 parts aggregate (gravel or crushed stone), using a bucket to measure the ingredients. Mix the sand and aggregate on a hard flat surface, then blend in the cement until the colour of the mixture is even. Make a depression for some water, scooping in the dry ingredients until the water has been absorbed; then mix the batch by chopping and turning the concrete with a shovel. Add more water until the concrete is smooth and holds ridges when you drag the shovel across it.

1 Mark out the area of the pad with string lines attached to pegs driven into the ground outside the work area. Remove them to excavate the site, but replace them afterwards to help position the formwork which will hold the concrete in place. Remove 150mm (6in) of topsoil within the site, to allow for a 75mm (3in) thick sub-base and a 75mm (3in) layer of concrete. Extend the area of excavation about 150mm (6in) outside the space allowed for the pad.

2 Cut back any roots you encounter. If there is any turf, put it aside to cover the infill surrounding the completed pad. Level the bottom of the excavation by dragging a board across it, and compact the soil with a garden roller.

3 For a straightforward rectangular pad, construct the formwork from softwood planks, 25mm (1 in) thick, set on edge. The planks, which must be as wide as the finished depth of concrete, are held in place temporarily with stout 50 x 50mm (2 x 2in) wooden stakes. Second-hand or sawn timber is quite adequate; if it is slightly thinner than 25mm (1 in), simply use more stakes to brace it. If you have to join planks, butt them end to end, nailing a cleat on the outside.

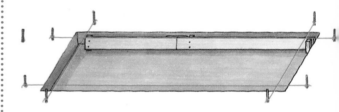

4 The finished pad should have a slight cross-fall to shed water. Using the string lines as a guide, erect one board at the 'high' end of the pad and drive stakes behind it at about 1m (3ft) intervals, or less, with one for each corner. The tops of the stakes and board must be level and correspond exactly to the proposed surface of the pad. Nail the board to the stakes.

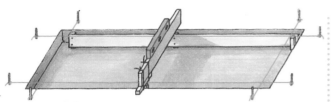

5 Set up another board opposite the first one – but before you nail it to the stakes, establish the cross-fall with a spirit level and straightedge. Work out the difference in level from one end of the pad to the other. For example, a pad which is 2m (6ft 6in) long should drop 25mm (1in) over that distance. Tape a shim of timber to one end of the straightedge and, with the shim resting on the 'low' stakes, place the other end on the opposite board. Drive home each low stake until the spirit level reads horizontal, then nail the board flush with the tops of the stakes.

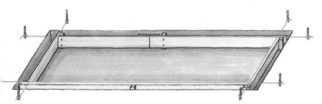

6 Erect the sides of the formwork, allowing the ends of the boards to overshoot the corners, which will make it easier to dismantle them when the concrete has set. Use the straightedge, this time without the shim, to level the boards across the formwork.

7 Hoggin – a mixture of gravel and sand – is an ideal material for a sub-base, but you can use crushed stone or brick hardcore provided you remove any plaster, scrap metal or similar rubbish.

Also remove large lumps of masonry, as they will not compact well. Pour hardcore into the formwork and rake it fairly level before tamping it down with a heavy balk of timber. If there are any stubborn lumps, break them up with a heavy hammer.

Fill in low spots with more hardcore or sharp sand, until the sub-base comes up to the underside of the formwork boards.

8 Mix the concrete as near to the site as practicable, and transport the freshly mixed concrete to the formwork in a wheelbarrow. If the ground is soft, set up firm runways of scaffold boards, especially around the perimeter of the formwork.

Dampen the sub-base and formwork with a fine spray, and let the surface water evaporate before tipping the concrete in place. Start filling from one end of the site and push the concrete firmly into the corners. Rake it level until the concrete stands about 18mm (¾ in) above the level of the boards.

9 *Tamp down the concrete with the edge of a plank, about 50mm (2in) thick, that is long enough to reach across the formwork. Starting at one end of the site, compact the concrete with steady blows of the plank, moving it along by about half its thickness each time.*

10 *Cover the whole area twice, then remove excess concrete, using the plank with a sawing action. Fill any low spots, then compact and level the concrete once more.*

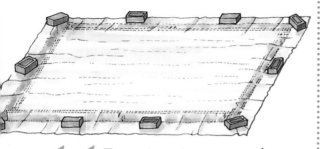

11 *To retain moisture, cover the concrete with a sheet of poly-ethylene, weighted down with bricks. Alternatively, use wet sacks and keep them moist for three days with a fine spray.*

Insulating concrete

Try to avoid laying concrete in very cold weather – but if it is unavoidable, spread a layer of earth or sand on top of the sheeting to insulate the concrete from frost.

You can walk on the concrete after three days, but leave it for about a week, to harden further, before removing the formwork and erecting the shed.

FINISHING THE EDGES

If any of the edges of the concrete are exposed, the sharp corners could cause a painful injury. Radius the corners with a home-made edging float, as described for rounding over the front edges of concrete steps. Run the float along the formwork as you finish the surface of the concrete.

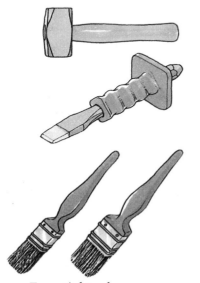

Essential tools

Bolster chisel

Club hammer

Cold chisel

Paintbrushes

Paint roller and extension

Plasterer's trowel or float

A NEW LIFE FOR THE GARAGE FLOOR

Concrete floors are the norm in many modern homes, particularly for utilitarian extensions and garages. In common with a lot of other building materials, concrete can suffer from the effects of damp, as well as cracking and crumbling of the surface. However, repairs are usually relatively easy to accomplish, and resurfacing prior to decorating with a floor paint is quite straightforward. It is the kind of job that takes at least one weekend, to allow sufficient time for materials to set.

Using floor paints

Floor paints are specially formulated to withstand hard wear, making them highly suitable for the concrete floor of a garage or workshop. You can also use them for painting paving stones or steps, and for other concrete structures. Although they come in a limited range of colours, floor paints make an attractive and durable finish for playroom floors, too.

The floor must be clean, dry and free from oil or grease. If the concrete is freshly laid, allow it to mature for at least a month before painting. Prime powdery or porous floors with a proprietary concrete sealer.

Covering a large floor

The best way to paint a large area is to use a paintbrush around the edges, then fit an extension to a paint roller to cover the bulk of the floor.

232

FIXING A CONCRETE FLOOR

An uneven or pitted concrete floor must be made flat and level before you apply floor paint. You can do this fairly easily, using a proprietary self-levelling screed, but you must ensure that the surface is free from damp. A new floor should be left to dry out for six months before any impermeable covering is applied, including paint.

Treating a damp floor

If you suspect that an existing floor is damp, make a simple test by laying a sheet of polyethylene on the concrete and sealing it all round with self-adhesive parcel tape. After one or two days, inspect it for any traces of moisture on the underside.

If this test indicates that widespread treatment is required, paint the floor with a bitumen-based waterproofer, priming the surface first with a slightly diluted coat. Brush on two full-strength coats, allowing each to dry between applications. If need be, you can lay a self-levelling screed over the waterproofer.

An isolated patch of damp suggests that the damp-proof membrane has a small puncture. Use a cold chisel to chop out the damp concrete down to the membrane, and clear away the dust and debris. Paint on two full coats of bitumen-based waterproofer; and when that is dry, seal round the edges of the hole with PVA bonding agent. Fill the hole flush with sand-and-cement mortar mixed with a little diluted bonding agent.

Patches of oil or grease

Wash a stained garage floor with a proprietary oil-and-grease remover. Soak up fresh oil spillages immediately with dry sand or sawdust, to prevent them becoming permanent stains.

APPLYING A SELF-LEVELLING COMPOUND

1 Fill holes and cracks that are deeper than about 3mm (⅛ in) by raking them out and undercutting the edges and then filling them with mortar mix.

2 Self-levelling compound is supplied as a powder that you mix either with water or with latex fluid.
Make sure the floor is clean and free from damp, then pour some of the compound onto the floor in the corner furthest away from the door. Spread the compound gently with a trowel or float until it is about 3mm (⅛ in) thick, and then leave it to seek its own level. Continue across the floor, joining successive applications of compound until the entire surface is covered.

You can walk on the floor after about an hour without damaging it, but leave the compound to harden for a few days before driving a car, or other vehicle, onto it.

TIP ● ● ● ● ● ● ● ● ● ● ● ● ● ●

Levelling small holes and cracks
For patching small holes and cracks in a concrete floor, a proprietary cement-based exterior filler is a useful alternative to self-levelling compound. After being mixed with water, the filler remains workable for 20 minutes. Just before it sets hard, smooth or scrape the filler level.

233

Essential tools

Banister brush

Bolster chisel

Club hammer

Cold chisel

Foam roller

Mallet

Pointing trowel

Wall brush

Wooden float

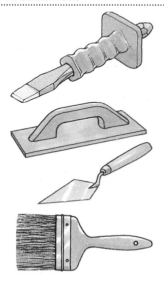

See also:
Brightening up a dull wall, page 118
Refurbishing an old wall, page 64

PATCHING UP RENDERED WALLS

Brickwork is sometimes clad with a smooth or roughcast cement-based render, both for improved weatherproofing and to provide a decorative finish. Render is susceptible to the effects of damp and frost, which can cause cracking, bulging and staining. Before you redecorate a rendered wall, make good any damage and clean off surface dirt, mould growth and flaky material, in order to achieve a long-lasting finish.

REPAIRING DEFECTS

Before you repair cracked render, have a builder check the wall for any structural faults that may have contributed to it. Apply a stabilizing solution if the wall is dusty. Ignore fine hairline cracks if you intend to paint the wall with a reinforced masonry paint.

Rake out larger cracks with a cold chisel. Dampen them with water and fill flush with an exterior filler. Fill any major cracks with a render made of 1 part cement, 2 parts lime and 9 parts builder's sand, plus a little PVA bonding agent to help it stick to the wall.

Bulges in render normally indicate that the cladding has parted from the masonry. Tap the wall gently with a wooden mallet to find out the extent of these hollow areas, then hack off the material to sound edges.

1 Use a bolster chisel to undercut the perimeter of each hole except for the bottom edge – which should be left square, so that is does not collect water.

2 Brush out debris, then apply a coat of PVA bonding agent. When it becomes tacky, trowel on a layer of 1:1:6 render, 12mm (½ in) thick, using plasterer's sand. Leave the render to set firm, then scratch it to form a key.

Next day, fill flush with a weaker 1:1:9 mix and smooth the surface with a wooden float, using circular strokes.

234

REINFORCING A CRACK

To prevent a crack in render opening up again, reinforce the repair with a glass-fibre membrane embedded in a bitumen base coat. Rake out the crack to remove any loose material, then wet it. Fill just proud of the surface with a mortar mix of 1 part cement to 4 parts builder's sand. When this has stiffened, scrape it flush with the render.

1 When the mortar has hardened, brush on a generous coat of bitumen base coat, making sure it extends at least 100mm (4in) on both sides of the crack. Embed strips of fibre-glass scrim (sold with the base coat) into the bitumen, using a stippling and brushing action.

2 While it is still wet, feather the edges of the bitumen with a foam roller, bedding the scrim into it. After 24 hours the bitumen will be hard, black and shiny. Apply a second coat and feather with the roller. When it has dried, apply two coats of a compatible reinforced masonry paint.

A QUICK PATCH FOR PEBBLEDASH

For additional weatherproofing, small stones are stuck to a thin coat of render over a thicker base coat, a process known as 'pebbledashing'. If water gets behind pebbledashing, one or both layers may separate. Hack off any loose render to a sound base, then seal it with stabilizer. If necessary, repair the scratchcoat of render.

You can simulate the texture of pebble-dash with a thick paste made from PVA bonding agent. Mix 1 part cement-paint powder with 3 parts plasterer's sharp sand. Stir in 1 measure of bonding agent diluted with 3 parts water to form a thick creamy paste. Load a banister brush and scrub the paste onto the bare surface. Apply a second generous coat of paste, stippling it to form a coarse texture. Leave it for about 15 minutes to firm up; then, with a loaded brush, stipple it to match the texture of the pebbles. Let the paste harden fully before painting the repair.

Essential tools

Banister brush

Paintbrushes

Paint roller and tray

Paint scraper

BRIGHTENING UP A DULL WALL

Although rendered walls were originally intended to simulate the appearance of cut stonework, the dull-grey colour of cement render is unacceptable to the majority of home owners. Consequently, rendered walls are usually decorated with an exterior-grade paint, as are brick walls in some areas of the country. The combination of heat, cold and rain is likely, to some degree, to cause staining, flaking and chalkiness, which need attention before repainting. Decorating an entire house is more than a weekend's work; but depending on the amount of preparation required, you may be able to paint the front or rear wall of a small terraced house in a weekend.

Paint walls in manageable sections

You can't hope to paint a large area in one session, so divide the wall into manageable sections to disguise the joins. Here the horizontal moulding divides the wall neatly into two sections, and the raised door and window surrounds form convenient break lines.

See also:

Patching up rendered walls, page 116
Refurbishing an old wall, page 64

PAINTS FOR EXTERIOR WALLS

Various grades of paint are produced for decorating and protecting exterior walls, taking into account economy, standard of finish, durability and coverage.

Cement paint

Cement paint is supplied as a dry powder to which water is added. It is based on white cement, but pigments are added to produce a range of colours. Cement paint is one of the cheaper finishes suitable for exterior use. Spray new or porous surfaces with water before applying two coats.

Shake or roll the container to loosen the powder, then add 2 parts powder to 1 of water in a clean bucket. Stir it to a smooth paste, then add a little more water to achieve a full-bodied creamy consistency. Mix no more than you can use in an hour, or the paint may start to dry.

To provide added protection for an exposed wall and help cover dark colours, add clean sand to the mix to give it body. If you find the sand changes the colour of the paint, add it to the first coat only. Use 1 part sand to 4 parts powder, stirring it in while the paint is still in its paste-like consistency.

Water-based masonry paint

Most masonry paints are water-based, being in effect exterior-grade emulsion paints with additives that prevent mould growth. Although they are supplied ready for use, it pays to thin the first coat on porous walls with 20 per cent water. Follow up with one or two full-strength coats, depending on the colour of the paint. Water-based masonry paints must be applied during fairly good weather. Damp or humid conditions and low temperatures may prevent the paint drying properly.

Solvent-based masonry paints

Some masonry paints are thinned with white spirit or with a special solvent – but unlike most oil paints, they are moisture-vapour permeable so that the wall is able to breathe. It is often advisable to thin the first coat with 15 per cent white spirit, but check the manufacturer's recommendations. Solvent-based paints can be applied in practically any weather conditions, so long as it is not actually raining.

Reinforced masonry paint

Masonry paint that has powdered mica or a similar fine aggregate added to it dries with a textured finish that is extremely weatherproof. Reinforced masonry paints are especially suitable for coastal districts and in industrial areas where dark colours are also an advantage. Although large cracks and holes must be filled before painting, reinforced masonry paint will cover hairline cracks and crazing.

Textured coating

A thick textured coating can be applied to exterior walls to form a thoroughly weatherproof self-coloured coating. The coating can also be overpainted to match other colours. The usual preparation is necessary, and brickwork should be pointed flush. Large cracks need to be filled, although a textured coating will cover fine cracks. The paste is brushed or rolled onto the wall, then left to harden, forming an even texture. However, if you prefer, you can produce a texture of your choice using a variety of simple tools; this is an easy process, but it pays to put in some practice on a small section first.

TACKLING PAINTING PROBLEMS

Before painting, it is always important to create a sound surface. Below are some common problems you may encounter when decorating previously painted walls.

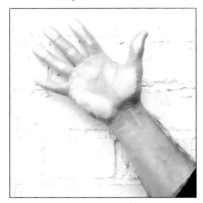

Chalky surfaces
Brush the wall with a stiff-bristle brush, then paint the entire wall liberally with a stabilizing primer, which binds the chalky surface so that paint will adhere to it. A white stabilizing primer can also act as an undercoat. If the wall is very dusty, apply a second coat of stabilizer after about 16 hours. Wait a further 16 hours before painting over it.

Flaking paintwork
Flaking is often the result of poor surface preparation or incompatible paint and preparatory treatments. Damp walls also cause flaking – so have them treated, then allow them to dry out before further treatment. Another cause could be too

many previous coats of paint. Use a paint scraper and stiff-bristle brush to remove all loose material. Finish the job with coarse glasspaper, or at least feather the edges of any stubborn patches. Stabilize the surface, as for chalky walls, before repainting.

Brown staining
A chimney stack that has the outline of brick courses showing through as brown staining is caused by a breakdown of the internal rendering. This allows tar deposits to migrate through the paintwork. To solve the problem, have a flue liner fitted, then cover the brown stains with a spirit-based aluminium sealer before applying a fresh coat of paint. Treat rust stains caused by faulty metal gutters and pipework with the same primer.

TIPS FOR PAINTING THE WALL

A paintbrush is the traditional tool for painting masonry. Choose a brush 100 to 150mm (4 to 6in) wide for painting walls, as larger ones are heavy and tiring to use. On rough walls, a good-quality brush with coarse bristles lasts longest. For good coverage, apply the paint with vertical strokes, crisscrossed with horizontal ones. You will find it necessary to stipple paint into textured surfaces. For faster coverage, use a paint roller with a deep pile for heavy textures and one with a medium pile for shallow textures and smooth surfaces.

Cutting in
Painting up to a feature such as the frame of a door or window is known as 'cutting in'. On a smooth surface you should be able to paint a reasonably straight edge following the line of the feature, but it's difficult to apply the paint to a heavily textured wall with a normal brushstroke.

Don't be tempted to apply more paint to overcome the problem – instead, touch the tip of the brush only to the wall, using a gentle scrubbing action, then brush excess paint away once the texture is filled.

Wipe splashed paint from the frames of doors and windows with a cloth dampened with the appropriate thinner.

A BANISTER BRUSH IS IDEAL FOR TACKLING DEEPLY TEXTURED WALL SURFACES

Painting with a banister brush
Use a banister brush to paint exceptionally deep textures such as pebbledash. Pour some paint into a roller tray and dip the brush in to load it. Scrub the paint onto the wall, using circular strokes to work it well into the uneven surface.

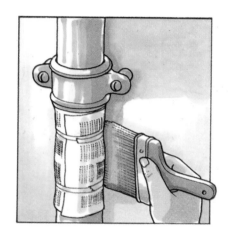

Painting behind pipes
Tape a roll of newspaper around rainwater downpipes to protect them from paint. Stipple behind the pipe with a brush, then slide the paper tube down the pipe to mask the next section.

Using a roller
Rollers apply paint three times faster than paintbrushes – but they wear out very quickly on rough walls, so have at least one spare sleeve handy. To ensure even coverage, vary the angle of the stroke when using a roller; and use a paintbrush instead to cut into angles and around obstructions.

GLOSSARY OF TERMS

Aggregate
Particles of sand or stone mixed with cement and water to make concrete, or added to paint to make a textured finish.

Airlock
A blockage in a pipe caused by a trapped bubble of air.

Architrave
The moulding around a door or window.

Ballast
Naturally occurring sand-and-gravel mix used as aggregate for making concrete.

Batt
A short cut length of glass-fibre or mineral-fibre insulation.

Batten
A narrow strip of wood.

Batter
Slope of the face of a wall that leans backwards or tapers from bottom to top.

Blown
To have broken away, as when a layer of cement rendering has parted from a wall.

Buttercoat
The top layer of cement-based render.

Cavity wall
A wall of two parallel separate masonry skins with an air space or insulation between them.

Countersink
To cut a tapered recess that allows the head of a woodscrew to lie flush with a surface; or, the tapered recess itself.

Cross-fall
The angle required to shed water from a flat surface.

Damp-proof course
A layer of impervious material which prevents moisture rising from the ground into the walls of a building.

Damp-proof membrane
A layer of impervious material which prevents moisture rising through a concrete floor.

Datum point
The point from which measurements are taken.

DPC
See damp-proof course.

DPM
See damp-proof membrane.

Drip groove
A groove cut or moulded in the underside of a windowsill to prevent rainwater running back to the wall.

Drop
A strip of paper cut ready for pasting to a wall.

Efflorescence
A white powdery deposit caused by soluble salts migrating to the surface of a wall or ceiling.

End grain
The surface of wood exposed after cutting across the fibres.

Fall
A downward slope.

Feather
To wear away or smooth an edge until it is undetectable.

Footing
A narrow concrete foundation for a wall.

Galvanized
Covered with a protective coating of zinc.

Hardcore
Broken masonry used to form a sub-base below paving and foundations.

Heave
An upward swelling of level ground caused by excess moisture.

Hoggin
A fine ballast, usually with a clay content, used to form a sub-base for concrete pads or paving.

Key
To abrade or incise a surface to provide a better grip for paint, adhesive or cement-based render.

Lath and plaster
A method of finishing a timber-framed wall or ceiling. Narrow strips of wood are nailed to the studs or joists to provide a supporting framework for the plaster.

Lead
A stepped section of brickwork or blockwork built at each end of a wall to act as a guide to the height of the intermediate coursing.

Marine plywood
Exterior-grade plywood.

Mastic
A nonsetting compound used to seal joints.

Microporous
See moisture-vapour permeable.

Mitre
A joint formed between two pieces of wood by cutting bevels of equal angle at the ends of each piece. *or* To cut the joint.

Moisture-vapour permeable
Used to describe a finish which allows moisture to escape from timber or masonry, allowing them to dry out, while protecting them from rainwater or condensation.

Mullion
A vertical dividing member of a window frame.

Muntin
A central vertical member of a panel door.

Nogging
A short horizontal wooden member between studs.

Nosing
The front edge of a stair tread.

Pargeting
The internal render of a chimney.

Party wall
The wall between two houses over which each of the adjoining owners has equal rights.

Pebbledash
See render.

Pilot hole
A small-diameter hole drilled prior to inserting a woodscrew to act as a guide for its thread.

Primer
The first coat of a paint system to protect the workpiece and to reduce absorption of subsequent undercoats and top coats.

Render
A thin layer of cement-based mortar applied to exterior walls to provide a protective finish. Sometimes fine stone aggregate is embedded in the mortar, a process known as pebbledashing.

Reveal
The vertical side of an opening in a wall.

GLOSSARY OF TERMS

Riser
The vertical part of a step.

Sash
The openable part of a window.

Scratchcoat
The bottom layer (undercoat) of cement-based render.

Screed
A thin layer of mortar applied to give a smooth surface to concrete etc.

Screed batten
A thin strip of wood fixed to a surface to act as a guide to the thickness of an application of plaster or render.

Set
A small rectangular paving block.

Soakaway
A pit or trench filled with rubble or gravel into which water is drained.

Spalling
Flaking of the outer face of masonry caused by expanding moisture in icy conditions.

Stile
A vertical side member of a door or window sash.

Stud partition
An interior timber-framed dividing wall.

Tamp
To pack down firmly with repeated blows.

Thixotropic
A property of some paints which have a jelly-like consistency until stirred or applied, at which point they become liquefied.

Trap
A bent section of pipe situated below a bath, washbasin or sink. A trap contains standing water that prevents the passage of gases.

Tread
The horizontal part of a step.

Undercoat
A layer or layers of paint used to obliterate the colour of a primer and to build a protective body of paint prior to the application of a top coat. See also – scratchcoat.

Vapour barrier
A layer of impervious material which prevents the passage of moisture-laden air.

Vapour check
See vapour barrier.

Wall tie
A strip of metal or bent wire used to bind sections of masonry together.

Waney edge
A natural wavy edge on a plank, which might still be covered by tree bark.

Warp
To bend or twist as a result of damp or heat.

Weathered
Showing signs of exposure to the weather. *or* Sloped so as to shed rainwater.

Weep hole
A small hole at the base of a cavity wall to allow absorbed water to drain to the outside.

Workpiece
An object in the process of being shaped, produced or otherwise worked upon.

INDEX

A

abrasives 12, 45, 47, 59, 75, 103
acetone 12
acidic soil 131
acrylic coating for tarmac 189
acrylic exterior wood stain 157, 158
acrylic lacquer 12
adhesives 59–60, 79, 120, 123
adhesive tape 20, 39, 41, 81
airing cupboard 19, 21
alcoves 71, 73, 110
algae 150, 222
alpine plants 205, 219, 226
aluminium spirit-based sealer 45, 57
aluminium weather trim 63
ammonia 12, 184
angle iron 200
arris rail 154
ashlar blocks 187
automatic latch 174–175

B

banister brush 187, 239
bank of shelving 72–73
base, tool shed 228–231
bathroom 21, 40–42, 117–123
battens 70–71, 119
beeswax polish 46
bib tap 179
bird feeder 156
bird nesting box 158–159
bird table 156–157
bitumen base coat 235
bitumen emulsion 189–191
bitumen-based waterproofer 233
black lead 25
blade seal 67
blanket insulation 78–79
blanking plug 23
bleach solution 44, 183
bleed valve 23
blinds 31–33
blockages 14–16
blockboard 69–70
blocked radiator valve 23
blocked sink 14

boiler 21, 23
bolts 35, 47, 51, 53
bonding stones 205–206
brackets 30, 32, 33, 70–73, 161, 163, 165, 198
branches, lopping 139
brass fittings 10–12
brass screws 159
brick
    climbing plants 137
    cracked 188
    efflorescence 185
    hardcore 154, 230
    incinerator 144–145
    painting 237
    patterns 215
    pavers 214–215
    piers 176
    refurbishing 182, 184
    repointing 150, 185–186
    retaining edges 193, 208, 216
    spacers 215, 217
    spalled 184, 188
    steps 193, 213
    terracing 208
    walls 236–237
British Standard 19, 34
brown staining of chimney stack 120
brush seal 63, 65, 67
builder's line 85, 88
burglars 50–53
butyl sealant 75
Bylaw 30 kit 80

C

cane and wire tent 143
capping strips 198
carnauba wax 46
carpet-fitting 38–39, 60
cars, parking 133, 193, 214–217
cascade 177–179, 223, 226–227
cast-iron door knocker 10, 13
cast-iron grate 25
cats 181
cavity fixings 30, 72
cedar wood 173
ceilings 30, 54–57, 78, 94, 104
cellulose fibre insulation 80
cement 185–186

cement paint 235, 237
cement render 234, 236
central-heating expansion tank 80
chalky soil 131
chalky surfaces 238
Chelsea catch 175
chemical drain cleaner 14
chemical paint remover 13, 47
chipboard 69, 78
chippings 189–191
circular landings 193
cisterns 17, 36–37, 42, 79–80
clay soil 131
cleaning agents 183
cleaning fluids 10
cleat 229
clematis 136–137
climbing plants 136–137, 142
cloche 143
coach screws 134
cobblestones 149
cold-cure tarmac 189
cold-water cisterns 79–80
compost 144–145, 168, 171
compost activator 171
compost bin 169–171
concrete floor 39, 41, 63, 90–91
concrete
    ballast 210
    base 228–231
    blocks 200–203, 208–209
    bricks 215
    cobblestones 149
    cracking 232
    fence post 152, 154, 197–198
    floors 232–233
    footings 200–202, 205, 208
    gateposts 172, 176, 228–231
    insulating 231
    kerbs 193
    mixing 229
    paving slabs 138, 193, 213, 228
    pierced blocks 200–203
    posts 176, 199
    retaining edges 216
    screening 200, 202
    sealer 232

spalling 151
spur 134
steps 151
condensation 80, 98
conservation area 139
control joint 228
coping slabs 200, 203
coping stones 206
cork granules 80
corners 106, 110
corrosion 11–13, 22–23, 25
corrugated iron 209
corrugated plastic sheet 135
coursing 204, 206
cracks 74–75
crazy paving 148, 210
cross-fall 216
crossways slope 199
curtain rails 28–30
cylinder jacket 80

D

damp 139, 185, 232, 234
damp-proof course (DPC) 41,
86, 183, 216, 233
Danish oil 47
datum pegs 87, 224
deadbolts 34
deathwatch beetle 78
decorative details 25
decorator's trestle 54
detached insulated lining 114
detergent 11, 15, 45
diaphragm valve 18, 36–37
disinfectant 15
distemper 57
doors
    aluminium sliding 53
    back 34
    draughtproofing 62–65
    exterior 62, 63
    fittings 10–13
    flush 97
    frame 11, 64, 98
    front 10, 24, 34
    furniture 10
    glazed 53, 98
    handles 97
    interior 62, 64
    kits 63
    knockers 10, 13
    mouldings 41

painting 10, 97–98
panelled 97
papering round 111
pull 10
right-handed opening 34
sealing 64
side 34
stile 34
surround 98
ways 42
double dressing 191
double glazing 81
double-seal non-return check
valve 180
double-sided adhesive tape
39, 41, 81
dowel pegs 164
drain auger 16
drainage 86, 135, 140–141,
144, 157, 161,180, 197, 210,
209
draincock 180
draught excluder 63–64, 67,
79
draughtproofing 60, 62–65
draughtproofing sealant 64
draughts 28, 60, 62–65,
66–67, 78
drawings 128, 132–133
dripping tap 21–22
driveway 133, 192–193, 214
dry-stone wall 204–206
dust sheets 56, 94
dwarf trees 219, 226

E

eaves 79–80
edging boards 216
edging float 231
edging stones 135, 181,
223–225, 227
edging trowel 151
efflorescence 185
electrical fittings 45, 78–79,
80, 110, 115
electricity supply (outdoors)
133, 135, 177, 226
energy saving 62, 66, 78, 81
epoxy-resin adhesive 165
erosion 185
escutcheons 35
evaporation 179
exfoliated vermiculite 80

expanded-metal mesh 76
expanding-foam filler 67
extension floor 232
exterior filler 233, 234
exterior walls 237
exterior-grade paint 236

F

facing blocks 213
fences
    fence-post spikes 152, 155
    interwoven panel 196
    larch 196
    panel 196–199
    posts 134, 152–155, 197
    rotting 134
    rustic larchlap 196
    waney-edged panel 196
fibre-glass scrim 235
fillers 74–75, 81
filter tank 226–227
filter 179, 226
finishing oil 47
fireplace 25, 110–111, 115
fish ponds 128, 181, 222, 225
flagstones 148
flaking paintwork 238
flap valves 36–37
float 17–18, 36
float arm 17–18, 36–37
float valve 36–37
floor paint 232–233
floorboards 38, 41, 58, 60,
114, 158, 169–170
floors 232–233
flue liner 238
flush joint 187, 209
flushing lever 36–37
foam filters 226
foam roller 235
foam strip insulation 64
foamed-plastic tubes 19–20,
38, 112
footings 200–202, 205–206,
208–209
formwork 228–230
formwork boards 230
fountains 177–179, 220
French polish 46
Frenchman 187

INDEX

frost 139, 142–143, 151, 184–185, 221, 234
fruit trees 142
fungicidal paste 106, 112
fungicide 150, 183
furniture beetle 78

G

galvanized mesh 200, 203
galvanized nails 159
gaps, filling 62, 64, 67, 75, 79–80, 114, 121, 123
garage floors 232
garages 163, 232
garden furniture 47
gardens
  bird table 156–157
  canes 142
  compost 144–145, 168–171
  cottage 129
  crazy paving 148
  driveway 133, 192–193, 214–217
  electric pump 133, 135, 177, 226
  features 131–132
  fish pond 128, 181, 222, 225
  formal 129
  gradients 131
  gravel 192–193
  incinerator 144–145
  Japanese-style 129
  lawn 148
  lighting 133, 135
  nesting box 158–159
  parking space 133, 193, 214–217
  patios 128, 132–133, 148, 177–179, 200–203, 214
  planning 128–133
  plants 128,136–137, 142–143, 205, 215, 219, 226
  ponds 128, 132–133, 135,181,218,220–225, 227
  rockery 130, 213, 218–219, 222–223, 225, 226–227
  romantic 129

safety 132–133, 141, 150–151, 211
screen 200–203
shed 163
sketching 128, 132
slopes 131, 193, 199,208–209,212–213, 219, 222
soil 128, 131, 168
stepping stones 148, 210
steps 150–151, 193, 211–213
sunlight 128, 131, 133, 183, 222
terracing 193, 208–209, 212, 227
tools 163–165, 228
trees 128, 132, 139, 142–143, 183, 210, 219, 222, 226
walls 136–137, 204–206
waste 168
water 130
water shortages 140–141
weather 131
gateposts 172–176
gates
  closeboard 173
  double 172, 174
  drive 173, 176
  entrance 173, 176
  five-bar 173
  frame-and-panel 173
  garden 172–176
  gateposts 172–176
  ground clearance 173
  hardware 175
  iron 173
  picket 173
  ranch-style 173
  side 173
  tongue-and-groove   173
  wooden 172
  wrought-iron 172–173
gauge stick 118–119
glass 69, 98
glass-fibre blanket 79–80, 115
glass-fibre membrane 235
glasspaper 238
goggles 13, 15, 121
gradients 131
graph paper 132
graphite 25

grate polish 25
gravel 86, 192–193,
gravel boards 198–199
gravel garden 192–193
grease stains 190, 233
gripper strips 39
grooved metal angle 70
grooved metal T-section 70
grouting 120–123
guide batten 119
guide lines 54, 72, 86–87, 91
guy ropes 197, 202

H

hairline cracks 75
hardcore 86, 149, 154, 176, 190, 193, 201, 209, 211, 216, 230
hardwood 176
hawk 186
headgear nut 21, 22
headrail 33
heat loss 62, 66, 78, 81
horizontal blinds 33
hinge stile 173
hoggin 230
hooks and eyes 164
hot-water cylinder 19, 21
hydrated lime 186
hydraulic guillotine 217
hydraulic pump 16

I

ice 213
immersion heater 21
incinerator 144–145
inlet valve 23
insulation 19–20, 28, 78–80, 115
internal rendering 238
interwoven panel fence 196
ivy 136–137

J

Japanese maple 226
jointer 187
joints 47, 59–60, 86
joints, mortar 186–187
joists 30, 77, 78, 80, 114

K

keyholes 35, 53, 65
kitchen cabinets 102–103

kitchen flooring 40–42
kitchen waste 168
knee kicker 38

L

laburnum trees 222
lacquers 10, 12
ladder storage 163
lagging 19–20, 80
landings 58
larch 196
larchlap panels 196
latch stile 173
latex fluid 233
lath 187
laths 76
lawn 148
lawn mower storage 164–165
leaking pipes 183
'laying off' 96
letter boxes 65
letter plates 10, 12–13
lichens 183
light fittings 55, 79
lighter fluid 12
lighting 133, 135
lippings 70, 73
liquid wax 46
living room, painting 92–101
locks 34–35, 50, 52–53, 65
loft 78–80
log path 210
logs 210–211
loop-over catch 175
loose-fill insulation 78, 80
lugs 118, 120

M

mall slipstone 121
man-made boards 69, 71
marking gauge 35
masking tape 12, 98
masonry
  cleaning 184
  climbing plants 136–137
  efflorescence 185
  leaking pipes 180
  mould 183
  paint 234–235, 237
  piers 176
  refurbishing 182–188
  repointing 185–188
  spalling 151, 188

steps 151
  wall plugs 161
masonry bit 72
mastic 79, 114–115
measurements 131–132
medium-density fibreboard
  (MDF) 69
metal bracket 163, 198
metal extrusions 70
metal gateposts 176
metal gutters 238
metal lintels 30
metal pipework 238
metal polish 11, 12
metallic inks 45
mica 80
microbes 171
mild-steel bar 173
mineral wool 80
mineral-fibre blanket
  insulation 19, 79, 115
mobile platforms 57
mortar 87, 91, 138, 150, 184,
  186, 193, 202–203, 204–205,
  208–209, 225, 233
mortar joints 186–181
mould growth 44, 47, 106,
  183
moulded pool 179
mouldings 47, 60, 97

N

nail punch 60
natural stones 84, 90
neighbours 139
nesting box 158–159
noggings 30, 72, 115
noise 28, 112, 114–116
non-return valve 180
nosing 60
nutrients 171

O

oak 173
oil finish 47
oil stains 190, 233
one-piece siphon 37
outlet valve 23
overflow 17–18, 36

P

paint
  acrylic 92, 96

  brushes 57, 95
  emulsion 45, 57, 75, 92,
    94–95, 104
  gloss 96, 103
  liquid 94, 96
  matt 13, 94, 103
  new-plaster emulsion 94
  oil 45, 96
  one-coat 92, 96
  satin 94, 96, 103
  solvent-based 92, 96
  stripping 13, 47
  rollers 95
  runs 97, 103
  shield 96, 98
  strippers 10
  textured 75
  thixotropic 94, 96
  tray 95
painted pressed steel 69
painting
  brush 232, 239
  casement windows 100
  ceilings 56–57
  doors 10, 97
  door surround 98
  exterior-grade paint 236
  flaking paintwork 238
  floor paint 232–233
  glass 98
  living room 92–101
  masonry 234–235, 237
  paint 236–237
  paint-roller 232, 239
  problems 238
  sash windows 101
  scraper 238
  stippling 239
  stripper 184
  walls 92, 94, 236–239
  woodwork 92
panel fences 196–199
panel-fixing bracket 198
paper-backed fabrics 106, 112
papering 54–55, 104–113
parking space 133, 193,
  214–217
partition wall 30, 75
passion flowers 137
patching 73, 74–77

INDEX

paths 90–91
pathways 192–193, 210
patios 84–90, 128, 132–133, 148, 177–179, 200–203, 214
paving slabs 84–88, 90, 138, 145, 150–151, 199, 213, 224, 228
pea gravel 193
pebbledash 235, 239
pebbles 179, 225
peephole viewer, fitting 24
pegged hanging rail 164
petrol stains 190, 233
piers 200–203
pilaster blocks 200, 202
pipes
    branch 15–16
    cold-water 20–21, 79–80
    downpipes 140–141
    drain pipes 201
    flush 36–37
    hot-water 19–20
    insulation 19, 79–80
    lagging 20
    leaking 183
    metal 238
    old water 80
    overflow 17–18
    painting behind 239
    plastic 209
    profile gauge 41
    rainwater 183
    tiling round 119, 122
    waste 14–15
planning 128–133
planters 160–162
planting crate 222
plants
    alpine 205, 219, 226
    cane and wire tent 143
    climbing 136–137, 142
    cloche 143
    compost 168
    dry-stone wall 206
    gravel 192
    log path 210
    planning 128
    planters 160–162
    pond 220, 225, 227
    protection 142–143

rockery 205, 219
shrubs 128,142, 219, 226
terracing 208, 212
trailing 181, 227
trellis 136–137
window boxes 160–161
plaster 74–77, 78, 104, 114
plasterboard 76, 115
plate vibrator 217
plumb line 72, 108, 110, 115
plunger 15
plywood 69–70, 80, 157, 162, 165, 171, 209
pointing 185–187, 188, 202–203
pointing trowel 187
polish 12, 25, 46
polyurethane foam 64
polyurethane varnish 161–162
pond liners 181, 220–225, 227
ponds 132–133, 137, 181, 218, 220–225, 227
post cap 154
post spikes 152, 155
post-hole auger 154, 196–197
potholes 189, 191
power supply 133, 135, 177, 226
pressure-treated logs 210–211
primer 13, 57, 92, 96, 117
profile boards 201–202
profile gauge 41
protection of plants 142–143
protective gloves 10, 13, 15, 78
pruning 137, 139
pruning sealant 139
PTFE tape 180
pumps 177, 179, 226
PVA bonding agent 151, 233–235
PVC 40, 64
PVC adhesive tape 20

Q

quadrant moulding 41
quarry stone 219

R

rack bolts 53
radiators 23, 110
rafter bracket 163

rainwater 138, 140–141, 144, 171, 185, 187, 213, 216, 236
rainwater diverters 140–141
raked joint 187
recycling waste 168
reed screening 142
reinforcing rods 200, 202, 208
rendered walls 137, 234, 236
repointing 114, 185–187, 188, 202–203
reproduction rocks 219
reservoir 226–227
residual-current device (RCD) 179
retaining edges 193, 216
retaining walls 199, 208–209, 212
revarnishing 102
ring latch 175
risers 150–151, 193, 211–213
risers, stairs 59–60
rising main 180
rock fibre 79
rockery 130, 213, 218–219, 222–223, 225, 226–227
rocks 192
roller blinds 32
roof timbers 78
rot 78, 134, 150, 152–153, 172–173, 198, 210, 228
rubbed joint 187, 209
rubble 204, 218
rust 172, 176, 238
rust-inhibiting primer 13
rustic larchlap panels 196

S

safety 132–133, 141, 150–151, 153, 183, 205, 211, 219
safety spectacles 121
salt and vinegar solution 11
sand base 86, 91, 179, 205, 210, 213, 216–217, 224, 228, 229
sandy soil 131
scaffold boards 230
scaffolding 54, 57
scoring 45
scraping 44–45, 75
screeding 41
screening 142–143, 200–203
screw hooks 157
screwed metal angle 70

screwed metal T-section 70
sealant 64, 75, 123
seam roller 109
secondary glazing systems 81
security 24, 34, 50–53
security bolts 173
security chain, fitting 24
self-levelling compound 233
self-tapping screws 165
sharp sand 138, 148, 216, 223, 229–230, 235
shaver socket 122
shelves 68–73, 115
shingle 209
shrubs 128, 142, 219, 226
silicone sealant 179
silicone-rubber caulking compound 123
silver sand 203
sink overflow 16
siphon 36
sketching 128, 132
skew-nailing 198
skirting board 39, 41, 75, 96, 109–110, 114–115, 119
slabs 138, 145, 150–151, 199, 213, 224, 228
sloping site 131,193, 199, 208–209, 212–213, 219, 222
sneck 175
softening 122
softwood 161–162, 170–162, 173, 229
soil 128, 131, 168, 171, 201, 205–206, 209, 218–219,
solar-powered panel 177
sole plate 44–45
soluble salts 185
solvent-based preservers 153
solvents 184
soundproofing 114–115
spacers 87, 118, 120, 215, 217
spalling 151, 184, 188
spare room, papering 104–113
spirit level 72–73, 91, 119–120
spirit-based aluminium sealer 238
spores 183
spraying equipment 184
spring strip 64, 67
spur 134
stabilizing primer 234, 238

stain removal 184
stairs 58–60
staples 52
stays 50, 52, 100
steam stripper 44–45
steel rods 200
step ladder storage 163
stepladder 54, 57, 94
stepping stones 148, 210
steps 150–151, 192, 211–213
stone chippings 189–191
stone pathway 90
stone paving 91
stone pointing 186
stonework 148, 182, 184–185, 192, 204–205, 208–209, 218–219
stopcock 21, 180
straightedge 77, 87, 91, 121
strap hinge 174–175
stratified rock 90
string lines 86, 87, 91
stripping 13, 44–45, 47
stud partition 115
studs 72, 77, 115
sub-base 193, 216, 230
submersible pumps 177, 179, 226
subsidence 201
sugar-soap solution 96
sump 179
sunlight 128, 131, 133, 183, 222

T
T-hinge 174
taped film 81
tapered-edge boards 115
taps 21–22
tarmac drive 189–191
teak oil 47
terracing 193, 208–209, 212, 227
textured coating 236
textured glass 69
textured surfaces 239
thatch screening 142
thixotropic paste 106
threshold bar 39, 41
thumb latch 175
tiles 115, 117–123
tinsnips 76
toilet cistern 17, 36–37, 42

tool shed 228
tool storage 163–165, 228
topsoil 154, 209, 210, 229
tracing paper 132
trailing plants 181, 227
training wires 137, 142
transformer 177, 226
traps 15–16
treads 193, 211–213
treads, stairs 59–60
tree resin 47
trees 128, 132, 138, 139, 142–145, 201, 219, 222, 226
trellis 136–137
trimming 108, 110–111

U
undercoat 92, 96
underlay 38–40
undressed stone 204
uprights 71, 73

V
VA woodworking adhesive 60
varnish 46–47, 102–103
vehicles, parking 133, 193, 214–217
veneer 69–70
Venetian blinds 33
ventilation 51–52, 62, 79, 81
vents 79–80
verdigris 11
vertical blinds 33
vinyl 40–42, 45, 94, 106–107, 112
Virginia creeper 136–137

W
walkway boarding 80
wall bracket 165
wallpaper
    backing 45
    cutting 108
    embossed 106
    flock 112
    hand-printed 108
    heavyweight 106
    lightweight 107
    lining 45, 56

INDEX

machine-trimmed 108
painted 45
paste 45, 104, 106
pasted 55, 106
pasting 107
patterned 106, 108
spare room 104
stripping 44–45
washable 45, 106, 112
walls
  'battered' 91, 205, 208
  brackets 72
  brick 236
  brush 107
  chalky surfaces 238
  climbing plants 137
  cracks 234–235, 237
  crazing 237
  'cutting in' 239
  designing 204
  dry-stone 204–208
  dull 236
  efflorescence 185
  exterior 237
  fixings 73
  garden 136–137, 204–206
  lath-and-plaster 75
  masonry 30, 72
  painting 92, 94, 239
  partition 30, 114–115
  party 115
  pebbledash 235, 239
  pointing 185–187, 188, 202–203
  plasterboard 77
  plugs 30, 72
  refurbishing 182–188
  rendered 234–235, 236
  retaining 208–209, 212
  soundproofing 114–115
  straight 108
  stain removal 184
  stud 76
  textured coating 237
  textured surfaces 239
  tiling 119–120
waney-edged panels 196
washbasin 14–16, 42
washers 21, 22
washing soda 11

water butt 140–141
water feature 177–179, 220, 223, 226–227
water garden 130
water pump 177, 179, 226
water shortages 140–141
water supply 180
water-based preservers 153
water-cylinder jacket 19
water-inlet valve 17
water-storage cistern 17
watercourses 226–227
waterfalls 220
waterproofing 232
wax polish 46
weather 131,
weather bar 63
weathering 47, 182
weatherproofing 234–235
weatherstruck joint 187
weedkiller 189, 191
weeds 189
wet rot 152–153, 172–173
wet-and-dry paper 96, 103
wheelbarrow storage 164
white spirit 46, 96, 103
wind 131, 142–143, 152, 185, 204
windbreak 131, 142–143
window boxes 160–161
window sills 160–161
windows
  bay 30
  burglars 50–53
  casement 30, 51, 66, 100
  catch 100
  curtain rails 28
  draughty 66–67
  fanlight 52
  flush 111
  frames 97, 100
  French 53
  handles 100
  keys 50–51
  locks 51
  metal 50, 52
  painting 96, 101
  panes 100
  papering 106, 111
  pivot 67
  recess 32–33
  reveal 111
  runners 101

  sash 30, 50–51, 66–67, 81, 101
  sloping 33
  tiling round 119–120
  wooden 50, 52
wire link 36–37
wire wool 11, 13, 46–47 103
wired glass 69
wiring 79
wood 35, 41, 46–47, 60, 69, 70–71, 96, 102–103, 118
wood-boring insects 153
wood
  cedar 173
  floorboards 158, 168–169
  hardwood 176
  larch 196
  oak 173
  plywood 157, 162, 164–165, 171, 209
  preserver 152–154, 161–162, 170, 210–211, 216
  rot 210
  softwood 161–162, 170–171, 173, 229
  stain 157–158, 162
wooden bracket 163
wooden float 234
wooden gateposts 176
woodworm 78
work platform 54–57, 94

NOTES

ACKNOWLEDGMENTS

The authors and producers
would like to thank the following for
their assistance in making this book:

STUDIO PHOTOGRAPHY
Paul Chave
Ben Jennings
Neil Waving
ARTWORK
Robin Harris
PAGE MAKEUP
Amanda Allchin
INDEX AND PROOF READING
Mary Morton
PICTURE RESEARCH
Ella Jennings

Special thanks to the following companies
and individuals who contributed additional photographs
and product information to this book:

BARLOW TYRIE LIMITED (TEAKWOOD OUTDOOR FURNITURE)
Braintree, Essex, pages 47, 89.
CUPRINOL LTD.(WOOD PRESERVATIVES)
Frome, Somerset, page 59.
DAVID DAY, pages 128, 178.
FIRED EARTH (TILES AND INTERIORS)
Twyford Mill, Oxford Road, Adderbury, Oxfordshire, pages 28, 77, 93, 99, 116, 117.
© JOHN GLOVER (The Garden Picture Library), page 129.
© HARCOSTAR GARDEN PRODUCTS,
Windover Road, Huntingdon, Cambridgeshire, page 141.
© SUNNIVA HARTE (The Garden Picture Library), page 207.
IDEAL STANDARD (BATHROOMS)
The Bathroom Works, National Avenue, Kingston upon Hull, pages 17, 31, 113.
© DAVID IRELAND, LANDSCAPE ARCHITECT,
David Mews, Greenwich South Street, London, pages 85, 89, 90.
ALBERT JACKSON, page 221.
SIMON JENNINGS, pages 130, 136, 151, 152, 182, 186, 188, 200, 214 top, 215, 220.
LANGLOWS (WOOD FINISHES)
Products Division, Palace Chemicals Ltd. Chesterton, Bucks, page 58.
NAIRN (CUSHION FLOORING)
Forbo-Nairn Limited, PO Box 1, Kircaldy, Scotland, page 43.
© Colin Philp (Photographer), page 85.
© PLYSU BRANDS LTD.,
Wolseley Road, Kempston, Bedfordshire, page 140.
SANDERSON (WALLPAPERS)
6, Cavendish Square, London W1, pages 105, 108.
© STAPELEY WATER GARDENS LTD.,
London Road, Stapeley, Nantwich, Cheshire, page 135.
SUNWAY/LUXAFLEX (BLINDS)
Hunter Douglas (Window Fashions)
Mersey Industrial Estate, Heaton Mersey, Stockport, Cheshire, page 31.
© RON SUTHERLAND (The Garden Picture Library), pages 149 left, 150.
© STEVEN WOOSTER (The Garden Picture Library), page 192.
© Inklink (Ben Jennings Photography),
Jacket & pages 2, 4, 7, 8, 9, 26, 27, 48, 49, 77, 82, 83, 118, 124, 125, 126, 127,
130, 146, 147, 156, 158, 160, 162, 167, 194, 195, 240, 244, 245, 252, 255, 256.